Frommer's

Grand
Canyon
National Park

2nd Edition

by Alex Wells

IDG Books Worldwide Inc.
An International Data Group Company
Foster City, CA • Chicago, IL • Indianapolis, IN
• New York, NY

ABOUT THE AUTHOR

A resident of Park City, Utah, **Alex Wells** has written for magazines including *Condé Nast Traveler, Men's Journal,* and *Outside.* When not on assignment, he enjoys backcountry skiing and backpacking. His idea of heaven is an eternal hike through the Grand Canyon—with weekly breaks for pizza and showers.

IDG BOOKS WORLDWIDE INC.

An International Data Group Company
919 E. Hillsdale Blvd.
Suite 400
Foster City, CA 94404

Find us online at **www.frommers.com**

ISBN 0-02-863623-6
ISSN 1093-9784

Editor: Vanessa Rosen
Production Editor: Christina Van Camp
Design by Michele Laseau
Staff Cartographers: John Decamillis, Roberta Stockwell
Additional cartography by: Nick Trotter
Photo editor: Richard Fox
Page creation by Natalie Evans and Angel Perez

SPECIAL SALES

For general information on IDG Books Worldwide's books in the U.S., please call our Consumer Customer Service department at 1-800-762-2974. For reseller information, including discounts, bulk sales, customized editions, and premium sales, please call our Reseller Customer Service Department at 1-800-434-3422.

Manufactured in the United States of America

5   4   3   2   1

Contents

List of Maps

AN INVITATION TO THE READER

In researching this book, we discovered many wonderful places—hotels, restaurants, shops, and more. We're sure you'll find others. Please tell us about them, so we can share the information with your fellow travelers in upcoming editions. If you were disappointed with a recommendation, we'd love to know that, too. Please write to:

Frommer's Grand Canyon National Park, 2nd Edition
IDG Travel
1633 Broadway
New York, NY 10019

AN ADDITIONAL NOTE

Please be advised that travel information is subject to change at any time—and this is especially true of prices. The authors, editors, and publisher cannot be held responsible for the experiences of readers while traveling. Your safety is important to us, however, so we encourage you to stay alert and be aware of your surroundings. Keep a close eye on cameras, purses, and wallets, all favorite targets of thieves and pickpockets.

WHAT THE SYMBOLS MEAN
✪ Frommer's Favorites

Our favorite places and experiences—outstanding for quality, value, or both.

The following abbreviations are used for credit cards:

AE	American Express	DISC	Discover
CB	Carte Blanche	MC	MasterCard
DC	Diners Club	V	Visa

FIND FROMMER'S ONLINE

Arthur Frommer's Budget Travel Online (www.frommers.com) offers up-to-the-minute travel information—including the latest bargains and personal articles updated daily by Arthur Frommer himself. No other Web site offers such comprehensive coverage.

Line drawings on pages 177 (Douglas fir), 179 (Indian paintbrush), 186 (bighorn sheep, coyote), 187 (elk), 188 (mule deer), 190 (bald eagle, golden eagle), and 191 (red-tailed hawk) by Jasper Burns.

Line drawings on pages 177 (white fir), 178, 179 (lupine, ponderosa pine, quaking aspen), 180–185, 186 (bat), 187 (desert cottontail), 188 (mountain lion), 189, 190 (common raven, great horned owl), 191 (peregrine falcon, violet-green swallow), 192–194 by Giselle Simons.

1

Welcome to the Grand Canyon

*Y*ears ago, upon completing a hike in the Grand Canyon, I stood at the rim, gazing one last time at the colors below, and vowed right then and there to inform everyone how lucky they were to be alive. My good intentions lasted for only a day, but it was an unforgettable one, and when it was over I realized that the canyon had moved me the way religion moves fervent believers. At the time I wasn't sure why. Only after I began work on this book did I begin to understand all those things that, for me, make the canyon not just a beautiful place, but a sacred one as well.

When I returned to the canyon to work on this book, I was awed by the terraced buttes and mesas, rising thousands of feet from the canyon floor and dividing the many side canyons. Early cartographers and geologists noticed similarities between these pinnacles and some of the greatest works of human hands. Clarence Edward Dutton, who scouted the canyon for the U.S. Geological Survey in 1880–81, began referring to them as temples and named them after eastern deities such as Brahma, Vishnu, and Shiva. François Matthes, who drew up a topographical map of the canyon in 1902, continued the tradition by naming Wotans Throne and Krishna Temple, among other landmarks.

The temples not only inspire reverence but tell the grandest of stories. Half the earth's history is represented in the canyon's rocks. The oldest and deepest rock layer, the Vishnu Schist, began forming 2 billion years ago, before aerobic life-forms even existed. The different layers of sedimentary rock that piled up atop the Schist tell of landscapes that changed like dreams. They speak of mountains that really did move, eroding away into nothingness. Of oceans that poured forth across the land before receding. Of deserts, swamps, and rivers the size of the Mississippi—all where the canyon now lies. The very evolution of life is illustrated by the fossils in these layers.

Many of the latest products of evolution—over 1,500 plant and 400 animal species—still survive at the canyon today. If you include

Grand Canyon Overview

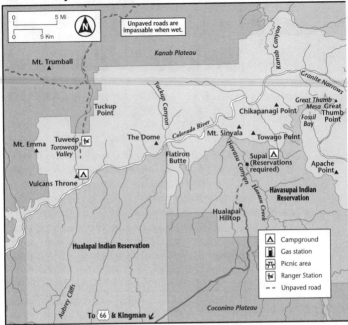

the upper reaches of the Kaibab Plateau (on the canyon's North Rim), this small area of northern Arizona includes zones of biological life comparable to ones found as far south as Mexico and as far north as Alaska. The species come in every shape, size, and temperament, ranging from tiny ant lions dwelling on the canyon floor to 1,000-pound elk roaming the rims. And for every species there is a story within the story. Take the Douglas fir, for example. Once part of a forest that covered both rims and much of the canyon, this tree has endured since the last Ice Age on shady, north-facing slopes beneath the South Rim—long after the sun-baked rim itself became too hot and inhospitable.

As much as I like the stories, I also enjoy the mysteries that can't be explained. The web of ecological cause-and-effect among the canyon's species is too complicated for any mortal to untangle. It leaves endless questions to ponder, such as why the agave blooms only once every 20-odd years. Similarly, the canyon's rocks withhold as much as they tell. More than a billion years' worth of sediment eroded away between the time the Vishnu Schist formed and the

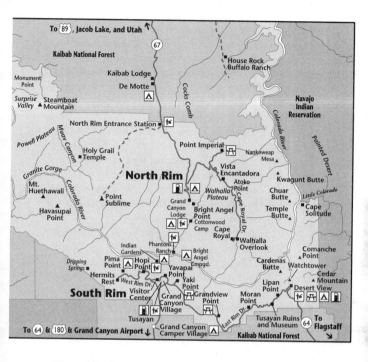

Tapeats Sandstone was deposited atop it—a gap in the geological record commonly referred to as The Great Unconformity. Other gaps—or unconformities—exist between other layers. And river gravels that would have explained how the canyon was cut have long since washed away.

The more time I spend inside the canyon, the better I hope to understand the first people who dwelt here. A number of different tribes have lived in or around the canyon, and the Navajo, Havasupai, Kaibab Paiute, Hopi, Zuni, and Hualapai tribes still live in the area. Before the white man arrived, they awakened to the colors of the canyon, made their clothes from its plants and animals, smelled it, touched it, tasted it, and felt it underfoot. The Hopi still regard the canyon as their place of emergence and the place to which their dead return. Their ancestors left behind more than 3,000 archaeological sites and artifacts that may be as old as 10,000 years. All this runs through my mind when I walk the canyon floor.

I also contemplate some of the first white people who came to this mystical place. The canyon moved them to do extraordinary, if not always productive, things. I think about the prospectors who clambered through the canyon in search of precious minerals, and then wonder about the ones who stayed here even after their mines proved unprofitable. I wish I could have met icons like Georgie White, who began her illustrious river-running career by *swimming* 60 miles down the Colorado River in the western canyon; and Mary Colter, the brilliant architect who obsessed over creating buildings that blended with the landscape, even going so far as to grow plants out of the stone roof at the Lookout Studio. I'd still like to meet David Brower, who, as executive director of the Sierra Club, helped nix a proposal to dam the Colorado River inside the Grand Canyon. He did so by running full-page ads in the *New York Times* that compared damming the canyon to flooding the Sistine Chapel. I admire these people, who felt blessed and inspired by the canyon.

Theodore Roosevelt would also belong in this group. During his 1903 visit, the canyon moved him to say: "Leave it as it is. You cannot improve on it. The ages have been at work on it, and man can only mar it. What you can do is to keep it for your children, your children's children . . . as the one great sight which every American . . . should see." That wasn't just talk. He backed up his words, using the Antiquities Act to declare the Grand Canyon a National Monument in 1908. Congress established Grand Canyon National Park in 1919.

Although Congress called it a "park," the canyon still has a daunting, even ominous side. Everyone, no matter how many times they enter it, must negotiate with it for survival. One look at the clenched jaw of a river guide as he or she rows into Lava Rapids will remind you that the canyon exacts a heavy price for mistakes. And the most common error is to underestimate it. Try to escape, and it becomes a prison 10 miles wide (on average), 277 (river) miles long, and with walls 4,000 feet high. The canyon's menace, for me, is part of its allure—a reminder that we're still animals who haven't completely conquered nature.

Clearly, you can suffer here, but reward is everywhere. It's in the spectrum of colors: The Colorado River, filled with runoff from a recent rain, runs blood red beneath slopes of orange Hakatai Shale; cactus flowers explode in pink, yellow, and red; and lichens paint rocks orange, green, and gray, creating art more striking than the works in any gallery. It's in the shapes, too—the spires, amphitheaters, temples, ramps, and cliffs—and in the shadows that bend across them before lifting like mist. It's in the myriad organisms and their individual struggles for survival. Perhaps most of all, it's in the constancy of the river, which, even as it cuts closer to a beginning, reminds us that all things break down, wash away, and return to the earth in time.

1 The Park Today

The years at the beginning of the new millennium find Grand Canyon National Park in transition. Visitation rose from just over 2 million in 1974 to 4.6 million in 1997 and is projected to top 7 million by 2010. Already, the park's resources are strained. On a typical summer day, some 6,500 vehicles drive to the South Rim, only to find 2,400 parking places. Faced with gridlock, noise, and pollution from emissions during high season, the park has had little choice but to make changes, many of which will be implemented in the next few years.

Under the park's **General Management Plan,** private vehicles will eventually be barred from most areas along the South Rim, including the historic district in Grand Canyon Village, the West Rim Drive, and all but one overlook (Desert View) on the East Rim Drive. Instead of driving, visitors will travel by light rail from a new transportation staging area in Tusayan (just south of the park's south entrance) to a larger orientation center—the Canyon View Information Plaza—inside the park near Mather Point. (The park's current visitor center will be converted to administrative space.) A second light rail line will link the Canyon View Information Plaza with the Village Transit Center, a bus depot near Maswik Lodge in Grand Canyon Village. At both the Canyon View Plaza and the Village Transit Center, visitors will be able to board buses powered by natural gas or electricity. These buses will transport them to other developed areas on the South Rim.

Private cars won't be banned altogether from this part of the park. Visitors camping or staying in lodges and campgrounds away from the rim will be allowed to drive directly to those areas. Those staying nearer the rim will have to take shuttles from parking areas farther out. Visitors will also be able to drive through the park on Highway 64, a through road connecting the towns of Williams and Cameron, Arizona. However, they will not be allowed to use the overlooks west of Desert View.

Future visitors to the park will also find an extensive "greenway" trail for cyclists (rental bicycles will be available), walkers, and equestrians. Paved in places, it will travel 33 miles on the South Rim between Hermit's Rest and Desert View. Another branch of the greenway will parallel the light-rail line linking Tusayan with the Canyon View Information Plaza.

The new transit and trails system should help the National Park Service achieve its goal of restoring the rim area to a quieter, less polluted state. Other parts of the master plan move commercial activity and housing away from the rim and, in some cases, out of the park. For starters, the rim-side Kachina and Thunderbird lodges will be razed; the area they occupy will become open space. Their guest rooms may be replaced by new ones away from the rim at Maswik Lodge and in historic buildings that now serve as employee dormitories. A net gain of 240 guest rooms is planned, and Mather Campground will be expanded slightly. To compensate for the loss of employee housing, Park Service employees will be given the chance to buy or rent homes in a new gateway community planned just outside the park's south entrance.

By September 2000, the National Park Service hopes to complete the **Canyon View Information Plaza** and a half-mile stretch of greenway linking the plaza and Yavapai Point. The light rail component may be in place as early as 2002. (Most sources close to the project deem 2003 more realistic.) Until the light-rail system is operating, automobile traffic into Grand Canyon Village probably won't be restricted. In the meantime, drivers can expect to see construction at Mather Point, along the East Rim Drive, and around Maswik Lodge.

The changes won't be limited to the park itself. A new development is also planned south of the park, where increased visitation has taxed the limits of the gateway community of Tusayan. In August 1999, the U.S. Forest Service approved a plan in which 282 acres of federal land just outside the park's south entrance would be traded to a Scottsdale-based developer in exchange for 2,118 acres of private lands located elsewhere in the national forest system. The developer, Canyon Forest Village, plans to use the 282 acres to build hotels totaling 1,220 rooms; 270,000 square feet of retail space; and 1,100 employee housing units. Business groups in Tusayan, Flagstaff, and Williams strongly opposed the Forest Service's decision and planned to appeal it.

The park's Master Plan is designed to let the South Rim accommodate the crowds expected in the future, and the National Park Service has no plans to limit visitation there. It may, however, limit North Rim visitation. Rather than expand North Rim facilities to accommodate larger crowds—in the process jeopardizing the peacefulness of this area—the Park Service may cap the number of day-use visitors sometime before 2010. Also, a new parking area near the North Kaibab trailhead may eventually be constructed. Visitors would park their cars in the lot and then take shuttles to Bright Angel Point, where Grand Canyon Lodge is located. During the next few years, however, few changes are in store at the North Rim.

2 The Best of the Grand Canyon

Choosing the best things at Grand Canyon is like naming the best thing about your true love. Especially when your true love—all 277 miles of it—is divine. But, since every vacation consists of smaller parts, I've done my best to isolate a few of the best places and ways to appreciate the larger beauty of Grand Canyon.

- **The Most Dramatic Rim View: Lipan Point** (on the East Rim Drive, South Rim). Located above a sweeping curve in the river and with views far downstream to the west, Lipan Point is the nicest easily accessible place to view the canyon and a great place to watch the sunset. From this overlook, you can barely make out the walls of schist and gneiss that make up the **Inner Gorge,** along the river to the west. The **Unkar Delta,** one of the most archaeologically rich areas in the park, is visible directly below the overlook. See chapter 3.
- **The Best Scenic Drive: East Rim Drive** (South Rim). You'll see more of the canyon on this drive than on the other two (The Cape Royal Road and the West Rim Drive). The westernmost overlooks open onto the monuments of the central canyon; the eastern ones have far-ranging views of the Marble Platform and the northeast end of the canyon. Along the way, you can stop at the 800-year-old Tusayan Ruin, which was once occupied by the Ancestral Puebloans. The Watchtower, a historic building artfully fashioned after towers built by the Ancestral Puebloans, is a perfect place to finish the drive. See chapter 3.
- **The Best Historic Building: Hermit's Rest** (at the western terminus of the West Rim Drive). On the outside, this 1913 building resembles a crude rock shelter like one built by a hermit. Inside, it has an enormous, cavelike fireplace, original furniture, and candelabras on the walls. Built as a rest stop for travelers en route to a camp inside the canyon, Hermit's Rest is still a great place to collect oneself before returning to Grand Canyon Village. See chapter 3.

- **The Best Bike Ride: The West Rim Drive in summer** (South Rim). During high season, when this road is closed to most private vehicles, motorized traffic consists mostly of the occasional shuttle bus. Between shuttles, you'll often have the gently rolling road and some of the overlooks to yourself. Before pedaling back to Grand Canyon Village, refresh yourself with a cold drink at Hermit's Rest. See chapter 3.

- **The Best Rim Trail: Widforss Trail** (North Rim). Easy enough for beginners but long enough to weed out the crowds, this 5-mile-long (one way) trail skirts the head of Transept Canyon, passes a balancing rock, then continues south through old-growth ponderosa pine forest to a canyon overlook. The picnic table near the end of the trail is perfect for a quiet lunch. The first 2 miles of the trail is a self-guided interpretive hike, for which brochures are available at the trailhead. See chapter 4.

- **The Best Day Hike Below the Rim: Plateau Point Trail** (accessible via the Bright Angel Trail). With views 1,300 feet down to the Colorado River, Plateau Point is a prime destination for fit, well-prepared day hikers. The hardest part of this 6.1-mile (each way) trip is on the Bright Angel Trail, which descends 4.6 miles and 3,060 vertical feet from Grand Canyon Village to Indian Garden. The trailhead for the Plateau Point Trail is a half mile west of Indian Garden on the Tonto Trail. From there, it's a smooth and relatively level stroll to the overlook. See chapter 4.

- **The Best Corridor Trail: North Kaibab** (North Rim). For people backpacking into the canyon for the first time, this is a scenic, less-crowded alternative to the South Rim corridor trails. It's easily my favorite of the three choices. During its 14-mile-long, 5,850-vertical-foot descent from rim to river, the trail passes through vegetation ranging from spruce-fir forest to Sonoran Desert. It ends near Phantom Ranch, the only lodging inside the canyon within the park boundaries. See chapter 4.

- **The Best Active Vacation: Oar-powered raft trips through Grand Canyon.** Expensive and worth it, these trips negotiate thrilling rapids on the Colorado River. Between the rapids, they move slowly and quietly enough to reveal the subtle magic of the canyon. During stops hikers have access to some of the prettiest spots anywhere. See chapter 4.

- **The Best Historic Hotel: The El Tovar Hotel** (Grand Canyon Village, ☎ 303/297-2757). Made of Oregon pine, this grand 1905 hotel rises darkly above Grand Canyon Village on the canyon's South Rim. Inside, moose and elk heads, copper chandeliers, and rooms with classic American furnishings add to its almost-spooky character. By far the most luxurious in the park, this hotel is the only one with room service. See chapter 5.

- **The Best RV Park: Kaibab Camper Village** (Jacob Lake, ☎ 520/643-7804). For once, an RV park that doesn't look like the lot at a drive-in movie. Old growth ponderosa pines and views of Jacob Lake (the tiny pond) make this RV park, located about 45 miles from the North Rim entrance, the best by far in the Grand Canyon area. Campers can pick up a few supplies at nearby Jacob Lake (the motel, store, gas station, and restaurant). The only thing missing is showers. See chapter 5.

- **The Best Car Campground in the Park: North Rim Campground** (☎ 520/638-2151). The campsites along the rim of Transept Canyon have pleasing views and are well worth the extra $5. Ponderosa pines shade all the sites, which are far enough apart to afford privacy. For hikers, the Transept Trail begins just a few yards away. If you're on the South Rim, try **Desert View Campground.** See chapter 5.

- **The Best Bar in the Park: Bright Angel Lounge** (inside Bright Angel Lodge in Grand Canyon Village, ☎ 520/638-2631). Every night, tourists from around the world perch atop the stools at this long bar, their backs to a mural by a renowned Hopi artist Fred Kabotie, their elbows resting atop a coated bar top displaying historic postcards, old horseshoes, and other canyon relics. During high season, you'll hear more languages here than at the United Nations—at least until the live music drowns everyone out. See chapter 5.

- **The Best Accessible Backcountry Destination: Waterfalls of Havasu Creek.** Surrounded by the red-rock walls of Havasu Canyon, these turquoise-colored falls seem to pour forth from the heavens into the cauldron of Grand Canyon. Travertine dams the creek in places, forming many seductive swimming holes. The 10-mile hike or mule ride from Hualapai Hilltop helps ease you into this area, home to the Havasupai Indians. See chapter 6.

- **The Best B&B: The Inn At 410 Bed & Breakfast** (410 N. Leroux St., Flagstaff, AZ 86001, ☎ 800/774-2008 or 520/774-0088). Your journey doesn't end at the door of this inn. Inside, each of the elegantly decorated rooms recalls a different setting. One room celebrates the cowboy way of life, another recalls a 19th-century French Garden, and a third is fashioned after a turn-of-the-century Mexican courtyard. The intriguing decor, together with the kindness of innkeepers Sally and Howard

Krueger, helps you travel the world—while catching up on your rest. See chapter 6.

- **The Best Expensive Hotel: Best Western Grand Canyon Squire Inn** (Tusayan, ☎ **800/622-6966** or 520/638-2681). Located just a mile outside the park, this hotel offers many of the amenities generally associated with resorts in big cities. Here, you'll find the town's best dining (in the elegant Coronado Room), its liveliest watering hole (downstairs, in the bar that locals call "The Squire"), and its only tennis courts for guests— not to mention luxuries such as a beauty shop and in-room massage. Located in the main building, the deluxe rooms equal the area's best. See chapter 6.

- **The Best Expensive Restaurant: Chez Marc Bistro** (Flagstaff, ☎ **520/774-1343**). This delightful country French restaurant, which showcases the cooking of chef Marc Balocco, could succeed in any city. Every course, from the smoked salmon crepes to the frozen Grand Marnier soufflé, not only looks divine, but tastes divine as well. The restaurant boasts an expansive selection of wines and after-dinner drinks, and the intimate, bistro-style room will make you want to fall (or stay) in love. See chapter 6.

- **The Best Midpriced Restaurant: Charly's** (Flagstaff, ☎ **520/779-1919**). With tables outside on the sidewalk and inside in a high-ceilinged, Victorian-style dining room, the atmosphere at this hotel restaurant is both casual and pleasant. Vegetarians and meat-eaters alike will enjoy the Southwestern dishes, which come with or without meat. There's also a nice choice of sandwiches, burgers, and steaks. The bar has live entertainment and a wide selection of domestic and imported beer. See chapter 6.

- **The Best Inexpensive Restaurant: The Black Bean Burrito Bar and Salsa Company** (Flagstaff, ☎ **520/779-9905**). Get a burrito as heavy as a hand weight, at a price that makes it feel like a handout. Wrapped in aluminum foil and served in plastic drive-in baskets, this may be the best food value in the whole Grand Canyon area. The food is ready within seconds after you order, making this a great place to get a quick fix after a long day. See chapter 6.

- **The Best Steak House: Rod's Steakhouse** (Williams, ☎ **520/635-2671**). Beef lovers won't want to miss this Route 66 landmark, identifiable by the cow-shaped sign out front. After 50 years, the tiny menus here are as laconic as cowboys—seems the restaurant would rather serve its giant steaks than write about them. Don't miss the creamy desserts, the perfect finish to a simple, yet delicious, meal. See chapter 6.

- **The Best Area Museum: Museum of Northern Arizona** (Flagstaff, ☎ **520/774-5213**). One of the most extensive collections of Native American art makes this museum unique. Both functional and striking, the artifacts are compellingly displayed, in exhibits that illuminate the close relationship between the indigenous people and the land of the Colorado Plateau. There's no better place to begin learning about the area. See chapter 6.

2

Planning Your Trip to Grand Canyon National Park

*A*ccording to Park Service studies, the average visit to Grand Canyon National Park lasts about 3 hours—and many people spend even less time than that. At the other end of the spectrum lies a handful of people who never really leave. Once they've seen the canyon, they spend lifetimes exploring it, logging thousands of miles on its hiking trails or weeks at a time on its river. How much time you allow depends on how well you'd like to know the canyon.

I recommend spending at least 1 full day and night on the rim or nearby. This will give you a chance to watch a sunset or (better still) a sunrise. It will also give you enough time to find a quiet place on the rim for writing postcards or listening to the canyon. If you spend 2 full days, you can hike 1 day and take a scenic drive the next. Another day is better still. A lifetime is best.

1 Getting Started: Information & Reservations

Grand Canyon National Park distributes a free trip planner that should answer most of your questions about the park. To get a copy of the planner, you can call ☎ **520/638-7888** or visit the park's Web site at: **www.thecanyon.com/nps**.

MULE TRIPS

Mule trips to Phantom Ranch fill up months ahead of time, so it's wise to make your reservations as early as possible. Reservations for the next 23 months can be made beginning on the first of the month. For example, dates in December 2002 would first go on sale on January 1, 2000. For advance reservations call ☎ **303/297-2757.**

MAPS

The best driving map of the Four Corners area is **AAA's Guide to Indian Country** ($3.95), which shows many of the more remote roads. **Trails Illustrated** publishes an excellent large-scale (1:73,500) topographical map of the Grand Canyon ($9.95). Waterproof and

Planning Tip

For every season but winter, reservations for campsites, raft trips, backcountry permits, motel rooms, and train and (South Rim) mule rides should be made in advance. Read below for specific information.

tear-proof, it shows both rims and all the canyon trails from Lee's Ferry to west of Havasu Canyon, with the eastern canyon displayed on one side and the western canyon on the other. These maps, as well as more than 200 titles about the canyon, are available through the **Grand Canyon Association,** P.O. Box 399, Grand Canyon, AZ 86023 (☎ **800/858-2808**).

Detailed topographical maps of the canyon are helpful for those hiking the canyon's wilderness trails. You can order **U.S. Geological Survey (USGS) 7.5-minute maps** of the canyon by calling the USGS directly (☎ **800/872-6277**). Cost for direct orders is $4 plus $3.50 shipping and handling. These maps are also usually available at **The General Store** (☎ **520/638-2262**) on the South Rim. The nearest North Rim outlet is at **Willow Creek Books** in Kanab, Utah (☎ **435/644-8884**). However, these stores, unlike the USGS, won't always have the map you need.

If you're planning to travel through the Kaibab National Forest to a remote campsite or trailhead, a map can be a lifesaver. The Kaibab National Forest Tusayan, Williams, and Chalender Ranger Districts map ($4) covers the Forest Service land along the South Rim. To order one, call ☎ **520/638-2443** or stop by the **Kaibab National Forest Tusayan Ranger District Office,** outside the park's south entrance. The Kaibab National Forest North Kaibab Ranger District map shows the Forest Service land along the North Rim, much of which extends to the rim itself. The **Kaibab Plateau Visitor Center** (☎ **520/643-7298**) at Jacob Lake sells these $4 maps.

USEFUL BOOKS & PUBLICATIONS

Among the hundreds of books written on the canyon, several stand out. For a general overview, page through *Grand Canyon: A Natural History Guide* (Houghton Mifflin Co., 1993) by Jeremy Schmidt. Schmidt reveals the larger beauty of the canyon by exploring the smaller relationships between its dwellers—human and otherwise.

If you're the type who leaves no stone unturned, you should consider buying *An Introduction to Grand Canyon Geology* (Grand Canyon Association, 1999) by L. Greer Price. The author explains the geology of Grand Canyon in terms anyone can understand.

The Man Who Walked Through Time (Vintage Books, 1967), by Colin Fletcher, provides a more personal look at the canyon. As he chronicles his own 300-mile walk through the canyon, the author explores how the land moves him. If people interest you most, look for *In the House of Stone and Light: A Human History of Grand Canyon* (Grand Canyon Natural History Association, 1978) by J. Donald Hughes. This meticulously researched book traces the canyon's human history from the prehistoric desert cultures through the 1970s. All of the above titles can be ordered through the Grand Canyon Association (☎ **800/858-2808**).

2 When to Go

The **South Rim** is open year-round. But don't plan on driving on the West Rim Drive from mid-March to October—during that period, if you don't want to walk, you'll have to rely on the park's free shuttles to move you from lookout to lookout.

Weather permitting, the North Rim is open from May 15 to October 16. After this date, the park remains open (without most services) until the first major snowstorm. The road from Jacob Lake into the park closes during the first storm and remains closed until spring.

AVOIDING THE CROWDS

When planning your trip, remember that July and August are the busiest months. To avoid the crowds, avoid the high season. If you can't come during the off-season, try to schedule your visit before 10am or after 2pm, so that you can avoid both the lines at the entrance gates and the parking problems inside the park. This advice holds true for both rims.

Although mass transit won't help you avoid the crowds, it might make those crowds more bearable. There's an hourly commercial shuttle from Tusayan to the South Rim, and there's also a train into the park from Williams. The park staff recommends that you park your vehicle outside the park and use these alternative modes of transportation.

Once at the South Rim, you can ride the park's free shuttles during high season. The free shuttles serve **Grand Canyon Village, Yavapai Point, Yaki Point, South Kaibab trailhead,** and the **West**

Packing Tips

A wide-brimmed hat, sunglasses, and sunscreen are standard equipment at the canyon in all seasons. If you're planning to hike in cool weather, you'll be most comfortable in a water-resistant, breathable shell and several layers of insulating clothing, preferably polypropylene, polar fleece, or other fabrics that remain warm when wet. The shell-and-layers technique works especially well in spring and fall, when extreme swings in temperature occur regularly. Even in summer, you'll still want a waterproof, windproof shell and at least one insulating layer (more on the North Rim) for cold nights or storms.

Rim Drive from mid-March to mid-October. When the shuttles run, the West Rim Drive, Yavapai Point, Yaki Point, and the South Kaibab Trailhead are closed to private vehicles.

CLIMATE

The climate at the Grand Canyon varies greatly not only from season to season but from point to point. At 8,000 feet and higher, the North Rim is by far the coldest, dampest part of the park. Its temperatures run about 30°F cooler than Phantom Ranch at the bottom of the canyon. Phantom Ranch is more than 4,000 feet lower and up to 25°F warmer than the South Rim. The North Rim averages 25 inches of precipitation per year, compared with just 8 inches at Phantom Ranch and 16 inches on the South Rim.

IF YOU'RE GOING IN SPRING   The North Rim doesn't open until mid-May, so in early spring your only choice is the South Rim, which is cool and breezy at this time of year. The South Rim's daily highs average 60°F and 70°F in April and May, respectively. Nights can be very cold, with lows in April around freezing. Travelers should be prepared for late-winter storms, which occasionally bring snow to the rim. Storms aside, this is an ideal time to hike the inner canyon, with highs in April averaging 82°F. It's also the most popular, so make reservations early. Many of the canyon's cacti bloom in spring, dotting the already colorful walls with lavenders, yellows, and reds and making this perhaps the prettiest time of year to visit.

IF YOU'RE GOING IN SUMMER   The South Rim seldom becomes unbearably hot, and the North Rim never does. During July, the average highs on the South and North rims are 84°F and 77°F, respectively. Although the temperatures on the rim are pleasant, the

Flood Warning

In mid-July, the monsoons usually begin. As hot air rises from the canyon floor, moist air from the oceans is swept up along with it. As this moist air rises, it condenses, forming towering thunderheads that unloose short-lived but intense afternoon thunderstorms. These localized storms frequently drench the park during August, the wettest month of the year, when nearly 2.25 inches of rain falls on the South Rim.

When rain threatens, hikers should avoid slot canyons, whose steep walls make climbing to safety nearly impossible. Even in wide, dry washes, hikers should be aware of the possibility of sudden, unexpected floods and be prepared to move to higher ground. Keep in mind that these floods can originate from storms that are miles away.

---

crowds there can feel stifling. Escaping into the canyon may not be an alternative—at this time of year, the canyon bottom can be torrid, with highs averaging 106°F, and considerably hotter along the dark-colored rocks near the river. However, on the North Rim especially, summer nights can be nippy. Even during July, low temperatures there average a chilly 46°F.

IF YOU'RE GOING IN FALL   After the monsoons taper off in mid-September, fall is a great time to be anywhere in the park. The crowds fall off before the red, orange, and yellow leaves on the rim-top trees follow suit. The North Rim, with its many aspens, is brightest of all. Highs on the South Rim average 76°F in September, 65°F in October, and 52°F in November. The North Rim has highs of 69°F in September and 59°F in October. (It closes in mid-October.) Highs average 97°F in the Inner Gorge in September. In October, however, the days cool off by 13°F, and backpackers can sometimes enjoy perfect weather. The first winter storms can hit the North Rim as early as mid-October.

Also in the fall, for 3 weeks every September, the **Grand Canyon Music Festival** brings together world-renowned classical musicians. The offerings, consisting primarily of chamber-music concerts, are held next to the park's visitor center, in the intimate, acoustically superb Shrine of the Ages Auditorium. Tickets for the 7:30pm concerts cost $15 for adults and $5 for children (park admission not included) and are available at the door or in advance through Grand Canyon Chamber Music Festival (☎ **800/997-8285** or 520/

638-9215), P.O. Box 1332, Grand Canyon, AZ 86023. A few concerts sell out. To ensure that you receive the tickets you want, order by early July.

IF YOU'RE GOING IN WINTER If you don't mind the cold, you'll love the canyon in winter. Winter is by far the quietest and most peaceful time to visit. Backcountry permits are easy to come by, the overlooks are virtually empty, and storms sprinkle snow across the red rocks. These storms, unlike summer monsoons, are not localized disturbances. Rather, they're the same large Pacific fronts that drop snow throughout the West. Closed in winter, the North Rim sometimes receives more than 200 inches of snow in a season. Although the South Rim gets considerably less, drivers should still be prepared for icy roads and occasional closures. When the snow isn't falling, the South Rim warms up nicely. High temperatures average 41°F in January and 45°F in February. The inner canyon can be pleasant during the coldest months. Even in January, its highs average a balmy 56°F, although snow does occasionally reach the floor.

3 Permits You Can Obtain in Advance

BACKCOUNTRY PERMITS & FEES Permits are required for all overnight camping in the backcountry. This includes all overnight stays below the rims (except in the cabins and dorms at Phantom Ranch) and on park land outside of designated campgrounds. Flip to the section "Preparing for Your Backcountry Trip," on p. 59 in chapter 4 for complete information on how to get a permit.

SKI PERMITS If you'd like to ski into the park and spend the night on the North Rim when the park is closed, you'll need to obtain a backcountry permit ahead of time from the **Backcountry Office** (☎ 520/638-7875).

4 Getting There

Las Vegas and Phoenix are the closest major cities to the North and South rims, respectively. You can save money by flying into these cities, but they're too far from the canyon to stay in during your visit. It's a 4-hour drive from Las Vegas to the North Rim and about a half hour longer to the South Rim. It's 4.5 hours from Phoenix to the South Rim. Flagstaff, Williams, Tusayan, and Kanab, Utah, are better choices for lodging near the Grand Canyon.

What Things Cost at the Grand Canyon	U.S. $
Local fare on Fred Harvey Taxi Service (between destinations on the loop drive of Grand Canyon Village, 1 person)	$4
(Each additional person)	$1
Shuttle from Tusayan to Grand Canyon Village (one-way fare for adults)	$4
(kids 16 and under)	free
Bottle of Budweiser beer inside the canyon	$3
Cup of coffee at Yavapai Cafeteria (inexpensive)	$1.20
Room with bed and sink only at Bright Angel Lodge (inexpensive)	$44
Double-occupancy high-end suite at El Tovar Hotel (expensive)	$279
Double-occupancy canyon-side room at Kachina Lodge (moderate)	$119
Double-occupancy room at Holiday Inn Express in Tusayan (moderate)	$139
(in low season)	$69
Double-occupancy room at Quality Inn Mountain Ranch Resort in Williams (in summer)	$109
(in low season)	$69
Site at Mather Campground in summer	$12–15
Water/electric hookup site at Grand Canyon Trailer Village	$20
Mule day trip to Plateau Point	$101
Gallon of gas in Tusayan (in summer 1999)	$1.60
(22¢ more than in Flagstaff)	
Park admission (per car)	$20
Backcountry permit	$20
(plus $4 per person per night)	
Big Mac burger at Tusayan McDonald's	$3.79

BY PLANE

Because Phoenix and Las Vegas are the closest gateway cities, many travelers opt to fly into either the **Phoenix/Sky Harbor International Airport,** 220 miles from the South Rim, or **McCarran International Airport** in Las Vegas, 263 miles from the North Rim.

Phoenix is served by **Aeromexico** (☎ 800/237-6639), **Air Canada** (☎ 800/776-3000), **America West** (☎ 800/235-9292), **American** (☎ 800/433-7300), **Continental** (☎ 800/525-0280), **Delta** (☎ 800/221-1212), **Delta Connection (Skywest)** (☎ 800/453-9417), **Northwest** (☎ 800/225-2525), **Southwest** (☎ 800/435-9792), **Sun Country** (☎ 800/752-1218), **TWA** (☎ 800/221-2000), **United** (☎ 800/241-6522), and **US Airways** (☎ 800/428-4322).

Las Vegas is served by **Air Canada** (☎ 800/776-3000), **Alaska Airlines** (☎ 800/426-0333), **America West** (☎ 800/235-9292), **American** (☎ 800/433-7300), **American Trans Air** (☎ 800/I-FLY-ATA), **Continental** (☎ 800/525-0280), **Delta** (☎ 800/221-1212), **Delta Connection (Skywest)** (☎ 800/453-9417), **Frontier** (☎ 800/432-1359), **Hawaiian** (☎ 800/367-5320), **Japan** (☎ 800/525-3663), **Midwest** (☎ 800/452-2022), **North-west** (☎ 800/225-2525), **Reno Air** (☎ 800/736-6247), **South-west** (☎ 800/435-9792), **Sun Country** (☎ 800/752-1218), **TWA** (☎ 800/221-2000), **United** (☎ 800/241-6522), and **US Airways** (☎ 800/428-4322).

For those who would like to fly in closer to the canyon, **America West Express** (☎ **800/235-9292**) has daily jet service (round-trip cost: $153) connecting Phoenix/Sky Harbor International Airport and **Flagstaff Pulliam Airport,** roughly 80 miles from the park.

Closer still is **Grand Canyon National Park Airport** in Tusayan, 1.5 miles south of the park's south entrance. **Arizona Professional Air Travel** (☎ **800/933-7590;** www.fly-in-america.com) offers commercial service between Flagstaff and Tusayan. Costing about $200 (round-trip) per person, the flights are on tiny four- or six-passenger aircraft. **Air Vegas** (☎ **800/255-7474** or 702/736-3599) and **Scenic Airlines** (☎ **800/634-6801** or 702/638-3300) both offer daily service between Las Vegas and Grand Canyon National Park Airport. Air Vegas, whose round-trip fare is $222, departs from **Henderson Executive Airport;** Scenic, which charges $200 round-trip, leaves from **Tropicana Airport** (part of McCarran International Airport).

BY CAR
RENTING A CAR

Major rental-car companies with offices in Arizona and Las Vegas include **Alamo** (☎ 800/327-9633), **Avis** (☎ 800/331-1212), **Bud-get** (☎ 800/527-0700), **Dollar** (☎ 800/800-4000), **Enterprise**

The Grand Canyon & Northern Arizona

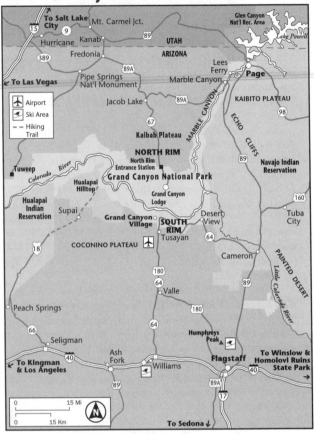

(☎ 800/325-8007), **Hertz** (☎ 800/654-3131), **National** (☎ 800/227-7368), and **Thrifty** (☎ 800/367-2277).

No rental cars are currently available in Tusayan.

In Flagstaff, car rentals are available through the following companies: **Avis** (☎ 800/831-2847 or 520/774-8421), **Budget** (☎ 800/527-0700 or 520/779-5255), **Enterprise** (☎ 800/325-8007 or 520/526-1377), **Hertz** (☎ 800/654-3131 or 520/774-4452), and **National** (☎ 800/227-7368 or 520/779-1975).

DRIVING TIPS Many of the dirt roads to remote areas on the rims are impassable in wet weather. During monsoon season, these roads can become too muddy or slippery to negotiate, and fallen

Driving Distances

Mileage from the South Rim of Grand Canyon National Park to:

Albuquerque, NM	407
Bryce Canyon National Park, UT	310
Cameron, AZ	57
Canyon de Chelly National Monument, AZ	243
Denver, CO	649
Flagstaff, AZ	78
Gallup, NM	273
Grand Canyon National Park Airport	9
Kanab, UT	222
Kingman, AZ	188
Las Vegas, NV	290
Los Angeles, CA	556
North Rim Grand Canyon National Park	215
Petrified Forest National Park	189
Phoenix, AZ	220
Williams, AZ	59
Zion National Park, UT	272

Mileage from the North Rim (entrance) of Grand Canyon National Park to:

Flagstaff, AZ	193
Fredonia, AZ	71
Jacob Lake, AZ	30
Kanab, UT	78
Las Vegas, NV	277
Phoenix, AZ	335
Salt Lake City, UT	438
Williams, AZ	225
Zion National Park, UT	119

trees can block the way any time. In winter, there's no snow removal on these roads. People using them in cold weather, even during spring and fall, should be aware that they could be stranded indefinitely by a heavy snowfall. Weather-related problems occasionally arise on the main roads as well. From late fall to early spring, visitors should be prepared for snowy or icy driving conditions and occasional road closures.

Renting an RV for Your Trip

Cruise America (☎ **800/RV-DEPOT**) rents RVs nationwide and has offices in Phoenix, Flagstaff, and Las Vegas. During July 1999, there was a weekly rate of $1,032 for a 25-foot, C-class motor home. Low-season weekly rates for the same vehicles dropped as low as $804. Thirty-foot motor homes went for $1,268 in high season, $997 in low season. Some campgrounds limit the size of RVs that they allow in. When making reservations at a campground, make sure that your RV meets its regulations.

BY TRAIN

Amtrak (☎ **800/872-7245** or 520/774-8679) regularly stops in downtown Flagstaff, where lodging, rental cars, and connecting bus service are available. Although there is no service from Phoenix, Las Vegas, or Salt Lake City to Flagstaff, you can take the train from Albuquerque to Flagstaff for $53 to $96 one way. If you're coming from the other direction, the one-way fare from Los Angeles to Flagstaff ranges from $56 to $102. Amtrak also serves Williams, where connecting bus and rail service (on the historic Grand Canyon Railway) are available. Cost is about $2 more than service to Flagstaff.

BY BUS

Daily bus service between the North and South rims is available from May 15 through October 15 on the **Trans-Canyon Shuttle** (☎ **520/638-2820**). The fare is $60 one way, $100 round-trip.

5 Learning Vacations & Special Programs

The Grand Canyon Field Institute, a nonprofit organization co-sponsored by the Grand Canyon Association and Grand Canyon National Park, lets you experience the canyon with those who understand it best. Every year it schedules dozens of backpacking trips and outings ranging in length from 2 to 9 days. Some explore broad subjects such as ecology; others hone narrow skills such as orienteering or drawing. All are guided by experts on the topics covered. Because the courses vary greatly, the Field Institute assigns a difficulty level to each and attempts to ensure that participants find ones suited to their skill levels and interests. If you love the canyon, there's no better way to pass a few days. To contact the Field Institute you can call ☎ **520/638-2485;** write to P.O. Box 399, Grand

Grand Canyon Driving Times & Distances

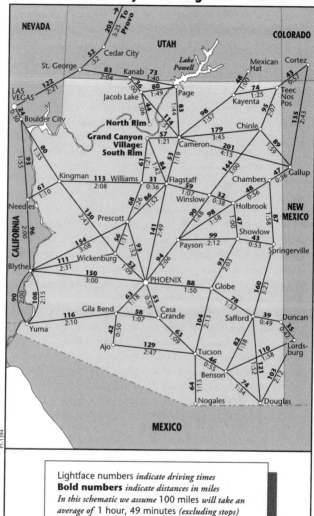

Lightface numbers *indicate driving times*
Bold numbers *indicate distances in miles*
In this schematic we assume 100 miles *will take an average of* 1 hour, 49 minutes *(excluding stops) at an average speed of 55 miles per hour*

P1-1394

23

Canyon, AZ 86023; or check out its Web site at **www.thecanyon.com/fieldinstitute**.

6 Tips for Travelers with Disabilities

The steep, rocky trails below the rim pose problems for travelers with disabilities. People with limited vision or mobility may be able to walk the Bright Angel or North Kaibab trails, which are the least rocky in the canyon. If you need to take a service dog on trails below the South Rim, check in with the ranger office at the corner of Center Road and Village Loop Road. On the North Rim, check in at the Backcountry Office.

On the rims themselves, many attractions are accessible to everyone. On the **South Rim,** the East Rim Drive is an excellent activity. Four of its overlooks—Yaki Point, Grandview, Moran Point, and Desert View—are wheelchair accessible, as are Tusayan Museum and Ruin. At Desert View, the bookstore and grocery are accessible, but no designated seating is available in the snack bar. Along this drive, rest rooms for the mobility impaired can be found at Tusayan Museum, Desert View (just east of Babbitt's General Store), and Desert View Campground.

The **West Rim Drive** poses more problems. For starters, most of the shuttles serving it are not accessible. Advance reservations are required for accessible shuttle service (☎ **520/638-0806**). It's easier for people in wheelchairs to drive themselves. The drive is closed to private cars when the shuttles are running, but people with disabilities can obtain permits for their vehicles at the visitor center. On the drive itself, Hopi Point, Pima Point, and Powell Memorial are all wheelchair accessible. The road also affords a number of nice "windshield views" of the canyon, from pull-outs where one need not leave the car. The gift shop at Hermit's Rest is accessible and worth a visit. It also houses wheelchair-accessible rest rooms.

Despite having many historic buildings, most of **Grand Canyon Village** is wheelchair accessible. The notable exceptions are Kolb Studio, Lookout Studio, and Verkamp's. Hopi House is accessible through a 29-inch-wide door on the canyon side of the building. Also, some hallways in Yavapai Lodge are too narrow for wheelchairs. Wheelchair-accessible rest rooms are found at the visitor center, Babbitt's General Store, Yavapai Observation Station, the El Tovar Hotel, Bright Angel Lodge, Mather Campground, and Maswik Lodge. Mather Campground has six sites for people with disabilities.

Those who have difficulty walking can usually negotiate the rim trail between Bright Angel Lodge and Yavapai Point (except when icy). This paved stretch has no grades exceeding 1:8.

On the **North Rim,** the gas station and grocery pose problems for people in wheelchairs, but most other buildings are wheelchair accessible. The two most popular North Rim overlooks—Point Imperial and Cape Royal—are each accessible, although neither has a designated parking space. Other wheelchair-friendly sites include The Walhalla Ruins, which are reached by a level gravel path; the east patio of Grand Canyon Lodge, which is accessible via both a lift and a ramp; and the North Rim Campground, which has two accessible sites. Wheelchair-accessible rest rooms are located at the Backcountry Office, Grand Canyon Lodge (assistance may be required), the North Rim Campground, and behind the visitor center.

The canyon's mule-trip concessionaires accommodate people with certain disabilities, as do many river companies. Also, **Fred Harvey** (☎ **303/297-2757** or 520/638-2631) can sometimes arrange for buses with lifts for its bus tours if it's informed in advance. For details about the accessibility of park buildings and facilities, pick up the park's free *Accessibility Guide* at the park's visitor centers.

As for raft companies, **Western River Expeditions** (☎ **800/453-7450**), **Arizona Raft Adventures** (☎ **800/786-RAFT**), **Grand Canyon Expeditions** (☎ **800/544-2691**), and **Canyon Explorations, Inc.** (☎ **800/654-0723**) are all good choices for people with disabilities.

7 Tips for Travelers with Pets

Hot weather and crowds make the canyon a bad place for pets. If you do bring your dog to the South Rim, you can take it on a leash on rim trails inside the park's developed areas, but not in the backcountry, below the rim, on buses, or inside public buildings. Rather than leave your dog in the car, use the **South Rim Kennel** (☎ **520/638-0534**), which is in Grand Canyon Village, near Maswik Lodge. Open daily 7:30am to 5pm, it will care for your pet during the day and overnight. Cost for day care is $9 for dogs, $6 for cats. Overnights cost $12.50 for dogs over 50 pounds, $10 for dogs under 50 pounds, and $7 for cats. Payment is by cash only. Be sure to call ahead for reservations, as this kennel frequently sells out. Upon arriving, you'll be asked to show proof that your pet's shots are up to date. There's no kennel on the North Rim, and the Park

Service discourages people from bringing pets there. On the North Rim, the only trail open to pets is the bridle path linking the lodge with the trailhead for the North Kaibab Trail.

8 Tips for Travelers with Children

The combination of heat, rough terrain, excitement, and crowds at the Grand Canyon can often leave children exhausted. Whether hiking or driving, take care not to push your children too hard. As you travel, make sure your kids (and you) get enough water and are protected from the sun.

The park's **Junior Ranger** program can help engage your kids during your stay. Pick up a Junior Ranger guide at these locations: South Rim Visitor Center, Yavapai Observation Station, Desert View Information Center, Tusayan Museum, or the North Rim visitor center. The guide outlines steps to become a Junior Ranger. These include attending a walk or talk by a ranger, completing the educational games and puzzles in the guide, and picking up litter or recyclables inside the park (or simply listing reasons for protecting the area). The activities are tailored to three age groups, together spanning ages 4 to 14. After completing the steps, your youngster will receive a certificate and be eligible to purchase (for $1.50) a Junior Ranger patch.

During summer the park offers additional programs aimed at children, including daily nature walks from the South Rim Visitor Center. For a complete listing of kids activities, consult the park's free newspaper, *The Guide*.

9 Protecting Your Health & Safety

While most visitors can enjoy a trip to the canyon without mishap, accidents can occur. Below is a list of guidelines to help make your trip as safe as possible.

- **Choose reasonable destinations for day hikes.** Although most park visitors quickly recognize the danger of falling into the canyon, they don't always perceive the danger of walking into it. Every year, the canyon's backcountry rangers respond to hundreds of emergency calls, most of them on the corridor trails (Bright Angel, and North and South Kaibab). Day hikers are lured deep into the canyon by the ease of the descent, the sight of other hikers continuing downward, and (sometimes) the goal of reaching the river. As they drop into the canyon's hotter climes in late morning, temperatures climb doubly fast. By the time they turn around, it's already too late. They are hot, fatigued, and literally in "too deep." When hiking in the canyon, particularly during the summer months, keep in mind that this is the wrong place to test your limits—even on the corridor trails. Pick a reasonable destination and, as the Park Service signs say, "Never attempt to hike to the river and back in a day."

- **Don't hike at midday during hot weather.** When hiking at temperatures over 100°F, you'll sweat fluids faster than your body can absorb them, no matter how much you drink. For this reason, hiking in extreme heat is inherently dangerous.

- **Drink and eat regularly.** During a full day of hiking, plan to drink more than a gallon of fluids—on the hottest days, make it more than two. Consume both water and electrolyte-replacement drinks such as Gatorade. Also, remember that eating carbohydrate-rich, salty foods is as important as drinking. If you consume large amounts of water without food, you can quickly develop an electrolyte imbalance, which can result in unconsciousness or even death.

- **Wear sunscreen and protective clothing.** Even during winter, the Arizona sun can singe unsuspecting tourists. To protect your skin and cool your body, wear long-sleeved white shirts, wide-brimmed hats, sunglasses, and high-SPF sunscreen.

- **Move away from rim overlooks during thunderstorms.** On the rim, you may be the highest point—and best lightning rod—for miles around.

- **Exercise caution on the rims.** Every year a few people fall to their death in the canyon. To minimize risk, don't blaze trails along the rim, where loose rock makes footing precarious. Use caution when taking photographs and when looking through the viewfinder of your camcorder. Be prepared for gusts of wind, and keep an eye on your children.

- **Yield to mules when hiking.** If you encounter mules, step off the trail on the uphill side and wait for instructions from the wranglers. This protects both you and the riders.

3

Exploring the Grand Canyon

At the edge of the Grand Canyon, even the breezes seem to take a deep breath. Sometimes the best thing to do at the canyon is to take one yourself. Find a quiet place on the rim or off a trail and sit for an hour or so on a nicely contoured rock. Feel the warm air rise, watch the shadows and light play across the monuments, and listen to the timeless hush. No matter how fast you drive, and no matter how many angles you see the canyon from, you'll never completely "do" the canyon. So relax.

1 Essentials

ACCESS/ENTRY POINTS

The park has three gated entrances—two on the **South Rim** and one on the **North Rim.** The one that's most convenient to travelers from Flagstaff, Williams, and Phoenix is the park's **South Entrance Gate,** 1 mile north of Tusayan on Highway 64. Traffic often backs up here during peak hours in high season. Many travelers from Flagstaff, as well as those from points east, prefer entering the South Rim area through its **East Entrance Gate,** near Desert View, 28.5 miles west of Cameron, Arizona, on Highway 64. From Flagstaff, the drive to the East Entrance Gate is about 8 miles longer than to the South Entrance.

The gate to the **North Rim** (separated from the South Rim by 210 highway miles) isn't convenient to anywhere, except perhaps the small store, motel, and gas station at Jacob Lake, Arizona, 30 miles north on Highway 67. (The North Rim is 14 miles south of the gate.) The closest real town is **Kanab, Utah,** on Highway 89A, 78 miles to the north on Highway 89A. Parts of the park can also be accessed via dirt Forest Service roads.

VISITOR CENTERS & INFORMATION

SOUTH RIM VISITOR CENTER For a park this size, this visitor center, located in Grand Canyon village, is hardly impressive. It's small, crowded, and offers little in the way of interpretation. One redeeming point is the slide show, which airs in the auditorium here

Exploring the Park Without a Car

CASSI Tours (☎ **520/638-0871** or 520/638-0821) offers a regular year-round service linking five Tusayan stops to Grand Canyon Village. To avoid parking problems inside the park, leave your car at **Grand Canyon National Park Airport** (or at your hotel) in Tusayan and take the shuttle into the park. Other Tusayan stops include **Best Western Grand Canyon Squire Inn, IMAX Theater, Babbitt's Village Store,** and **Moqui Lodge.** The adult one-way fare is $4 (16 and under free). The shuttle schedule is posted at each stop.

The best time to be car-less inside the park is from mid-March to mid-October, when the park's free shuttle service is running. Departing regularly from 7:30am to sunset, the shuttle buses serve **Grand Canyon Village, Yavapai** and **Yaki points,** and the **West Rim Drive.** When the shuttles are operating, most cars are banned from the West Rim Drive and Yaki Point. (Cars carrying people with disabilities are allowed, but the drivers will need to obtain a permit at the park's visitor center.) You can board a shuttle at any of the marked stops, including the West Rim Interchange bus stop, just west of the Bright Angel Lodge; at the Maswik Transportation Center; or near Yavapai Lodge. Consult the park's free publication, *The Guide,* for detailed information on shuttle stops and schedules.

When the shuttles aren't running, you may need to take advantage of **Fred Harvey's 24-hour taxi service** (☎ **520/638-2631**). These taxis do not have meters, and their fares vary according to distance and the number of passengers. For example, a trip between destinations on the loop drive through Grand Canyon Village costs $4 for the first person, $1 for each additional person; a trip from Grand Canyon Village to the South Kaibab Trailhead (at Yaki Point) runs $8 for the first passenger, $3 for each additional one.

every 30 minutes and features a number of scenic photos of the canyon. A few rangers staff a very busy information desk, and many ranger activities originate here. In fall 2000, this center is scheduled to be replaced by a large new information plaza at Mather Point.

While waiting to attend the slide show, be sure to wander through the center's courtyard, home to a number of historic river-running boats. Unfortunately, parking is scarce. If you can't find a space here, try across the street in the parking lot between the General Store and

Yavapai Lodge. If *that* lot seems full, check the "hidden" spaces on the southeast side of the store.

YAVAPAI OBSERVATION STATION   Roughly a mile east of the South Rim Visitor Center, this station on Yavapai Point has an observation room where you can identify many of the monuments in the central canyon. Rangers lead interpretive programs. (For more information, see the information on the East Rim Drive later in this chapter.)

DESERT VIEW CONTACT STATION   Staffed by volunteers, this small station 26 miles east of Grand Canyon Village sells books and has information on the canyon. This station is just inside the park's East Entrance, 28.5 miles west of Cameron on Highway 64.

NORTH RIM VISITOR CENTER   This visitor center near Grand Canyon Lodge has a small bookstore and information desk.

FEES

Admission to Grand Canyon National Park costs $20 per private vehicle and $10 for those on foot or bicycle. The receipt is good for a week and includes both rims.

SPECIAL DISCOUNTS & PASSES

A number of special passes are available at the park's entrance stations. **Golden Eagle Passports** entitle holders to unlimited use of all National Park Service sites, including Grand Canyon, for 1 year from the date they make this $50 purchase. A **Grand Canyon Passport** ($40) entitles the holder to free admission to Grand Canyon for 1 calendar year. For $10, U.S. residents aged 62 and older can purchase a **Golden Age Passport,** which admits the holder, free of charge, for life at all National Park Service sites. Another card, the **Golden Access Passport,** entitles U.S. residents with permanent mental or physical disabilities to the same privileges afforded by the Golden Age Passport. This card is free, but the applicant must apply in person at the visitor center (not available at the entrance gate).

CAMPING FEES

Camping at **Mather Campground,** the largest on the South Rim, costs $12 per site from September to May and $15 per site from June to August. **Desert View Campground,** open from mid-May to mid-October, costs $10 per site. And the **North Rim Campground,** also open from mid-May to mid-October, costs $15 per site. At all three campgrounds, no more than two vehicles and six people can share a site. **Trailer Village,** an RV park on the South

Especially for Kids

Anyone who's ever watched *The Brady Bunch* knows that the Grand Canyon is a great place for a family vacation. Just make sure that your kids don't wander off too far from the campsite. The following is list of activities that kids will especially enjoy.

- **Involve your kids in the Junior Ranger program.** Pick up a free Junior Ranger newspaper at the visitor center. Let your children complete the fun, educational activities in the paper, then take it back to the visitor center, where they'll be certified as Junior Rangers.

- **Look for deer.** At sunset, take a quiet walk in the grass along the train tracks by Grand Canyon Village, or watch a meadow along the entrance road on the North Rim. See how many deer you can count. But please don't feed them.

- **Hike a rim trail.** If your kids are too small to make the steep descent into the canyon, take them walking on a rim trail. This gets them away from the car and into less developed areas. The West Rim Trail is the best choice on the **South Rim,** though it does have a number of sections that would be dangerous for small children. (Be cautious near the edges.) On the **North Rim,** the Transept or Cliff Springs trails are both fine for kids.

- **Attend a Ranger program especially for kids.** These programs, held daily during summer on the South Rim, are open to everyone, but they're simple enough for children. Meeting times are listed in the park's free newspaper, *The Guide.*

- **Go birding.** During daytime, sit on the rim and watch raptors and ravens ride the thermals. See if you can identify eagles, hawks, or vultures. Watch swifts and swallows dart around the rim. At dusk, see who can spot the first bat. Use chapter 7, "A Nature Guide to Grand Canyon National Park," to help identify many of the different animals and plants.

- **Watch the wranglers prepare the mules for the trip into the canyon every morning.** At 8am daily (9am in winter), the wranglers bring the mules to the corral on the South Rim just west of Bright Angel Lodge. While the mules entertain the kids, the wranglers will entertain the adults with their humorous lecture on mule-ride protocol.

- When the canyon fails to entertain your young ones, show it to them on video at the **IMAX Theater** outside the park in Tusayan. The footage on the 82-foot-high screen is sure to impress the young ones.

Rim, charges $20 per hookup. For more information, see chapter 5.

PARK RULES & REGULATIONS

The following list includes a set of rules established to protect both the park and its visitors:

- Bicycles must stay on roads. That means no mountain biking on the trails.
- It's illegal to remove any resources from the park. This can be anything from flowers to pot shards. Even seemingly useless articles such as bits of metal from the canyon's old mining operations have historical value to the park's users and are protected by law.
- Dogs must be leashed at all times. They're allowed on rim trails in developed areas of the park, but are banned from trails below the rim, buses, or in park lodging. The only exceptions are certified service dogs.
- Fires are strictly prohibited except at North Rim, Desert View, and Mather campgrounds. In the backcountry, you can use a small camp stove for cooking.
- Weapons including guns, bows and arrows, crossbows, slingshots, and air pistols are all prohibited, as are fireworks. If, by chance, you have a hang glider and are considering jumping into the canyon, forget it. It's illegal, and you'll be fined.
- An Arizona State Fishing Permit is required for fishing. (For more information, see chapter 4.)

FAST FACTS: The Grand Canyon

ATM The lone ATM in the park is on the South Rim at Bank One, adjacent to the General Store and across the road from the visitor center.

Fuel There is only one gas station inside the park on the South Rim. **Desert View Chevron,** on Highway 64, 25 miles east of Grand Canyon Village, is open daily 7am to 7pm from late April to September. If you're entering from the park from the south and you're running low on fuel, make sure to gas up in **Tusayan,** 1 mile south of the park's south entrance. On the North Rim, the **Chevron Service Station** is open daily 8am to 5pm (7am to 7pm in summer), also seasonally. You can also get gas at the general store across from Kaibab Lodge, 18 miles north of the North Rim on Highway 67.

Garages   A garage with 24-hour emergency towing service (☎ **520/638-2631**) currently operates inside the park on the South Rim, though it may be removed in the near future. The garage itself is open from 8am to noon and 1pm to 5pm daily. The nearest automotive service to the North Rim is at **Judd Auto** (☎ **520/643-7107**) in Fredonia. Judd Auto has 24-hour towing and a reputation for being honest.

Health Services   On either rim, dial ☎ **911** (or 9911 from hotel rooms) for medical emergencies. On the South Rim, a **health clinic** (☎ **520/638-2551**) and **pharmacy** (☎ **520/638-2460**) are located on Clinic Road, off Center Road between Grand Canyon Village and the South Rim entrance road. The clinic is open Monday to Friday 8am to 5:30pm, Saturday 9 am to noon. After-hours emergency service is available. Pharmacy hours are Monday to Friday 8:30am to 12:30pm and 1:30 to 5:30pm, Saturday 9am to noon. On the **North Rim,** a small **walk-in clinic** (☎ **520/638-2611,** ext. 222) operates out of a cabin near Grand Canyon Lodge. Check at the lodge or visitor center for its hours of operation.

Laundry   Laundromats can be found inside the park on both rims. Open 6am to 11pm daily, the **South Rim's Laundromat** is in the Camper Services building near Mather Campground. Open 7am to 9pm daily, the **North Rim's Laundromat** is near the North Rim Campground.

Lost & Found   For items lost in or near the park's South Rim lodges, call ☎ **520/638-2631,** ext. 6503. For those lost elsewhere on the South Rim, call ☎ **520/638-7798** Tuesday to Friday 8am to 5pm. Found items can be returned at the South Rim Visitor Center or Yavapai Information Station. On the North Rim, report lost and found items in person at the visitor center.

Outfitters   On the South Rim, **The General Store** (☎ **520/ 638-2262,** open daily 8am to 8pm in summer, 9am to 7pm in winter) in Grand Canyon Village rents and sells camping and backpacking equipment. There is no equipment for rent on the North Rim, but the **North Rim General Store** (☎ **520/638-2611,** ext. 270), sells a very limited supply of gear.

Police   For emergencies dial ☎ **911** (9911 from motel rooms).

Post Offices   There are post offices on both rims. On the **South Rim,** you'll find the main post office (☎ **520/638-2512**) next to The General Store, across the road from the visitor center.

Window hours are Monday to Friday 9am to 4:30pm and Saturday 11am to 3pm. On the **North Rim,** a tiny post office at Grand Canyon Lodge is open Monday to Friday 8 to 11am and 11:30am to 4pm and Saturday 8am to 2pm.

Supplies   There are three grocery stores inside the park. The largest, **The General Store** (☎ 520/638-2262), is in Grand Canyon Village across the street from the visitor center (on the South Rim). Its hours are usually 8am to 8pm in summer, 9am to 7pm the rest of the year. **Desert View Store** (☎ 520/638-2393), at Desert View (25 miles east of Grand Canyon Village on Highway 64), is open daily 8am to 7pm in summer, 9 am to 5pm the rest of the year. On the North Rim, the only provisions are at the **North Rim General Store** (☎ 520/638-2611, ext. 270), adjacent to North Rim Campground. It's usually open daily 8am to 8pm.

Weather Updates   Recorded weather information, updated every morning, is available by calling ☎ **520/638-7888.** Forecasts are also posted at the main visitor centers.

2   How to See the Park in Several Days

IF YOU HAVE 1 OR 2 DAYS

Remember, the rims are 210 highway miles apart.

ON THE SOUTH RIM   After stopping at the visitor center, hike a short distance down the **Bright Angel** in the morning (If the weather is hot or if your condition is not top-notch, a rim trail may be preferable.) During midday, attend a ranger presentation, for which times and locations are posted at the visitor centers. Later in the day, go on a scenic drive. Your best choice on the first day would be the **East Rim Drive,** which is open to cars year-round and has expansive views of the central and northeastern canyon. Catch the sunset at **Lipan Point.**

The next morning, watch the sun as it rises back up at **Desert View** on the South Rim. Later in the morning, visitors should drive or take the shuttle on the **West Rim Drive.** From any of the stops on the drive, you can walk a short distance along the **West Rim Trail** to quiet spots where you can rest, snack, and take time to savor the canyon. Strong hikers should consider a short walk down the **Hermit Trail,** near Hermit's Rest, at the terminus of the West Rim Drive. (This trail can be very hot in late afternoon.)

ON THE NORTH RIM   In the morning after checking in at the visitor center, hike down the beginning part of **North Kaibab.** In

How Grand Is the Grand Canyon?

Size: 1,904 square miles (more than 1¹/₂ times the size of Rhode Island)

Length of River in Canyon: 277 miles

Vertical Drop of River in Canyon: 2,215 feet

Average Width of Canyon: 10 miles

Widest Point: 18 miles

Narrowest Point: 600 feet (in Marble Canyon)

Average Depth: 1 mile

Lowest Point: 1,200 feet (at Lake Mead)

Highest Point on South Rim: 7,400 feet

Highest Point on North Rim: 8,801 feet

Colorado River Facts (as it flows through the canyon)

Length: 277 miles

Average Width: 300 feet

Average Depth: 40 feet

Average Gradient: 8 feet per mile

the afternoon, drive down the **Cape Royal Road.** To complete your scenic drive, watch the sunset from **Cape Royal.**

For those willing to drive before dawn, head to **Point Imperial** before dawn the next day to watch the sun rise. Then head for one of the rim trails—**the Transept Trail, the Uncle Jim Trail** (to Uncle Jim Point), or, my favorite, **the Widforss Trail** (to Widforss Point).

IF YOU HAVE 3 OR 4 DAYS

With 3 or 4 days at the canyon, three day hikes may be in order.

ON THE SOUTH RIM   Choose from the Bright Angel, South Kaibab, Grandview, Hermit, and West Rim trails.

ON THE NORTH RIM   Try the North Kaibab Trail and two rim trails. There are fewer diversions on the North Rim, so be prepared for deep relaxation on the third and fourth days.

ON BOTH RIMS   Consider riding a mule into the canyon, accompanying a ranger on a guided walk, or sitting and reading on the porch of one of the canyon's lodges.

3 Driving Tours

The South Rim is easily accessible by car off Highway 64, which connects Williams and Cameron. Inside the park's southern gates, the South Entrance Road diverges from Highway 64 and leads to **Grand Canyon Village.** A National Historic District, the village feels like a small town, with hotels, restaurants, shops, and a train depot. The loop road can be confusing, so take your time, watch carefully for signs, and use the village map included in the park newspaper, *The Guide.*

Scenic drives hug the canyon rim on either side of the village. **The West Rim Drive** heads west for 8 miles to its terminus at Hermit's Rest. **The East Rim Drive** covers 25 miles between Grand Canyon Village and the Desert View overlook on the eastern edge of the park. Two of the 25 miles are on the park's entrance road, 23 are on Highway 64. The two scenic drives have numerous pull-offs that open onto the canyon, some with views of the river. These drives, and walks around Grand Canyon Village, are popular with visitors.

Some 210 highway miles and 4 hours of driving separate the North Rim from the South Rim. On the way, Highway 89A crosses the Colorado River near the canyon's northeastern tip, where the river begins cutting down into the rocks of the Marble Platform and the Grand Canyon begins. As you drive west from Lee's Ferry, you'll see where rocks make a single fold along a fault line and rise more than 4,000 vertical feet from the Marble Platform to the level of the Kaibab Plateau—the canyon's North Rim.

The North Rim is more than 4,000 feet higher than the Marble Platform and 1,000 feet above the busier South Rim. Highway 67 travels south 44 miles from Highway 89A at Jacob Lake to where it dead-ends at Bright Angel Point, site of the Grand Canyon Lodge. A 23-mile-long paved scenic drive travels from Highway 67 southeast to the tip of the Walhalla Plateau, a peninsula east of Bright Angel Point. This drive, which ends at Cape Royal, has overlooks of the eastern Grand Canyon. On this curvy road, signs appear quickly. Pay attention, as there are few places to turn around. The 3-mile-long road to Point Imperial, the highest point on the North Rim, forks to the northeast off this road.

The rims at the **western end of the canyon** are lower, rockier, and more remote than those in the central canyon. Only a few roads cross these lands. The canyon ends abruptly at the Grand Wash cliffs at the eastern end of Lake Mead. To drive from rim to rim around

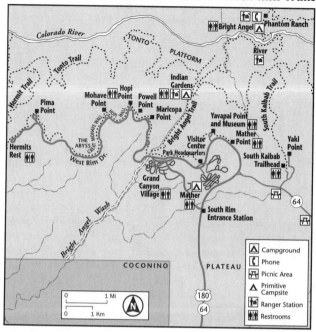

the western end of the canyon, you'd have to cross the Colorado River at the Hoover Dam, near Las Vegas.

WEST RIM DRIVE

Highlights: Closed to private cars (except for those carrying people with physical disabilities) during high season, the overlooks are more quiet than those on the East Rim drive and afford excellent river views.

Drawbacks: Occasional long waits for buses.

The 8-mile-long road from Grand Canyon Village to Hermit's Rest is open to private cars when the shuttles aren't running. (The shuttles run from mid-March through mid-October.) Allow a half day for this drive.

Stop #1: Trailview 1 & 2. These viewpoints en route to Maricopa Point are a great place to look back at Grand Canyon Village. Below the village, the switchbacks of the Bright Angel Trail descend along a natural break in the cliffs. This break was created by the

Bright Angel Fault, one of many fault lines that crisscross the main canyon.

Looking north across the canyon, you can see down the fault all the way to the North Rim. Runoff seeps into the cracks along fault lines, beginning the process by which side canyons such as these are formed. Below, Indian Garden, where Havasupai Indians farmed for generations, is identifiable by the lush vegetation that grows around the spring there. Past Indian Garden a trail travels straight out to the edge of the Tonto platform, where it dead-ends. This is not the Bright Angel Trail, which descends another side canyon to reach the Inner Gorge, but a spur known as the Plateau Point Trail. From Plateau Point, hikers and people on mule trips can gaze 1,300 feet down to the river.

Stop #2: Maricopa Point. The Orphan Mine southwest of this point produced some of the richest uranium ore anywhere during the 1950s. Below and to the west, you can see some of the metal framework of the tramway that moved ore to the rim from 1956 to 1959. Later, a 1,500-foot-high elevator replaced the tramway. A metal headframe from that elevator remains visible on the rim, directly above the old shaft. Mining continued here, sometimes at night, through 1966.

Stop #3: Powell Memorial. Here you'll find a large memorial to John Wesley Powell, the one-armed Civil War veteran who is widely believed to have been the first person to float through the canyon. Funded in part by the Smithsonian Institute, Powell first drifted into the canyon on August 5, 1869. He and his crew of eight portaged around rapids when the walls were gradual enough to allow it. In parts of the canyon's Inner Gorge, however, the walls became too steep to climb, and the men were forced to float blindly, in wooden boats, through some of the world's most dangerous waters.

Parts of the Inner Gorge are visible below this point, but only a tiny stretch of the river can be seen. Where Powell saw those dark-colored, steep rocks lining the water, he thought not of their beauty but of the peril they represented. He called the gorge "our granite prison" and described his men "ever watching, ever peering ahead, for the narrow canyon is winding and the river is closed in . . . and what there may be below, we know not."

When the men stopped above what appeared to be another set of dangerous rapids after 3 weeks in the canyon, three of them left the expedition by walking out into what is now known as Separation Canyon, but were never seen again. The irony here was that the expedition had already passed most of the worst rapids. The remaining crew negotiated the last white water and soon arrived at a small Mormon outpost bearing the first records of the inner canyon's rocks, geography, and life-forms. Powell later fleshed out these records and notes in a lengthy diary, "The Exploration of the Colorado River and its Canyons."

✪ **Stop #4: Hopi Point.** Because it projects far into the canyon, the tip of Hopi Point is the best place on the West Rim Drive to watch the sunset. As the sun drops, its light will play across four of the canyon's loveliest temples. The flat mesa almost due north of the point is Shiva Temple. The temple southwest of it is Osiris; the one southeast of it is Isis. East of Isis is Buddha Temple.

Named for a destructive yet popular Hindu god, Shiva Temple was the site of a much ballyhooed 1937 mission by a team of scientists from the American Museum of Natural History. Believing that the canyon isolated the forest atop Shiva Temple the same way oceans isolated the Galapagos Islands, the team set out to find species that had evolved differently from those on the rim. The East Coast press drummed up sensationalistic stories about the trip, even going so far as to hail it as a search for living dinosaurs. Alas, the search didn't turn up any new species, let alone dinosaurs. Rather, the team learned that cliffs and desert didn't bar the movements of most Grand Canyon species. (The Colorado River poses a more significant barrier.) The most noteworthy discovery: an empty Kodak film box and soup cans deliberately left behind by canyon local Emery Kolb, who was upset when the expedition declined his offer to help. Kolb easily made the first ascent, proving that the cliffs were hardly a barrier.

Stop #5: Mohave Point. This is a great place to observe some of the Colorado River's most furious rapids. Farthest downstream (to your left) is Hermit Rapids. Above it, you can make out the top of the dangerous Granite Rapids, one of the steepest navigable rapids in the world. Just above Granite Rapids, the bottom of Salt Creek Rapids is visible. As you look at Hermit Creek Canyon and the rapids below it, you can easily visualize how flash floods washed rocks from the side canyon into the Colorado River, forming the natural dam that creates the rapids.

Straight below Mohave Point, a red landform resembles an alligator's back and head. Sure enough, it's called The Alligator.

Stop #6: The Abyss. The walls in this side canyon steeply fall 2,600 feet to the base of the Redwall Limestone. The best way to experience the steepness is to follow the rim trail a few hundred yards west of the overlook, where the cliffs are most sheer.

Stop #7: Pima Point. Three thousand feet below Pima Point you can see some of the foundations and walls from the old Hermit Camp, a tourist destination built in 1912 by the Santa Fe Railroad. Situated alongside Hermit Creek, the camp featured heavy-duty tents, each with stoves, Indian rugs, and windows. An aerial tramway connected this point with the camp below. Used to lower supplies, it made the 3,000-foot descent in roughly a half hour.

To get to Hermit Camp, tourists traveled 51 miles by train from Williams to Grand Canyon Village, 9 miles by stagecoach from the village to the top of the Hermit Trail trailhead, and 8 miles by mule to the camp. After the Park Service wrested control of the Bright Angel Trail from Ralph Cameron in the 1920s, Phantom Ranch became a more popular tourist destination, and Hermit Camp closed its doors in 1930.

The Hermit Trail, however, remains popular. North of the overlook, below the fin of rock known as Cope Butte, you can see it zig-zagging down the blue-green Bright Angel Shale.

✪ **Stop #8: Hermit's Rest.** Before descending to Hermit Camp, tourists rested at this Mary Colter–designed building, built in 1914. Here, Colter celebrated the "hermit" theme, making the building look as if an isolated mountain man had constructed it. It resembles a crude rock shelter, with stones heaped highest around the chimney. A large fireplace dominates the interior. Colter covered the ceiling above it with soot, so that the room had the look of a cave warmed by fire—much like the nearby Dripping Springs overhang where "The Hermit of Hermit Canyon," Louis Boucher, once passed time. Colter had a knack for finding the perfect details. Note the anthropomorphic rock above the fireplace, the candelabras, and the hanging lanterns. Some of the original hand-carved furniture are still used.

A snack bar sells sweets, chips, and soda. (Don't count on getting a meal.) Two heavily used rest rooms are behind the main building. Before leaving for good, take one last look at the canyon. The three-pronged temple across the canyon to the north is the Tower of Ra, named for the always-victorious Egyptian sun god. Seen from above, each prong points to a different set of rapids: the near arm to Hermit Creek, the middle to Boucher, and the far one to Crystal— waters that have triumphed over more than a few river guides.

○ EAST RIM DRIVE

Highlights: Spectacular views of both the central and northeastern canyon.

Drawbacks: Packed parking lots in summer.

The drive begins at Yavapai Point, about a mile east of Grand Canyon Village. It travels 2 miles on the South Entrance Road, which links Tusayan and Grand Canyon Village. The remaining 23 miles are on the stretch of Highway 64 linking the South Entrance Road and the Desert View overlook, near the park's east entrance. The Yavapai and Mather overlooks are on the South Entrance Road; the remaining seven stops are accessible from Highway 64. In all, eight pull-offs lead to overlooks with views of the central and northeastern canyon and the Colorado River, and one leads to historic Tusayan Museum and Ruin. Past Desert View, the scenic drive ends, but the highway continues for another 28 miles to Cameron, Arizona, on the Navajo Indian Reservation. Allow 4 hours for the East Rim Drive—one more than for the West Rim Drive.

Stop #1: Yavapai Observation Station. Yavapai Point features some of the most expansive views both up and down the canyon. A historic observation station here has huge plate glass windows overlooking the central canyon, along with interpretive panels identifying virtually all the major landmarks.

From here you can spot at least four hiking trails. To the west, the Bright Angel trail can be seen descending to the lush Indian Garden area. The straight white line leaving from this general area and eventually dead-ending, is the Plateau Point Trail. Directly below the overlook and to the north, the Tonto Trail wends its way across the blue-green Tonto Platform. Across the Colorado River, find the verdant area at the mouth of Bright Angel Canyon. The North Kaibab Trail passes through this area yards before ending at the river, just below Phantom Ranch. Looking just east of Bright Angel Canyon, you may also be able to make out a thread of the Clear Creek Trail just above the Tapeats Sandstone, on the Tonto Platform. Turning to face east, find the saddle just south of O'Neill Butte. The South Kaibab Trail crosses this saddle.

You may have noticed that some trails are wider than the others. This is no optical illusion. Rather, the Bright Angel and North and South Kaibab Trails are corridor trails, which means that they're wide, regularly maintained, and heavily traveled. The Tonto and Clear Creek trails, meanwhile, are narrow, rarely maintained wilderness trails, which see far less foot traffic than the corridor trails. (The Plateau Point Trail, while technically not a corridor trail, is trampled by mules, which makes it wide and dusty.)

Stop #2: Mather Point. If there's such a thing as a bad overlook, this is it. Visitors who see the canyon only once, seem to do it from here. Although it's against the law, tour buses often idle in the parking lot while the throngs they unload snap photos. People entering the park from the south generally catch their first glimpse of the canyon in this area. Many of them immediately steer off the highway, sometimes onto the dirt alongside the road, and rush to the overlook. It's a clamorous place, epitomizing the "industrial tourism" that the late author Edward Abbey so dreaded. Its one redeeming point is its panoramic vista, similar to the one at the Yavapai Observation Station.

Grand Canyon National Park, perhaps sensing that this was a natural stopping point (and already ruined), plans to finish construction on a large orientation center near this overlook in fall 2000. This plaza will be a hub for the new light-rail system and will replace the park's current visitor center. (Turn to "The Park Today," in chapter 1, for more information.)

Stop #3: Yaki Point. Accessible by car when the shuttles aren't running, this overlook is one of the best places to see some of the canyon's most notable monuments, including Vishnu Temple, Zoroaster Temple, and Wotan's Throne. As erosion and runoff cut side drainages into the land around the larger canyon, pinnacles such as these are sometimes isolated between the drainages. Eventually, these monuments will erode away altogether, as will more of the rims. The South Kaibab trailhead is located nearby.

Stop #4: Grandview Point. At 7,406 feet, this is one of the highest spots on the South Rim. In the 1890s, it was also one of its busiest. In 1890, one of the canyon's early prospectors, Pete Berry, filed a mining claim on a rich vein of copper on Horseshoe Mesa, visible to the north of the overlook. To remove ore from the mine, Berry built—and in some cases hung—a trail to it from Grandview Point. He erected cabins and a dining hall on the mesa, then, as visitors began coming, added a hotel a short distance away from Grandview Point. Built of ponderosa pine logs, the Grand View Hotel flourished in the prerailroad days. To reach the hotel, which for a brief period was considered the best lodging at the canyon, tourists took a grueling all-day stagecoach ride from Flagstaff.

In 1901, however, the Santa Fe Railroad linked Grand Canyon Village and Williams, putting an end, almost immediately, to the

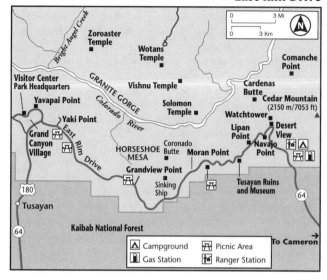

Flagstaff-to-Grandview stagecoach run. Once at Grand Canyon Village, few tourists wandered 11 miles east to Grandview Point, and the hotel went out of business in 1908. The mine fared no better. Plagued by high overhead, it shut down shortly after the price of copper crashed in 1907. Only a trace of the foundation remains of the Grand View Hotel, but the historic Grandview Trail is still used by thousands of hikers annually (see chapter 4 for details), and debris from the old mine camp still litters Horseshoe Mesa.

Stop #5: Moran Point. This point is named for landscape painter Thomas Moran, whose sketches and oil paintings introduced America to the beauty of the canyon in the years before landscape photography. After accompanying Maj. John Wesley Powell on a surveying expedition in 1873, Moran illustrated Powell's book, *The Exploration of the Colorado River and its Canyons.* Moran's painting, *The Grand Chasm of the Colorado,* later adorned one wall of the nation's capitol. These and other works helped lure some of the first tourists to the canyon in the 19th century.

Moran Point is the best place from which to view the tilting block of rock known as **The Sinking Ship.** Standing at the end of the point, look southwest at the rocks level with the rim. Looking a bit like a warship going down, the Sinking Ship can be seen beyond the horizontal layers of Coronado Butte (in the foreground). It's part of the Grandview Monocline, a place where rocks have bent in a single fold around a fault line. Looking down the drainage below Coronado Butte, you'll see the red splotches of Hakatai Shale that give Red Canyon its name.

The first white people to see the canyon probably saw it from somewhere on the rim between here and Desert View. In 1540, Spanish explorer Francisco Vásquez de Coronado was scouring the Southwest for the mythical Seven Cities of Cíbola, with its equally mythical fortune in gold. After hearing of a great river and settlements north of the Hopi pueblo of Tusayan, he sent a small force led by Garcia Lopez de Cardenas to explore the area. Hopi guides led Cardenas and his men, who began the journey in armor, to the South Rim between Moran Point and Desert View. Upon seeing the Colorado River, the Spaniards initially estimated it to be 6 feet wide. (It's closer to 200 in this area.) When Cardenas asked how to reach it, the Hopi, who had made pilgrimages to the bottom of the canyon for generations, professed not to know. For 3 days Cardenas's men tried unsuccessfully to descend to the river. In the process they learned what many canyon hikers would later discover: "What appeared to be easy from above was not so, but instead very hard and difficult." They gave up, and no white people returned to the canyon for 200 years.

✪ **Stop #6: Tusayan Ruin.** By studying the tree rings in the wood at these dwellings, archaeologists determined that parts of this 14-room stone-walled structure were built in 1185 by the Ancestral Pueblo People. Among the pueblos that have been excavated near Grand Canyon, Tusayan Ruin was the most recently occupied. By 1185 most of the Ancestral Puebloans had already left the canyon. For unknown reasons, however, the dwellers of this pueblo stayed on, despite a prolonged drought (also known from tree rings) and despite the nearest year-round water source being up to 7 miles away.

A self-guided tour takes you through this small pueblo, which includes the stone foundations of two kivas, living areas, and storage rooms, all connected in a U-shaped structure.

This dwelling, like many Ancestral Pueblo abodes in present-day northern Arizona, has a clear view of the San Francisco peaks, including Mt. Humphreys, which at 12,643 feet is the highest point in Arizona. These peaks formed when volcanoes boiled up through weak spots in the earth's crust between 1.8 million and 400,000 years ago. The descendants of the Puebloans, the modern Hopi, believe these peaks are home to the spirit beings known as Kachinas.

Built in 1932, **Tusayan Museum** celebrates the traditions of the area's indigenous people. Displays in this dimly lit historic building include traditional jewelry, attire, and tools, as well as historic photos. It's worth coming here just to see the 3,000-year-old split-twig figurines, made by members of a hunter-gatherer clan known as the **Desert Culture.** These mysterious figurines of deer or sheep were found under cairns (piles of stones) in caves inside the canyon.

Note: There are bathrooms at Tusayan Ruin.

✪ **Stop #7: Lipan Point.** With views far down the canyon to the west, Lipan Point is a supreme place to catch the sunset. It also overlooks the Colorado River where the river makes two sweeping curves. Between those curves, on the opposite bank, Unkar Creek has deposited a large alluvial fan. From A.D. 800 to 1150, the Ancestral Pueblo People grew beans and corn in this rich soil. Archaeologists have found many granaries and dwellings in the area—not to mention evidence of the use of astronomy. At least some of the Puebloans migrated to the rim during summer, to hunt the abundant game and farm there.

Stop #8: Navajo Point. Like Lipan Point, this one offers fine views of the Grand Canyon Supergroup, a formation of igneous and sedimentary Precambrian rocks that has eroded altogether in many other parts of the canyon. The long, thin streaks of maroon, gray, and black, which tilt at an angle of about 20 degrees, are layers of this formation. They're visible above the river, directly across the canyon. As you look at these rocks, note how the level, brown Tapeats Sandstone, which in other canyon locations sits directly atop the black Vishnu Formation, now rests atop the Supergroup—hundreds of feet above the schist. Where the Supergroup had not yet eroded away, the Tapeats Sandstone was often deposited atop it, protecting what remained. In scattered locations, the Supergroup rocks formed islands in the ancient Tapeats Sea, and no sandstone was deposited atop them.

✪ **Stop #9: Desert View.** Here you'll find the **Watchtower,** a 70-foot-high stone building designed by Mary Colter. Colter modeled it after towers found at ancient pueblos such as Mesa Verde and Hovenweep. To get an idea for the shape she wanted, she made a clay model of the building, atop an exact replica of the land at Desert View. Her model seems to have worked. Like Colter's other buildings, this one seems to emerge from the earth, the rough stones at its base blending seamlessly with the rim rock.

The Watchtower is connected to a circular observation room fashioned after a Hopi kiva—a ceremonial room that often adjoined the real pueblo towers. To climb the Watchtower, you'll first have to pass through this room, currently being used as a gift shop. Admission to the Watchtower costs 25¢. Inside, narrow stairways along the walls connect floors that are open in the middle. The walls are decorated with traditional Native American art. Some of the finest work is by Hopi artist Fred Kabotie, whose depiction of the Snake Legend, the story of the first person to have floated down the Colorado River, graces the Watchtower's Hopi Room. At the top is an enclosed observation deck, which at 7,522 feet is the highest point on the South Rim.

The rim at Desert View offers spectacular views of the northeast end of the canyon. To the northeast you'll see the cliffs known as the Palisades of the Desert, which form the southeastern wall of Grand Canyon proper. If you follow those cliffs north to a significant rock outcropping, you're looking at **Comanche Point.** Beyond Comanche Point, you can barely see the gorge carved by the Little Colorado River. In 1956, at the point where that gorge intersects the Grand Canyon, two planes collided and crashed, killing 128 people. Most of the debris was removed from the area around the confluence of the rivers, but a few parts, including a wheel from one of the planes, remain. (None are visible from the rim.)

The flat, mesalike hill to the east is **Cedar Mountain.** This is one of the few places where the story told by the rocks at Grand Canyon *doesn't* end with the Kaibab Limestone. Cedar Mountain and Red Butte (a hill just south of Tusayan along Highway 64) were both deposited during the Mesozoic Era (245 to 65 million years ago). They linger, isolated, atop the Kaibab Limestone, remnants of the more than 4,000 feet of Mesozoic deposits that once accumulated in this area. (Sedimentary rock like this is usually deposited when the land is near or below sea level, as the land in this area was for long periods in the past. It erodes when elevated, the way the Grand Canyon is now.) Though nearly all of these layers have eroded off Grand Canyon, they can be seen nearby in the Painted Desert, the Vermilion Cliffs, and at Zion National Park.

This is the last overlook on the East Rim Drive. Past Desert View, Highway 64 continues east, roughly paralleling the gorge cut by the Little Colorado River. It leaves the Grand Canyon, which follows a more northerly course upstream of Desert View. About 10 miles above the confluence, the canyon narrows and the walls begin to drop, eventually disappearing below river level at Lee's Ferry (68 miles upstream of where the river passes Desert View), where the canyon begins.

NORTH RIM: CAPE ROYAL DRIVE

Highlights: Sparse crowds and lovely views of the eastern canyon.
Drawbacks: Has only one viewpoint (Cape Royal) from which to see the central canyon. The Colorado River is not visible from as many points on this drive as on the South Rim drives.

From the Grand Canyon Lodge, I recommend driving 23 miles directly to Cape Royal, on the Walhalla Plateau. Make your stops on the way back to the Grand Canyon Lodge. That way, you can do the short hikes near Cape Royal while your legs are fresh, then stop at the picnic areas, closer to the lodge, on your way back.

As with the other scenic drives, the Cape Royal Road is best done in low light. Most of the overlooks look east, so it may be nicest at sunrise. The drive will probably take around 4 hours—more if you do any hiking.

⚪ **Stop #1: Cape Royal.** Lined by cliff rose and piñon pine, a gentle, paved .3-mile (each way) trail opens onto some of the most stunning views in the park. It first approaches a natural bridge, Angel's Window, carved into a rock peninsula along the rim. Through the square opening under the bridge, a part of the lower canyon, including a slice of the Colorado River, can be seen from the trail. This opening in the Kaibab Limestone was formed when water seeped down through cracks and then across planes between rock beds, eventually eroding the rock from underneath.

The left fork of the trail travels about 150 yards, ending at the tip of the peninsula above **Angel's Window.** With sheer drops on three sides, Angel's Window is a thrilling place to stand.

The right fork of the trail goes to the tip of Cape Royal. From here, Wotan's Throne, a broad mesa visible in the distance from many South Rim overlooks, looms only 1.5 miles to the south. Also to the south, and nearly as close, is Vishnu Temple. Closer still is Freya Castle, a pinnacle shaped like a breaking wave. Across the canyon, the tiny nub on the rim is the 70-foot-high Watchtower at Desert View.

Optional stop: The **Cliff Springs Trail** (3 miles north of Cape Royal, in a small pull-out). This half-mile walk ends at a small spring in a side canyon. (See "Rim Trails: North Rim" in chapter 4.)

Stop #2: Walhalla Overlook and **Walhalla Glades.** Ancestral Puebloans no doubt enjoyed the views from here. Follow the tan line of Unkar Creek as it snakes down toward Unkar Delta. Enriched by the river deposits of the creek, the soil and abundant water at the delta made for excellent farming. Many Ancestral Puebloans lived there, growing corn, beans, and squash on terraces that caught run-off and left deposits of rich soil.

When the canyon heated up, they also spent time on the North Rim, at dwellings such as the ones across the street from this overlook. A flat dirt path leads to this Walhalla Ruin, which includes the foundations of two small pueblos. In this area, the Ancestral Puebloans could farm, taking advantage of the extra moisture and a growing season that was lengthened by the warm breezes blowing out of the canyon. In addition to farming, the Puebloans also gathered food and hunted the abundant game on the rim.

Optional stop: Cape Final Trail (4.9 miles south of Roosevelt Point). This gentle, 1.5-mile-long (one way) hike follows an old Jeep trail to an overlook at Cape Final. (See "Rim Trails: North Rim," in chapter 4.)

Stop #3: Roosevelt Point. This is one of the best places in the canyon to see the confluence of the gorge of the Little Colorado River and the Grand Canyon. They meet at nearly a right angle, unusual in that most tributaries enter at close to the same direction as the larger rivers. Geologists have used this observation to buttress arguments that the ancestral Colorado River exited the canyon via the Little Colorado gorge, but little evidence supports this theory. The cliffs south of this junction, which form the southeast wall of Grand Canyon proper, are known as the Palisades of the Desert. Those north of the confluence are called the Desert Facade.

Stop #4: Vista Encantadora. By starting your driving tour of the Walhalla Plateau early in the day, you can reach Vista Encantadora in time for a late picnic lunch. You'll find several tables, one on the rim. From there you can look down an upper drainage of Nankoweap Creek and at the rock pinnacle known as Brady Peak.

✪ **Stop #5: Point Imperial.** A 3-mile spur road leads from the Cape Royal Road to Point Imperial, which at 8,803 feet is the highest point on the North Rim and the best place on either rim to view the northeastern end of the park. To the northeast, 3,000 feet below the overlook, you'll see the brownish-green plane known as the Marble Platform. The Colorado River cleaves this platform between Lee's Ferry and where Grand Canyon proper yawns open just east of here. Because the Marble Platform has the same rock layers as Grand Canyon, **Marble Canyon** is considered by geologists to be the uppermost section of Grand Canyon.

Cape Royal Drive & North Rim Area

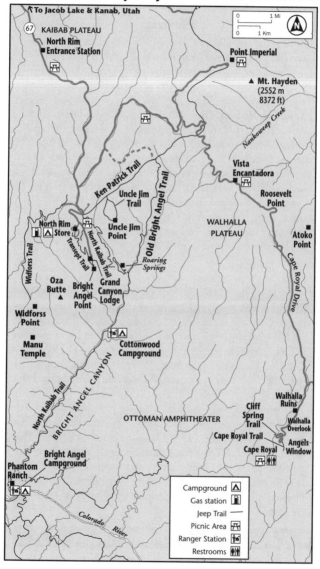

To Jacob Lake & Kanab, Utah

0 — 1 Mi
0 — 1 Km

(67) KAIBAB PLATEAU

North Rim Entrance Station

Point Imperial

▲ **Mt. Hayden** (2552 m 8372 ft)

Nankoweap Creek

Ken Patrick Trail

Uncle Jim Trail

Old Bright Angel Trail

Vista Encantadora

Roosevelt Point

North Rim Store

Uncle Jim Point

WALHALLA PLATEAU

Atoko Point

Widforss Trail

Transept Trail

North Kaibab Trail

Roaring Springs

Oza Butte ▲

Bright Angel Point

Grand Canyon Lodge

Cape Royal Drive

Widforss Point

Manu Temple

Cottonwood Campground

North Kaibab Trail

BRIGHT ANGEL CANYON

OTTOMAN AMPHITHEATER

Cliff Spring Trail

Walhalla Ruins

Walhalla Overlook

Cape Royal Trail

Cape Royal

Angels Window

Bright Angel Campground

Phantom Ranch

Colorado River

Campground	△
Gas station	⬛
Jeep Trail	—
Picnic Area	⊞
Ranger Station	⬛
Restrooms	⬛

Wild Things

If you watch carefully, you'll see wildlife everywhere during your stay. Even during the day, **raptors** soar above the canyon, **lizards** sun themselves on rocks, and **squirrels** scurry across the rim. The best time to view larger animals is at dawn or dusk, when they become more active. To see large animals such as elk, drive into the **Kaibab National Forest** near Grandview Point. **Deer,** which often graze alongside the train tracks near Grand Canyon Village, are hard to miss—especially when you're driving. On the North Rim, the meadows alongside the entrance road on the North Rim are frequented by **wild turkey, deer,** and (less often) **coyotes.** If you're serious about wildlife watching, bring binoculars. Sit a few hundred yards downwind of one of the small water holes (in this arid country, they're called "lakes") in these meadows and wait quietly for the animals. To learn more about the species in this area, turn to the "Fauna" section of chapter 7.

Bordering the Marble Platform on the north are the **Vermilion Cliffs.** Located along the Utah-Arizona border, these cliffs are also the next steps up in the Grand Staircase, a geological formation in which progressively younger rock formations rise like steps from Marble Canyon to Bryce Canyon in southern Utah. The Vermilion Cliffs run southwest to northeast. Where this formation turns toward the south near Lee's Ferry, the cliffs are known as the Echo Cliffs.

Looking southeast, you can see where the gorge of the Little Colorado River intersects the Grand Canyon. Past that confluence, the landforms of the Painted Desert stain the horizon a rich red. This desert, made up of badlands and other erosional features carved from the soft clays of the Chinle Formation, surrounds the Little Colorado River and one of its tributaries, the Puerte River. Like the Vermilion Cliffs, the Painted Desert is made up of "younger" rocks than are found in Grand Canyon.

4 Ranger Programs & Organized Tours

The South Rim Visitor Center has a free slide show designed to introduce visitors to the park.

On both rims, the park offers a host of ranger programs whose schedule changes seasonally. A typical schedule includes guided hikes and walks, kids' programs, and discussions of geology, native plant and animal species, and natural and cultural history. Evening programs are offered nightly, all year-round. The South Rim cuts back on its programs in winter, and the North Rim closes. All the programs are free and open to everyone. You just need to show up at the meeting places, which are scattered around the park (overlooks, trailheads, archaeological sites, and so on). For an up-to-date schedule, consult the park newspaper, *The Guide.*

BUS TOURS

Of the many private companies that offer bus tours, **Fred Harvey** has the most extensive schedule. Among the choices are East Rim and West Rim tours ($24.50 and $13.50, respectively, for adults; under 16 free), sunset tours to Hopi or Mojave Point ($10), and all-day outings ($29.50) that combine two of the shorter tours. Unlike the drivers on the free shuttles, Fred Harvey drivers narrate the tours. Don't believe everything they say. Though they mean well and have undergone some training, they have been known to skew facts terribly. At least kids 16 and under ride free. For advance reservations, call ☎ **303/297-2757.** Once at the canyon, visit the Fred Harvey desks at Yavapai, Maswik, or Bright Angel lodges, or call ☎ **520/638-2631,** ext. 6015.

Nava-Hopi Tours (☎ **520/774-5003**) offers 1-day guided canyon tours that depart from Flagstaff at 8:30am and return by 5:30pm. Total cost for adults is $46. For kids ages 5 to 15, it's $19. The tour stops at Cameron Trading Post on the Navajo Indian Reservation before entering the park through the South Rim's East Entrance. The coach then pauses at several overlooks on the East Rim Drive and visits Grand Canyon Village. It exits the park via the South Entrance gates. Its last stop is the IMAX Theater in Tusayan.

5 Historic & Man-Made Attractions

Please refer to the map "Grand Canyon Village" on p. 99 in chapter 5 to find the exact locations of the historic buildings in the South Rim.

SOUTH RIM

Most of the historic buildings on the South Rim are concentrated in Grand Canyon Village, a National Historic District. Outside of the village, **Hermit's Rest** on the West Rim Drive and The **Watchtower** on the East Rim Drive are also of historical significance. For information on these two sites, refer to the West Rim (p. 37) and East Rim (p. 41) driving tours. Strange and beautiful, these historic buildings, like the canyon itself, take time to appreciate.

More than a half dozen of these historic buildings were designed by Mary Colter, a Minneapolis schoolteacher who in 1902 began decorating the shops that sold Indian art on the Santa Fe Railroad line. As both a decorator and self-trained architect, Colter later designed these Grand Canyon landmarks: Hopi House (1905), the Lookout (1914), Hermit's Rest (1914), Phantom Ranch (1922), Watchtower (1932), and Bright Angel Lodge (1935). Colter's work drew heavily on the architectural styles of Native Americans and Spanish settlers in the Southwest, long before these styles were fashionable among Anglos. The most noteworthy historic buildings in Grand Canyon Village are detailed below.

THE BRIGHT ANGEL LODGE   In the 1930s, the Santa Fe Railroad asked Mary Colter to design moderately priced accommodations for the tourists flocking to the canyon by rail and automobile. Colter laid out a number of cabins, as well as this rustic log-and-stone lodge, which would house a lounge, restaurant, and curio shop. Completed in 1935, the lodge, located near the west end of Grand Canyon Village, looks low from outside but has a spacious lobby with wood walls, flagstone floors, and a high ceiling with an exposed log framework. A remarkable hearth is found in what was once the lounge and is currently the site of the Fred Harvey Museum. Known as "the geologic fireplace," it features the rock layers found in the canyon, stacked in the same order in which they occur there. Rounded, smooth river stones lie at the bottom of this bell-shaped hearth and Kaibab Limestone, the rim rock, is on top.

The museum tells the story of Harvey Girls—young women who came west during the years from 1883 through the 1950s to staff the Fred Harvey restaurants and hotels along the rail lines. In a building where employees still wear Fred Harvey name tags, the wall boasts: "Harvey established standards that were astonishingly above anything seen from Kansas to California up to that time." How times change.

BUCKEY O'NEILL CABIN   This is the second-oldest structure in Grand Canyon Village (the oldest being Red House Station, which was moved to the rim in 1890). It was the home of Buckey O'Neill, who in the 1890s worked at a number of jobs, including sheriff, judge, reporter, and prospector, in the area. After discovering what he believed to be a rich copper vein in Anita, 14 miles south of the canyon, he pushed for the construction of a railroad line connecting Williams with Grand Canyon—via Anita. A Chicago mining company bought out O'Neill, but the project collapsed when the mine turned out to be less than rich. In 1901, the Santa Fe Railroad bought the line and laid the remaining track. When Mary Colter designed cabins for Bright Angel Lodge, she fought for the preservation of the O'Neill Cabin, eventually building her own ones around it. Today, this cabin, a few feet west of Bright Angel Lodge, is the most luxurious guest suite in the park.

✪ **THE EL TOVAR HOTEL**   A year after the Santa Fe Railroad linked the South Rim with Williams, Fred Harvey commissioned Charles Whittlesey, an architect who had worked alongside Mary Colter on the Alvarado Hotel in Albuquerque, to build a large luxury hotel on the rim. Whittlesey fashioned the El Tovar after the northern European lodges of that period. Built of Oregon pine, this 100-room hotel offered first-class luxury accommodations at the canyon, attracting luminaries such as George Bernard Shaw and Theodore Roosevelt. To find it, walk 200 yards east along the rim from Bright Angel Lodge. (For more on the El Tovar, see chapter 5.)

GRAND CANYON DEPOT   Built in 1909, this is one of three remaining log train depots in the United States. It closed after the last train from Grand Canyon departed in 1968, then reopened in 1990, roughly a year after the railway resumed service. Located about 100 yards south of the El Tovar, this two-story depot is built of logs that are flat on three sides, making for smooth interior walls and a rounded, rustic exterior. Once home to the station agent and his family, the upstairs of the depot now houses Park Service offices.

✪ **HOPI HOUSE**   Aware that travelers were captivated by the idea of meeting Native Americans, Fred Harvey brought a group of Hopi artisans to Grand Canyon Village. At the same time that it was erecting the El Tovar Hotel on the rim, the company commissioned Mary Colter to design a structure 100 feet east of the hotel that could serve as both a dwelling for the Indians and a place to market their wares.

Colter fashioned Hopi House after the pueblos in Oraibi, Arizona. Completed in 1905, this faux adobe structure rises in tiers, with each level connected by exterior wood ladders (and interior stairways). The roof of each level serves as the porch for the one above. Inside, low doorways and nooks in the walls recall the snug quarters found in real pueblos. The concrete floors are made to look like dirt, the plaster walls to look like adobe. Log beams support thatched ceilings.

Through 1968, the Hopi artisans lived on the top floor of this building while they created and sold their pottery, rugs, and jewelry on the lower floors. They chanted and danced nightly on a platform behind the building. Today, Hopi House still sells Native American art on the lower two floors. Once used for religious purposes, the kiva on the second floor remains off-limits to non–Native Americans.

✪ KOLB STUDIO   In 1902, two brothers, Emery and Ellsworth Kolb, began photographing tourists descending the Bright Angel Trail on mules. After snapping the photos, they ran to Indian Gardens, where they had water to develop their plates, then raced back to the rim in time to sell the photos. Flush with profits from the business, they built this home and studio alongside the trailhead of the Bright Angel Trail, along the rim at the westernmost edge of Grand Canyon Village, in 1904. Several years later the brothers launched a more ambitious project: a motion picture of a raft trip through Grand Canyon. Completed in 1912, the film earned them international fame and drew throngs of people to the studio's viewing room.

After clashing regularly throughout the years, the two brothers eventually flipped a coin to see which one would have the privilege of remaining at their beloved Grand Canyon. Emery won two out of three tosses. So while Ellsworth moved to Los Angeles, Emery continued to live and work at Kolb Studio, introducing the brothers' film to audiences each day until his death at age 95 in 1976, after which the Park Service took over the building. Today, Kolb Studio houses a bookstore and gallery (located in the former viewing room), which features exhibits year-round. Photos and clips from the Kolbs' films are shown in an interactive video (a must-see) inside the store.

LOOKOUT STUDIO   Seeing the crowds drawn to Kolb Studio, The Fred Harvey Company decided to launch a similar business, only nearer the railroad terminus. Mary Colter was hired to design the building, which she eventually named The Lookout. Unlike some of her buildings, which were fashioned after occupied pueblos or well-preserved ruins, this one, on the canyon rim about 100 yards east of Kolb Studio, resembled a collapsed ruin. Its original chimney and low-slung roof looked like a pile of rocks and seemed barely higher than the canyon rim. To add to the effect, Colter planted indigenous plants on the roof. After its completion in 1914, tourists came here to buy souvenirs or to photograph the canyon from the deck, where a high-power telescope was placed. Today, Lookout Studio still serves much the same purpose.

VERKAMP'S CURIOS   A true visionary, John G. Verkamp may have been the first to sell curios at the Grand Canyon. In 1898, before the railroad even reached Grand Canyon Village, Verkamp was hawking souvenirs out of a tent on the grounds of the Bright Angel Lodge. Although his first attempt at the business failed, Verkamp returned in 1905, after the trains began running, and opened a curio shop in a wood-shingled building 200 feet east of Hopi House. This time he succeeded. His descendants still run the store, making it one of the last privately held businesses in the park.

NORTH RIM

GRAND CANYON LODGE & CABINS   This lodge sits quietly on the North Rim, gracefully blending into its surroundings. Built in 1928 by the Pacific Railroad, this hotel burned down in 1932 and was rebuilt in 1937. Inside, an expansive 50-foot-high lobby opens onto an octagonal sunroom with three enormous windows offering picturesque views of the canyon. You can also enjoy the views in a rocking chair on one of two long decks outside the sunroom. For more information see chapter 5.

4

Hikes & Other Outdoor Pursuits in the Grand Canyon

*T*here's no better way to enjoy the canyon than by walking right down into it and seeing all the rock layers and the plant and animal life up close. You can day-hike part of the way into the canyon on a number of trails.

Although hiking below the rims is the best way to experience the canyon, it's not always a smart idea, especially at midday during summer. If it's hot out or you aren't up to climbing, consider walking on one of the rim trails. These can often be as pleasant, and less crowded, than walks inside the canyon. They're especially nice in the forests on the North Rim.

On the South Rim, the wide, lush **Bright Angel Trail** is the least dangerous canyon trail for day hikers. It has toilets, emergency phones, and water (some of it seasonal). A few well-prepared hikers will be comfortable traveling 6 miles one way to the end of the ✪ **Plateau Point Trail,** which departs from the Tonto Trail just north of where the Tonto crosses the Bright Angel Trail. This is the farthest anyone should day-hike into the canyon.

Other popular day hikes on the South Rim include the **South Kaibab Trail** to Cedar Ridge, the **Hermit Trail** to either Dripping Springs (via the Dripping Springs Trail) or Santa Maria Spring, and the **Grandview Trail** to Horseshoe Mesa. Because it is steeper and has no water and little shade, the South Kaibab Trail is considered more strenuous than the Bright Angel Trail, but the views are spectacular. The Hermit and Grandview trails, which are unmaintained and very steep in places, are considerably more taxing than the South Kaibab.

On the North Rim the **North Kaibab Trail,** which has seasonal water and abundant shade, is the best option for day hikers descending into the canyon. Day hikers, as a rule, shouldn't go any farther than Roaring Springs, 4.7 miles and 3,000 vertical feet below the trailhead.

The trail descriptions later in this chapter cover all these hikes, including turn-around points for day hikers. Because of remote locations and/or rugged conditions, the **South Bass, North Bass,** and **Nankoweap** trails are not covered in this book.

Wherever you hike, carry plenty of water and know where the next water sources are. Eat and drink regularly. If you hike into the canyon, allow yourself twice as much time for the trip out as for the descent.

RECOMMENDED HIKING DISTANCES

The following is a list of trails recommended for day hikers, and the farthest point that day hikers should try to go on them.

FOR FIT, WELL-PREPARED HIKERS:

South Kaibab Trail to Cedar Ridge
North Kaibab Trail to Roaring Springs
Bright Angel Trail to Plateau Point

FOR EXPERIENCED DESERT HIKERS ONLY:

Grandview Point to Horseshoe Mesa
Hermit Trail to Santa Maria Spring
Hermit and Dripping Springs trails to Dripping Springs

1 Exploring the Backcountry

BACKPACKING FOR BEGINNERS

In the Grand Canyon, most of the rim trails and all of the canyon trails are considered part of the backcountry.

By camping inside the canyon, you can give yourself time to explore the lower elevations of the park. However, the extreme changes in temperature and elevation can make the Grand Canyon a nightmare for backpackers. The jarring descent strains your knees; the climb out tests your heart. Extreme heat often precludes hiking during the middle of the day, and water is scarce. Because of these hazards, a first-time backpacker should consider hiking on gentler terrain before venturing into the canyon.

CORRIDOR TRAILS   When descending into the canyon for the first time, even experienced backpackers should consider one of the **corridor trails:** North Kaibab, South Kaibab, or Bright Angel, discussed in detail below. Well maintained and clearly marked, these are regularly patrolled by park rangers. Each has at least one emergency phone and pit toilet. Drinking water is available at several sources along both the Bright Angel and the North Kaibab trails, but not on the South Kaibab. (Some of these sources are seasonal.) Check at the Backcountry Office for current water availability before starting your hike. While hiking the corridor trails, you can spend your nights at **Bright Angel, Cottonwood, or Indian Garden** campgrounds, each of which has a ranger station, running water, and toilets.

WILDERNESS TRAILS   By hiking on corridor trails, you can acclimate yourself to the conditions in the canyon without having to negotiate the boulder-strewn and sometimes confusing **wilderness trails,** which also go into the canyon. Rangers are seldom encountered on these trails, which are not maintained by the park. These trails have washed away in some places; in others, they descend very steeply through cliffs. They can also be very faint; hikers not accustomed to following trails like these risk becoming lost. These trails allow little margin for error, especially during the summer months. A seemingly minor injury like a sprained ankle can easily lead to a life-threatening situation, especially when people hike alone.

Unlike the Bright Angel and North Kaibab trails, which provide access to backcountry campgrounds, most wilderness trails accommodate only **at-large camping,** meaning that it's up to each hiker to find his or her own campsite. Unlike the campgrounds, the campsites along wilderness trails do not have purified water or ranger stations nearby, and only a few of them have pit toilets. On the busiest wilderness trails, campers may be limited to **designated sites.**

PACKING TIPS   What you carry (or don't) in your pack is almost as important as your choice of trails. Warm temperatures and dry weather make the canyon an ideal place for traveling light. You can lighten your load by carrying dry food such as instant beans and ramen noodles. In summer, you can go lighter still by leaving the stove at home and preparing cold meals such as tabouli and hummus. Some foods that are usually heated, like ramen noodles or couscous, will soften in cold water—even inside a water bottle—over time. During summer, carry a light shelter or tarp instead of a tent. At this time of year, you're more likely to die of problems related to heat—and heavy packs—than from the cold. Just be sure you know how to rig your shelter, in case rain does fall.

Also, make sure you have enough water containers. I usually carry 6 to 8 quarts in summer and sometimes, for long, waterless walks, bring even more. Drink all the time—start before you get thirsty—

and fill up your bottles whenever you have the chance. Eating carbohydrate-rich, salty food is just as important. If you guzzle too much water without eating, you run the risk of developing an electrolyte imbalance that can result in unconsciousness or death. Loss of appetite is common during a hike. So try to eat, even if you don't feel hungry. Also, carry powdered Gatorade or another electrolyte replacement drink.

LOCATIONS OF RANGER STATIONS

Backcountry ranger stations are found at **Indian Garden, Phantom Ranch,** and **Cottonwood Campground** (in summer). Emergency phones, connected to the park's 24-hour dispatch, are at the rest houses along the Bright Angel Trail and near the intersection of the South Kaibab and Tonto trails. On the **North Kaibab Trail,** an emergency phone is near Roaring Springs.

CAMPING ETIQUETTE & SPECIAL REGULATIONS

First, the standard camping etiquette: Pack out all your garbage, including uneaten food and used toilet paper. Stay on designated trails. Don't disturb plants, wildlife, or archaeological resources. Camp in obvious campsites—off the vegetation and cryptogamic soils. If pit toilets are not available, bury human waste in holes 4 inches deep, 6 inches across, and at least 200 feet from water and creek beds. When doing dishes, take water and dishes at least 200 feet from the water source, and scatter the waste water. When bathing, take water away from the water source, and use a biodegradable soap (or, better yet, none at all). Hang food and trash out of reach of wildlife.

There are also a few canyon-specific regulations. No campfires are allowed (only camp stoves). Also, be sure to camp inside the use areas specified on your permit. These are shown on the Trails Illustrated topographical map of the canyon. Finally, pay attention to trail-specific rules provided by the Backcountry Office. If you have any questions about the hike—especially water sources—ask a ranger. The Backcountry Office can't determine whether a hike suits you. It's up to you to ask the necessary questions.

2 Preparing for Your Backcountry Trip

Permits are required for all overnight camping in the backcountry that falls within the park's boundaries. This includes all overnight stays below the rims (except in the cabins and dorms at Phantom Ranch) and on park land outside of designated campgrounds. Good

Equipment Checklist

- ☐ Tent or light shelter
- ☐ Ground cloth
- ☐ Sleeping bag (lightweight in summer)
- ☐ Sleeping bag stuff sack (can be used to hang food)
- ☐ Sleeping pad
- ☐ Bicycle tube patch kit (if pad is inflatable)
- ☐ Backpack (external frame is better)
- ☐ Binoculars
- ☐ Walking stick or ski pole (optional)
- ☐ Signal mirror
- ☐ Compass
- ☐ Headlamp with batteries
- ☐ Spare batteries and bulbs
- ☐ First-aid kit (adhesive tape, supportive elastic wrap, moleskin, mole foam, iodine, bandages, aspirin)
- ☐ Water-purifying tablets (pumps quickly clog in the Colorado River)
- ☐ Four 1-quart unbreakable plastic water bottles plus one or two 4-liter nylon water bags
- ☐ Extra gallon jug for water cache (depending on hike, and don't bank on it being there)
- ☐ Small plastic or collapsible metal shovel for burying human waste
- ☐ Waterproof matches
- ☐ Stove repair kit and spare parts (if carrying stove)
- ☐ Topo maps
- ☐ Trail descriptions published by the Backcountry Office
- ☐ Camp stove (optional during summer) and fuel
- ☐ Swiss army knife
- ☐ Eating utensils
- ☐ Lightweight cooking pot
- ☐ Hiking boots

- ☐ Two T-shirts
- ☐ One pair shorts
- ☐ Thick socks
- ☐ Breathable water-resistant shell
- ☐ Polypropylene underwear (top and bottom)
- ☐ Polar fleece leggings and uppers (seasonal)
- ☐ Winter cap and gloves (seasonal)
- ☐ Wide-brimmed hat
- ☐ 100% UV protection sunglasses
- ☐ High SPF sunscreen and lip balm
- ☐ Extra plastic freezer bags
- ☐ Toilet paper
- ☐ Notebook and pen (optional)
- ☐ Lightweight camera and film (optional)
- ☐ $1/4$-inch nylon rope (if necessary for hike)
- ☐ Trail mix
- ☐ Ramen noodles
- ☐ Dehydrated beans
- ☐ Dried tabouli mix
- ☐ Dried hummus mix
- ☐ Granola bars
- ☐ Power or Cliff bars
- ☐ Dried milk
- ☐ Cold cereal
- ☐ Raisins
- ☐ Crackers
- ☐ Hard cheese
- ☐ Salted peanut butter (in plastic jar)
- ☐ Bagels

Note: Dried or freeze-dried food is fine only if you have access to plenty of water. If not, take food that doesn't require water during preparation.

Backcountry Permit Waiting List

If you show up at the park without a permit and find the backcountry booked, you may be able to obtain one by putting your name on the waiting list. During the spring, summer, and fall you should expect to spend one or more days on the waiting list before obtaining a permit. To do this, show up in person at the Backcountry Office. The ranger will give you a number at that time. To stay on the waiting list, you'll have to show up at the Backcountry Office at 8am every morning until you receive an opening. Usually permits are for the next night, but occasionally ones for that night are issued. Even though cancellations don't always happen, the office sometimes sets aside a spot or two at the Bright Angel Campground or Cottonwood Campground for people on the list.

for up to 11 people, each permit costs $20 plus an additional $4 per person per night.

Regular hikers can purchase a **Frequent Hiker Membership,** which costs $50 but waives the $20-per-permit fee for a year from the date of purchase.

Permits for the month desired go on sale on the first of the month, 4 months earlier. For example, permits for all of May go on sale January 1; permits for June go on sale February 1, and so on. By using a **Backcountry Permit Request Form,** included in the free Backcountry Trip Planner mailed out by the park, you can make sure that you provide all the necessary information. The Backcountry Trip Planners also suggest itineraries for first-time Canyon hikers and offer advice on safe, low-impact hiking. To receive one, call the park's main extension at ☎ **520/638-7888** and choose the "backcountry information" option. Or write to Grand Canyon National Park, P.O. Box 129, Grand Canyon, AZ 86023, and request a **Backcountry Trip Planner** (not to be confused with one of the park's regular trip planners). To increase your odds of receiving a permit, be as flexible as possible when filling out the Backcountry Permit Request Form. It helps to request three alternative hikes, in order of preference, and more than one starting date. Keeping your group small also helps.

Once you fill out your Permit Request Form, you can take it in person to the Backcountry Office on either rim; fax it to ☎ **520/638-2125** no earlier than the date the permits become available, or mail it postmarked no earlier than that date. No requests are taken by phone.

If you have questions about a trail or about the process itself, the Backcountry Office, at ☎ **520/638-7875,** takes calls weekdays between 1 and 5pm mountain standard time. You can visit the office in person from 8am to noon and 1 to 5pm daily. The **North Rim Backcountry Office,** which keeps the same hours as the main (South Rim) office but closes seasonally, can be reached at ☎ **520/638-7868.**

3 Backcountry Campgrounds

Permits to **Bright Angel Campground, Cottonwood Campground,** and **Indian Garden Campground** are available through the park's Backcountry Office at P.O. Box 129, Grand Canyon, AZ 86023. All three campgrounds have toilets, running water, and picnic tables.

BRIGHT ANGEL CAMPGROUND

The **River Trail** (which begins at the foot of the Bright Angel Trail), the **South Kaibab Trail,** and the **North Kaibab Trail** all converge below Bright Angel Campground. The River Trail crosses the Colorado River on the Silver Suspension Bridge just west of the campground; the South Kaibab Trail crosses on the Kaibab Suspension Bridge just east of the campground. The lowest section of the North Kaibab Trail parallels the campground on the opposite side of Bright Angel Creek.

This long, narrow campground lies in a purgatory between the cool waters of Bright Angel Creek and black cliffs of the Vishnu Formation, which are hot as grills in the summer. A few hundred yards away, the Colorado River rumbles past, eddying against a beach that is a popular stopping point for raft trips. A walkway divides the campground, which is open all year. Roughly half of the 31 campsites are on the cliff side; the other, nicer half are on the creek side. Most are shaded by cottonwood trees, initially planted in the 1930s by Civilian Conservation Corps (CCC) workers whose camp was here. (Many, if not all, of the ones planted by the CCC washed away in a 1966 flash flood.) Phantom Ranch is a half mile to the north.

COTTONWOOD CAMPGROUND

As you hike up the North Kaibab Trail from the Colorado River, the walls of Bright Angel Canyon part like the Red Sea below this campground. Between them rests a valley floor soft enough and damp enough to support a few cottonwood trees, most of which grow by the ranger station. The 14 campsites are surrounded by shrub oak, whose low-slung branches barely shade tents and picnic tables. Bright Angel Creek flows past the west side of the campground. On a hot summer day, it's the only cool place around.

Halfway between the North Rim and the Colorado, Cottonwood Campground is a great place to camp while en route to (or from) the river. For a nice 4-day hike from the North Rim, schedule 2 nights here around a night at Bright Angel Campground.

INDIAN GARDEN CAMPGROUND

You can use this campground, 4.6 miles from the Bright Angel trailhead and 3,100 vertical feet below the rim, to break up hikes from the South Rim to the Colorado River (and Bright Angel Campground). The 14 sites are surrounded by lush riparian vegetation that taps into Indian Garden Spring, just a short walk down the canyon. For a nice 4-day hike from the South Rim, schedule 2 nights here around one at Bright Angel Campground.

4 Rim Trails: South Rim

For a map of the South Rim trails, please see p. 37 in chapter 3.

West Rim Trail and South Rim Trail. 8 mi. to Hermit's Rest; 1.5 mi. to Yavapai Point. Access: Grand Canyon Village, along the rim behind the El Tovar Hotel. Water sources at Grand Canyon Village, Hermit's Rest, visitor center, Yavapai Point. Easy to moderate. Maps: Trails Illustrated Topo Map or Village Area Map (included in the *Guide*).

From Grand Canyon Village, you can follow the rim trail 8 miles west to Hermit's Rest or 1.5 miles northeast to Yavapai Point.

WEST RIM TRAIL Walking instead of driving along this trail is a great way to see the canyon without the crowds. It travels near the West Rim Drive and passes through all the same scenic overlooks, described in the driving tour (see chapter 3). The 1.3-mile stretch from the village to Maricopa Point is paved with one 200-vertical-foot climb. Past Maricopa Point, it planes off somewhat and the pavement ends. For the rest of the way to Hermit's Rest, the trail meanders through piñon-juniper woodland along the rim (when not crossing overlooks). Sagebrush roots and loose rocks make for tricky footing, but the scenery is lovely, and the crowds thin as you move farther west.

As 16 miles might be too much hiking for 1 day, I recommend hiking out on this trail from Grand Canyon Village and taking the shuttle back (mid-March through mid-October). By hiking out, you

Note About Trail Descriptions

The trail descriptions in this chapter are not intended for use in route finding. It's up to each hiker to hike smart, be physically fit, and have the skills and equipment needed to stay on the trail. Also, more detailed trail descriptions are available. The Grand Canyon Association publishes a number of guides to the most popular trails, and the Sierra Club offers a book, *Hiking the Grand Canyon* (by John Annerino), which is devoted to canyon trails and hiking.

can avoid revisiting the same overlooks on the shuttle ride back—the shuttles stop at every turnout while en route to Hermit's Rest, but only stop at Mohave Point and Hopi Point on their way back to Grand Canyon Village.

If you don't want to walk the whole 8 miles, here's a list of distances, which will help determine how far you've gone and if it's worth it to walk to the next lookout. People who are tired should catch the shuttle at the **Abyss,** about halfway to Hermit's Rest. The next stop, **Pima Point,** is nearly 3 miles farther.

Trailhead to Trailview I:	.6 miles
Trailview I to Maricopa Point:	.7 miles
Maricopa Point to Powell Point:	.5 miles
Powell Point to Hopi Point:	.3 miles
Hopi Point to Mohave Point:	.8 miles
Mohave Point to the Abyss:	1.1 miles
The Abyss to Pima Point:	2.9 miles
Pima Point to Hermit's Rest:	1.1 miles

SOUTH RIM TRAIL   This smooth, paved trail connects Grand Canyon Village and Yavapai Point. Around the lodges, the path is a flat sidewalk teeming with people. The crowds dissipate somewhat between the east edge of the village and Yavapai Point. Near Yavapai Point you'll find many smooth flat rocks along the rim—great places from which to contemplate the canyon. Located 5 miles north of the park's south entrance, **Yavapai Point** has a historic (1928) observation station with large windows overlooking the canyon. From here, you can take a shuttle back to near your starting point.

5 Rim Trails: North Rim

To familiarize yourself with the lay of the land on the North Rim, start with either the **Transept Trail** or the **Bright Angel Point**

Trail, which are different sections of the same pathway. At the bottom of the stairs behind Grand Canyon Lodge, the Bright Angel Point Trail goes to the left, while the Transept Trail goes right.

The Bright Angel Point Trail and the Transept Trail. Bright Angel Point Trail .25 mi. each way; Transept Trail 1.5 mi. Access: Behind North Rim General Store (near the campground), or by descending the back steps off the patios at Grand Canyon Lodge. Easy. Map: *The Guide.*

Highlights: Views of Transept and Bright Angel canyons, easy access from Grand Canyon Lodge and North Rim Visitor Center.
Drawbacks: Big crowds, especially at Bright Angel Point.

THE BRIGHT ANGEL POINT TRAIL   This paved trail travels .25 mile along a narrow peninsula dividing Roaring Springs and Transept canyons. On the way it passes a number of craggy outcroppings of Kaibab Limestone, around which the roots of wind-whipped juniper trees cling like arthritic hands. Although the trail stays at about the same level as the rim, junipers supplant ponderosa pines here because of the warm winds that blow out of the canyon. The trail ends at 8,148-foot-high Bright Angel Point. From this overlook you can follow Bright Angel Canyon (with your eyes) to its intersection with the larger gorge of the Colorado River. On a quiet day you can hear Roaring Springs, a tributary of Bright Angel Creek and the water source for both the North and the South rims of the canyon.

THE TRANSEPT TRAIL   Traveling 1.5 miles northeast along the rim of Transept Canyon, this trail connects the lodge and the North Rim Campground. Passing through old-growth ponderosa pine and quaking aspen, it descends into, then climbs out of, three shallow side drainages, with ascents steep enough to take the breath away from people unaccustomed to the 8,000-foot altitude. A small Indian ruin sits alongside the dirt trail.

Ken Patrick Trail. 10 mi. each way. Access: From the south side of the parking area for Point Imperial or from the parking area for the North Kaibab Trail (on the North Rim entrance rd., 2 mi. north of Grand Canyon Lodge). Difficult. Maps: Trails Illustrated Topo Map.

Highlights: The stretch between Cape Royal Road and Point Imperial skirts the rim, with nice views of Nankoweap Creek drainages.
Drawbacks: Trail is mule-trampled near North Kaibab Trailhead parking lot, faint in other spots, and steeply rolling near Point Imperial.
This long, steeply rolling trail travels through ponderosa pine and spruce-fir forest between the head of Roaring Springs Canyon and

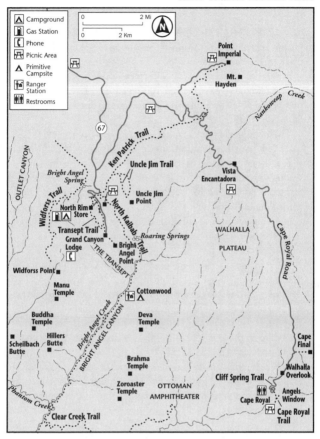

Point Imperial. Along the way, it poses a number of challenges. Starting at the North Kaibab end, the first mile of the trail has been pounded into a dustlike flour (where not watered down into something resembling cake batter) by mules. Where the mules turn around after a mile, the trail becomes faint. It becomes even less distinct about 4 miles in, after passing the trailhead for the old Bright Angel Trail.

After crossing the Cape Royal Road (the one and only road that you encounter, about two-thirds of the way to Point Imperial), the trail descends into, then climbs out of, a very steep drainage overgrown with thorn-covered New Mexican locust. While challenging, the 3-mile stretch between the road and Point Imperial is also the

Shooting the Canyon: Tips for Photographers

It's not easy to capture the canyon's spirit on film. Here are some tips to help you take the best possible photos:

A **polarizing filter** is a great investment if you have the kind of camera that will accept lens filters. It reduces haze, lessens the contrast between shadowy areas and light areas, and deepens the color of the sky.

The best times to photograph the canyon are at sunrise and sunset, when filtered and sharply angled sunlight paints the canyon walls in beautiful shades of lavender and pink. At these times the shadows are also at their most dramatic. To capture these ephemeral moments it's best to use a tripod and a long exposure. The worst time to photograph the canyon is at noon when there are almost no shadows, and thus little texture or contrast. *The Guide,* the park's official visitor newspaper, includes a table with sunrise and sunset times.

Something else to keep in mind is that the Grand Canyon is immense. A wide-angle lens may leave the canyon looking on paper like a distant plane of dirt. Try zooming in on narrower sections of the canyon to emphasize a single dramatic landscape element. If you're shooting with a wide-angle lens, try to include something in the foreground (people or a tree branch) to give the photo perspective and scale.

When shooting portraits against a sunrise or sunset, use a flash to illuminate your subjects; otherwise your camera meter may expose for the bright light in the background and leave your subjects in shadow.

—*By Karl Samson*

prettiest on the trail, skirting the rim of the canyon above upper drainages of Nankoweap Creek. In these areas you'll see plenty of scarlet bugler, identifiable by tubular red flowers with flared lower petals, as well as a number of Douglas firs interspersed among the ubiquitous ponderosa pines.

Uncle Jim Trail. 5 mi. round-trip (including Ken Patrick Trail). Access: 1 mi. down Ken Patrick Trail from North Kaibab trailhead parking area. Moderate.

Highlights: Views of Bright Angel and Roaring Springs canyons, and easy access make this a great place for a picnic.

Drawbacks: Mule traffic.

A lasso-shaped loop accessible via the Ken Patrick Trail, the Uncle Jim Trail circles Uncle Jim Point, which divides Roaring Springs and Bright Angel canyons. By taking the right branch of the lasso, you'll soon reach an overlook near the tip of Uncle Jim Point, named for a former game warden, Jim Owens, who slaughtered hundreds of mountain lions on the North Rim in the early 1900s. (Owens's handiwork, part of a misguided predator-control program, may have contributed to an explosion in the deer population and an ensuing famine.) From here, you'll have views across Roaring Springs Canyon to Bright Angel Point and up Roaring Springs Canyon, to where the upper switchbacks of the North Kaibab Trail are visible. This overlook is a scenic, easily accessible spot for a picnic lunch. After passing it, the trail skirts the edge of Bright Angel Canyon before looping back.

Cape Final Trail. 1.5 mi. (each way). Access: An unmarked dirt parking area off the Cape Royal Rd., 4.9 mi. south of Roosevelt Point. Easy. Map: Trails Illustrated Topo Map.

Highlights: An uncrowded, flat, boulder-free walk to a canyon overlook.

Drawbacks: Parking area is tough to find.

Because this trail is relatively flat and boulder free, it's a good choice for a first hike in the backcountry. It meanders through ponderosa pine forest on an old Jeep trail, ending on the north side of Cape Final, where you'll have partial views of the northern canyon and Juno Temple.

Cliff Springs Trail. .5 mi. (each way). Access: A small pullout .3 mi. north of Cape Royal on the Cape Royal Rd. Moderate. Map: Trails Illustrated Topo Map.

Highlights: This short walk down a shady drainage of Grand Canyon passes springs and an Ancestral Pueblo granary.

Drawbacks: Rocky stretches make this trail a bit difficult for people lacking agility.

Both scenic and fairly short, this is a nice hike for most families. Although this dirt trail seems at first to head into forest *away* from the canyon, it quickly descends into a narrow, rocky canyon that drains into the larger one—a reminder that the Walhalla Plateau is a peninsula in Grand Canyon. Spruce and fir trees dominate the northern exposures in this side canyon, while ponderosa pines and even piñon and juniper trees grow in the sunnier spots. Roughly .25 miles from the trailhead, the trail passes a small Ancestral Pueblo granary. After crossing a small drainage, it hugs the north wall of the side canyon, passing under limestone overhangs, in light colored green by the canopies of box-elder trees (identifiable by their leaflets in groups of three and by their double-winged fruit). The springs drip from one of these overhangs, where mosses carpet the fissures in the rock. A waist-high boulder marks the end of the trail.

✪ **Widforss Trail.** 5 mi. (one way). Access: A dirt road .25 mi. south of the Cape Royal Rd. Follow this road .7 mi. to the parking area, which is well marked. Moderate. Map: Trails Illustrated Topo Map.

Highlights: A nice escape into ponderosa pine forest, culminating with canyon views from Widforss Point.

Drawbacks: Markers on self-guided interpretive trail (the first mile of trail) are missing or damaged.

This trail, named for Gunnar Widforss, a landscape painter, may be the nicest rim hike in the park. It curves around the head of Transept Canyon before venturing south to Widforss Point. A brochure, available at the trailhead, explains points of interest in the first 2 miles, during which the trail undulates through ponderosa pine and spruce-fir forest. Unfortunately, most of the wooden posts marking these points seem to have burned or otherwise disappeared.

At the head of Transept Canyon, about halfway to Widforss Point, you'll pass several nice overlooks that make for good resting spots. You'll also see a balancing rock, formed when water seeping across planes in the rock eroded beds of Kaibab Limestone from underneath the ones above.

Past the head of Transept Canyon, the trail heads south through a stand of old-growth ponderosa pine. Under the red-orange-trunked trees, lupine blankets the forest floor with blue flowers. You'll also note a number of badly singed pines. In the late '90s the National Park Service conducted prescribed burns in this area, eliminating excess deadfall and undergrowth from the forest floor. Burns like these are designed to bring the forest closer to its natural state. Before the park existed, natural fires swept through the ponderosa pine forest an average of every 7 to 10 years. (For more on prescribed burns, see chapter 7.)

The trail, remaining hilly most of the way, reaches the rim again at Widforss Point. There, you'll have a nice view of five temples. The three to the southeast are Zoroaster (farthest south), Brahma (north of Zoroaster), and Deva (farthest north); to the southwest, Buddha Temple sits like a sphinx with two long legs. Out of one of those legs rises Manu Temple. Near the rim are a picnic table and several good campsites.

A Note About Difficulty of Trails

Because of the huge elevation changes on the canyon trails, none should be called easy. (More people are rescued off the Bright Angel Trail, generally considered the "easiest" trail into the canyon, than off any other trail.) In general, please note that rating a trail easy, moderate, or difficult oversimplifies the situation. For example, the **Hermit Trail** is wide and relatively gradual between the rim and just above Santa Maria Spring, but it's considerably more rugged after that; the **Tonto Trail** is easy to walk on in places, but has almost no water and very little shade. The following is a very subjective ranking of some of the most popular trails that go from the rim into the canyon from **least to most difficult.**

South Rim	North Rim
Bright Angel	North Kaibab
South Kaibab	Thunder River
Grandview	Bill Hall/Thunder River
Hermit	Nankoweap
Hermit/Dripping Spring/Boucher	North Bass

6 Corridor Trails: South Rim

Bright Angel Trail. 4.6 mi. to Indian Garden; 7.8 mi. to Colorado River; 9.3 mi. to Bright Angel Campground. Access: Trailhead is just west of Kolb Studio, near Grand Canyon Village. 6,860 ft. at trailhead; 3,800 ft. at Indian Garden; 2,450 ft. at Colorado River. Water sources at Mile-and-a-Half Rest House (seasonal), Three-Mile Rest House (seasonal), Indian Garden, Colorado River, Bright Angel Campground. Maps: Grand Canyon (7.5 min.), Phantom Ranch (7.5 min.).

Highlights: With water sources, ample shade, and a wide smooth surface, this is the least dangerous South Rim Trail into the canyon. It follows a route created by Mother Nature along a large fault line.
Drawbacks: During high season, you'll pass hundreds of hikers and a few mules.

Both Native Americans and early settlers recognized this as a choice location for a trail into the canyon. First, there's an enormous fault line, along which so much erosion has taken place that even the usually sheer Redwall Limestone holds vegetation. Then there's the water—more of it than anywhere on the South Rim. The springs at Indian Garden supplied Grand Canyon Village as late as 1970.

For centuries, the Havasupai used this trail to descend from the rim, where they hunted in winter, to Indian Garden, where they farmed year-round. This went on until the 1920s when the Park Service expelled the remaining tribe members. Although most of the Havasupai now live on a reservation in the central canyon, a few of their pictographs (rock paintings made with mineral dyes) remain along the trail. Some are on display high on the rocks just past the first tunnel; others can be seen on a sandstone overhang above Two-Mile Corner, the first switchback below Mile-and-a-Half Rest House.

When Pete Berry, Niles Cameron, and Ralph Cameron prospected for minerals here in the late 1800s, they improved the trail to the point where most people could descend it. As more visitors came to the canyon, Ralph Cameron realized that the trail might be worth more than gold. He bought out his partners, then used mining law to take control of the land near and below Grand Canyon Village. Although the Santa Fe Railroad challenged his authority in the early 1900s, it wasn't until the 1920s that Cameron lost the trail. By then he had charged countless hikers the $1 fee to go down it.

If Cameron earned a dollar for every hiker on this trail today, he'd be doing just fine. More than 500,000 people hike on the Grand Canyon's three corridor trails (South and North Kaibab, and Bright Angel) every year, and the Bright Angel is the most popular. It's a freeway: wide, dusty, relatively gradual, with some occasional mule manure thrown in.

On a day hike, walk down to **Mile-and-a-Half House** or **Three-Mile House,** each of which has shade, an emergency phone, and seasonal drinking water. Or continue down to the picnic area near the spring at Indian Garden, where lush vegetation will surround you and large cottonwood trees provide shade.

Watch the layers on this trail as you descend. As you move from the Kaibab Formation to the Toroweap Formation, the wall on your left will gradually turn from cream-colored to pinkish-white. After the second tunnel you'll start down through the steep buff-colored cliffs that form the Coconino Sandstone. As you do, compare the elevations of the cliffs on either side of the fault. The ones to the west have been offset and are 189 feet higher. At the bottom of the Coconino Sandstone, the Hermit Shale, deep red in color, is visibly eroding out from under the harder cliffs above it. This weakens the cliffs, which then break off along joints.

After dropping through the Supai Group and Redwall layers, the trail begins its long, direct descent to Indian Garden. As you near

Bright Angel & South Kaibab Trails (South Rim)

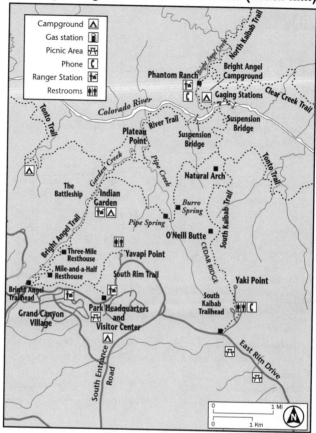

Indian Garden, you'll begin seeing species found near water, including willow, mesquite, catclaw acacia, and even Arizona grape, a native species that grows tart but edible grapes. In spring, the purple blooms on the redbud are bright enough to be seen from the rim. Fit, well-prepared day hikers may wish to hike an additional 1.5 miles past Indian Garden on the Tonto and Plateau Point trails. The Plateau Point Trail eventually crosses the Tonto Platform to an overlook of the Colorado River, 1,300 feet below.

Below Indian Garden, the Bright Angel Trail follows Garden Creek down a narrow canyon in the Tapeats Sandstone. After leaving the Garden Creek drainage, the trail descends through much of the Vishnu Formation in a series of switchbacks known as the

Hiking Tip

This route on the South Kaibab trail is steeper and shorter than the Bright Angel Trail. While the Bright Angel follows narrow side canyons below Indian Garden, the South Kaibab stays on ridge lines, with expansive views, for much of the way to the river. And while the Bright Angel offers ample shade and water, the South Kaibab has no water and little shade. So hikers planning to do a loop hike to Phantom Ranch should descend the South Kaibab Trail and climb out on the easier Bright Angel Trail.

Devil's Corkscrew. It then follows Pipe Creek to the Colorado River and the junction with the River Trail. There you'll find a small rest house with an emergency phone and pit toilet—but no pretreated drinking water. After skirting the river for 1.7 miles on the River Trail, you'll reach the Silver Suspension Bridge. When you cross it, you'll be near **Bright Angel Campground.**

South Kaibab Trail. 6.3 mi. to Colorado River; 7.3 mi. to Bright Angel Campground. Access: Trailhead at Yaki Point (Hwy. 64, E. Rim Dr., 5 mi. east of Grand Canyon Village). 7,260 ft. at trailhead; 2,450 ft. at Colorado River. Water sources at Colorado River and Bright Angel Campground. Maps: Phantom Ranch (7.5 min.) quadrangle.

Highlights: By following ridge lines, this relatively smooth trail affords panoramic views for much of the distance from the rim to the river.

Drawbacks: You won't find water, shade, or shelter atop these ridge lines, so the trail is more dangerous than the Bright Angel. It's also steeper.

Note: From mid-March through mid-October, a free shuttle ferries hikers to the trailhead daily beginning before sunrise. During other months, backpackers who want to start hikes from Yaki Point can either drive or use **Fred Harvey's 24-Hour Taxi Service** (☎ 520/638-2631), which costs $8 for one person and $3 for each additional passenger.

The South Kaibab Trail was the Park Service's way of bypassing Ralph Cameron, who controlled the Bright Angel Trail in the early 1900s. Cameron used mining law to lay claim to the land around the Bright Angel Trail and charged $1 to every person descending it. Later, as a senator, he pushed to deny funding for the Park Service. In 1924, exasperated by Cameron's maneuverings, the Park Service began to build the South Kaibab Trail, which like the Bright

Angel Trail linked Grand Canyon Village with the Colorado River and Phantom Ranch. Unlike the Bright Angel Trail, which follows natural routes into the canyon, this one was built using dynamite and hard labor.

The South Kaibab Trail begins by making a series of switchbacks through the upper rock layers. As you descend the Kaibab Formation, note the Douglas firs, remnants of the last Ice Age. After that Ice Age ended 10,000 years ago, the firs retreated off the South Rim, clinging only to a few due-north slopes where they received almost no direct sunlight. As the trail descends the Coconino Sandstone, watch for evidence of cross-bedding—diagonal lines formed by windblown sand in an ancient desert.

Below the Coconino, the trail descends onto Cedar Ridge, a platform that has pit toilets and a hitching post for mules. This is an excellent place for day hikers to picnic and rest before hiking the 1.5 miles back out. Continuing northward down the ridge, it then reaches a saddle underneath O'Neill Butte, with views a thousand feet down to the Tonto Platform on either side. The trail then rounds the east flank of the butte, eventually reaching another saddle. It descends in steep switchbacks through the Redwall, then slices downhill across the Tonto Platform toward the Inner Gorge. From the Tonto Platform, make sure to glance back at the natural rock bridge in the cliffs. At the tip-off, where the trail begins its drop into the Inner Gorge, an emergency telephone and toilet are available.

As you begin your descent of the Tapeats Sandstone, you'll see the Colorado River between the dark, sheer walls of the Inner Gorge. The pink in the otherwise black walls is Zoroaster Granite, formed 1.2 billion years ago when molten rock was squeezed into fissures in the Vishnu Schist. From here it's an hour's walk to the Kaibab Suspension Bridge and Bright Angel Campground.

7 Corridor Trail: North Rim

✪ **North Kaibab Trail.** 2.7 mi. to Supai Tunnel; 4.7 mi. to Roaring Springs; 6.8 mi. to Cottonwood Campground; 14.4 mi. to the Colorado River. Access: On North Rim entrance rd., 2 mi. north of Grand Canyon Lodge. 8,250 ft. North Kaibab trailhead; 5,200 ft. at Roaring Springs; 4,080 ft. at Cottonwood Campground; 2,400 ft. at Colorado River. Water sources at Roaring Springs (seasonal), Bright Angel Creek, Cottonwood Campground (seasonal), Phantom Ranch, Bright Angel Campground. Maps: Bright Angel Point (7.5 min.) and Phantom Ranch (7.5 min.) quadrangles.

Highlights: Less crowded than the Bright Angel Trail, and with ample water and shade. Great for a first backpack trip into the canyon.

Drawbacks: At 14.4 miles and with a vertical drop of 5,850 feet, it's much longer, and drops farther, than the South Rim corridor trails.

Forget the myth about corridor trails being easy. At 14.4 miles long and with a vertical drop of 5,850 feet, the North Kaibab Trail will test any hiker who attempts to go from rim to river (or vice versa) in a day. By comparison, the South Rim corridor trails, the Bright Angel and South Kaibab, travel 9.2 and 6.7 miles, respectively, and fall about 4,800 vertical feet from rim to river. Despite the length and the big vertical drop, the North Kaibab Trail may be the nicest place for backpackers to first experience the canyon. The scenery is lovely, the grades on the trail manageable. The North Kaibab has beautiful views down two side canyons—Roaring Springs and Bright Angel—but unlike the South Rim trails, you see less of the gorge cut by the Colorado River. Another benefit of the North Kaibab is the chance to camp at Cottonwood Campground on the way to and from the river; backpackers can use stopovers here to extend their trips while hiking reasonable distances. It's also less crowded than the South Rim corridor trails.

The trail begins with a long series of switchbacks down the head of Roaring Springs Canyon. At over 8,000 feet, the first switchbacks are in thickly forested terrain that could just as easily be found in the Rocky Mountains. Aspen, Douglas fir, and Gambel oak shade the trail and hide many of the rocks in the Kaibab and Toroweap layers. The Coconino Sandstone, whose sheer cliffs hold too little soil for these trees, stands out against the greenery, its white rocks streaked tan and black by mineral deposits.

The next major landmark is **Supai Tunnel.** At 2.7 miles from the trailhead, and with seasonal water, shade, and rest rooms available, this is an excellent turnaround point for day hikers. Beyond the tunnel the canyon warms up, and heat-tolerant plants such as squaw-bush, pale hoptree, piñon pine, and juniper appear. The trail descends in relatively gradual switchbacks through the Supai Group, then crosses a bridge over a creek bed. Past the bridge, the creek plummets. The trail travels along the south wall of Roaring Springs Canyon, on ledges above Redwall cliffs. A spire of Redwall Limestone known as **"The Needle"** marks the point where the trail begins its descent of the Redwall.

North Kaibab & Clear Creek Trails (North Rim)

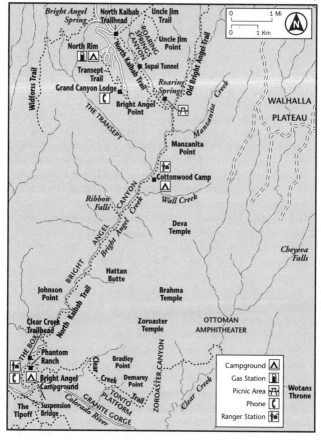

Roaring Springs, the water source for both rims, becomes audible just above the confluence of Bright Angel and Roaring Springs canyons. A .2-mile-long spur trail descends to the springs, where water pours from an opening in the Muav Limestone and cascades downhill, pooling at the bottom of the creek bed. Around those pools grow Arizona grape, scouring rushes, and box elder and cottonwood trees. You'll find drinking water, shade, and picnic tables here. This is the farthest a day hiker should go.

Below the springs are a pump house, a heliport, and a residence for the pump house operator. In this area, the trail begins a long, gradual descent to the Colorado River, traveling on or near the floor of Bright Angel Canyon for most of the way. The rocks along this stretch can be difficult to sort out. In addition to the layers seen everywhere in the canyon, you'll find members of the Grand Canyon Supergroup, including the reddish-brown Dox Sandstone, purplish Shinumo Quartzite, orange-red Hakatai Shale, and numerous dikes and sills—places where lava filled cracks in the earth.

About a mile past Cottonwood Campground, a spur trail leads to **Ribbon Falls,** the centerpiece of a large natural amphitheater. The waterfall is usually a short detour off the North Kaibab trail. But when the water level is high, you'll need to backtrack to the bridge after seeing the falls, instead of fording the river farther downstream. Even so, don't pass up a chance to hike to the base of these falls, which roll off a high sandstone ledge and arc gracefully to earth, skimming an apron of travertine on the way. This apron formed when calcium carbonate precipitated out of the water as rock. You may see small, brown birds known as dippers (the name alone describes them) fishing in the pools around these falls.

About 2.5 miles past the falls, the trail enters a long stretch of narrows known as "The Box" and remains there, winding alongside Bright Angel Creek, until just above Phantom Ranch. To keep hikers dry in these narrows, the CCC in the 1930s built three bridges over the creek and blasted ledges in the cliffs of the Vishnu Formation. An immense flash flood swept away most of the originals— steel and all—in 1966. A more recent flood, in July 1999, damaged the trail so badly that it was closed for more than 2 months.

8   Wilderness Trails: South Rim

Hermit Trail. 2.5 mi. to Santa Maria Spring; 7.8 mi. to Hermit Creek; 9.3 mi. to Colorado River. Access: Parking area west of Hermit's Rest. 6,640 ft. at trailhead; 4,880 ft. at Santa Maria Spring; 2,400 ft. at Colorado River. Water sources at Santa Maria Spring, Hermit Creek, and Colorado River. Maps: Grand Canyon (7.5 min.) quadrangle.

Highlights: Once the best-built trail in the canyon, it's still in relatively good shape between the rim and upper Hermit Basin. Late-afternoon sun feels good on cold days.

Drawbacks: Past Santa Maria Spring, washouts and rock fall complicate route-finding.

Note: Backpackers planning overnight trips on the Hermit Trail can receive special permits to drive on the West Rim Drive, at the Backcountry Office.

Hermit Trail/Dripping Springs/Boucher Trails (South Rim)

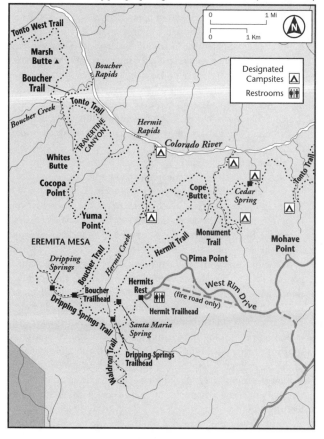

In 1912, the Santa Fe Railroad sought to establish a route into the canyon that Ralph Cameron, the "owner" of the Bright Angel Trail, couldn't control. So it built the Hermit Trail 8 miles west of Grand Canyon Village. Paved with sandstone slabs and with low walls on the outside, the Hermit Trail was generally regarded as the nicest in the canyon in the 1910s. The vine-covered shelter at Santa Maria Spring was built at about the same time, as was Mary Colter's new building known as Hermit's Rest.

Today the Hermit Trail remains wide at the top, with long, gradual switchbacks descending to the bottom of the Coconino

Sandstone and onto the expanse of upper Hermit Basin. Because the upper trail is on west-facing cliffs, it's cool in the morning and hot in the afternoon. Below the Coconino Sandstone, the trail, passing a few low-lying piñon and juniper trees, intersects both the Waldron and the Dripping Springs trails. Go right both times. Near the head of the brick-red Hermit Gorge, the trail makes a few switchbacks down into the Supai Group, eventually reaching a delicious water source, Santa Maria Spring. At 2.5 miles down, this spring is a nice turnaround point for day hikers. To be safe, treat the water before drinking.

Past the spring, the trail heads toward the tip of Pima Point, remaining fairly level—except when negotiating areas covered by rockfall or when making short descents, via switchbacks, lower into the Supai Group rocks. Finally, reaching a break in the Redwall, it careens downhill in tight switchbacks known as the Cathedral Stairs. Below the Redwall, the trail slices downhill, then makes a series of long switchbacks onto the Tonto Platform.

At the junction with the Tonto Trail, the Hermit Trail continues west (left) toward Hermit Creek. Later you'll reach another junction. The trail forking to the right from here descends to Hermit Creek between the Hermit Creek campsites and the Colorado River. Hikers camping at Hermit Rapid should take this shortcut. Others, including those using the Hermit Creek sites, should continue straight, passing this turnoff. In this area you'll also find remnants of the old Hermit Camp. Guests here in the 1920s were shuttled around the camp in a Model T that had been transported to the camp in pieces and reassembled on site—a luxury you may pine for by this point.

If you do walk the 1.5 miles down the creek to the beach at Hermit Rapids, you'll pass several nice pour-overs and small pools that are perfect for soaking. Along the walls, watch for sacred datura, identifiable by its large, teardrop-shaped leaves and white, lilylike flowers. You may have company at the beach—river trips frequently stop here to scout the rapids below the confluence.

Dripping Springs Trail. 3 mi. from Hermit trailhead to Dripping Springs. Access: Located off of the Hermit Trail at the head of Hermit Gorge. 6,640 ft. at Hermit trailhead; 5,600 ft. at Dripping Springs; 5,300 ft. at junction Dripping Springs trail (off Hermit Trail). Water sources at Dripping Springs (purify before drinking). Map: Grand Canyon (7.5 min.) quadrangle.

Highlights: This uncrowded trail ascends gradually to springs in a deep alcove.

Drawbacks: Does not afford expansive views.

Although this trail doesn't have expansive views of the inner canyon, it offers the peace and solitude needed to appreciate the desert's sounds, smells, and lighting. The most physically demanding part is the 1,340-vertical-foot descent from the Hermit Trail trailhead to the junction with the Dripping Springs Trail. On the Dripping Springs Trail, it's a gradual westward climb to the springs themselves. (There are however, a few sections of trail near the head of Hermit Gorge that roll steeply and are narrow and exposed.) The trail eventually curves into an upper drainage of Hermit Basin, rounding the base of Eremita Mesa. The springs are partway up this drainage.

The 30-foot-deep rock overhang at Dripping Springs looks like a great place for a hermit to live. Perhaps this is why everyone assumed that Louis Boucher, the prospector who lived in this area in the early 1900s, *was* a hermit. It even looks a bit like the oversized fireplace of Hermit's Rest, the building Mary Colter designed as her own tribute to a loner's way of life. Not much remains of Boucher's camp. But the springs still trickle out of the overhanging rock, through moss and Maidenhair fern, and drip into a pool below. If you fill up, purify the water.

Note: Dripping Springs is also accessible via a short, steep trail from the rim directly above it. To purists, this is the real Dripping Springs Trail. Because the road to the original Dripping Springs trail is now closed a mile or so from the trailhead, the above route is preferable for most hikers.

✪ **Boucher Trail.** 10.5 mi. from Hermit trailhead to Boucher Rapid; 8 mi. from Boucher trailhead to Boucher Rapid. Access: Follow the Hermit Trail to the Dripping Springs Trail. The trailhead for the Boucher Trail is roughly a mile down the Dripping Springs Trail. 6,640 ft. at Hermit trailhead; 5,200 ft. at Boucher trailhead; 2,325 ft. at Boucher Rapid. Water sources at Boucher Creek and Colorado River. Map: Grand Canyon (7.5 min.) quadrangle.

Highlights: Starts with a relatively level stroll atop the Supai Group rocks, with expansive views.

Drawbacks: Challenging descents down boulder-covered slopes follow the stroll. Aircraft in Dragon Flight Corridor buzz around this area.

This trail is named for Louis Boucher, the hermit for whom Hermit Canyon may have been named. Despite his reputation, Boucher probably wasn't the most reclusive of the canyon's early settlers. Generally regarded as generous, he hired a few men to help him mine for copper and graphite in Boucher Canyon and even guided tourists at times before leaving the canyon for Utah in 1919. Far from hating people, he may have shunned the rims simply because he relished life inside the canyon. The shallowness of his mines seems to indicate that he did plenty of relaxing.

Although sightseeing planes in the Dragon Flight Corridor frequent this area, this trail, with its dual personality, is still one of my favorites. The trail's upper section consists of a long, relatively level stroll atop the Supai Group rocks—an elevated stretch that can make you feel weightless. The trail's lower section is its nettlesome alter ego. It's dauntingly steep—so steep that most people prefer to descend it as part of a Boucher/Tonto/Hermit loop. I prefer climbing it, which is easier on the knees. This precipitous stretch makes the Boucher Trail suitable only for the strongest hikers.

From its junction with the Dripping Springs Trail, the Boucher Trail contours for almost 3 miles atop the Supai Group rocks, traveling below the tip of Yuma Point to near the head of Travertine Canyon. While you amble around Yuma Point, you can look just past your feet into the depths of Hermit Gorge or across the canyon at the pronged **Tower of Ra,** among other inner canyon features.

After descending steeply (a good deal of scrambling and use of hands is required) through the Supai Group rocks to the bed of Travertine Canyon, the trail stays on the west side of the drainage. Another, equally steep section starts after the trail veers left out of the drainage and traverses to a saddle below Whites Butte. From here, it plummets down a rocky chute, passing through the Redwall, Temple Butte, and Muav layers. On the Bright Angel Shale, the trail continues to drop steeply, only with fewer boulders for footholds. At the junction with the Tonto Trail, go left (west) to Boucher Creek.

You can choose from several nice campsites near the confluence of Boucher and Topaz creeks, a short distance downstream from where Louis Boucher once grew oranges, peaches, and figs (the historic Boucher Cabin is closed to camping, though the sites around it remain open). Or you can walk an additional 1.5 miles down the creek bed to Boucher Rapids. Here, white-sand beaches border schist polished smooth by the Colorado River.

Grandview Trail. 3 mi. from Grandview Trail trailhead to Horseshoe Mesa; 6.8 mi. to Tonto Trail (via the East Horseshoe Mesa Trail). Access: From Grandview Point (on Hwy. 64, 12 mi. east of Grand Canyon Village). 7,400 ft. at Grandview trailhead; 4,800 ft. at Horseshoe Mesa; 3,760 ft. at Tonto Trail Junction. No water sources on Horseshoe Mesa. Water source at Miner's Spring (off the east

Horseshoe Mesa Trail, well below the rim of Horseshoe Mesa). Maps: Grandview Point (7.5 min.) and Cape Royal (7.5 min.) quadrangles.

Highlights: This historic trail, itself worth seeing, is in good shape to Coconino Saddle, which provides views down into two side canyons.

Drawbacks: No water on or above the mesa. Steep ramps on the trail become slippery when wet or icy. In winter, near the top, crampons and even an ice ax might be required.

Hiking the Grandview Trail is a great way to take in human history along with the canyon scenery. Strong day hikers can descend the 2,600 vertical feet over 3 miles to Horseshoe Mesa, look over the remnants of Pete Barry's turn-of-the-century copper mine, and still make it back to the rim for dinner. Backpackers can use it to begin or close out loop hikes.

The trail itself is part of the history. All but the top 430 feet of it was built in the 1890s. (The current upper section was completed around 1910.) In some places, the trail builders used dynamite to blast away rock from sheer cliffs, forming ledges where none had been. In others they pinned a trail against the walls. To do this, they drilled holes into the rocks, pounded metal rods into the holes, then laid logs lengthwise above the rods. They then crammed rocks and dirt into openings and, as a finishing touch, paved the trail with a layer of cobblestones. Be sure to look at the trail from below to admire its structure.

As you walk down the cobblestone ramps below Grandview Point, you'll find that this area is especially slick in wet weather. For day hikers who are agile but not particularly strong, a smart place to turn around is at the saddle between upper Hance and Grapevine canyons. Known as the Coconino Saddle, it's about .75 mile from the rim. Here, you'll find shade, flat spots for resting, and views of both canyons. At the bottom of the Coconino Sandstone, the trail traverses east, then turns north, descending through the Hermit Shale and the Supai Group and onto Horseshoe Mesa. On the mesa, it intersects the Horseshoe Mesa Trail.

Whether you go right, left, or straight at this junction, you'll eventually intersect the Tonto Trail. By going right, you'll descend 700 feet through the Redwall Limestone on the southeast side of the mesa. Steep and rocky, this is the most precarious route off the mesa. It's also the quickest path to water. Below the Redwall, a short spur trail leads to the perennial Miner's Spring. (Purify it for safety.) You'll also find several mines here, including the New Tunnel (new in 1906), with a boiler and a compressor outside. In addition to being unstable, the mines have high levels of radon, so it's best to stay out of them.

By going left, you'll descend the west side of the mesa to the ephemeral Cottonwood Creek, where the first miners lived. By going straight, you'll travel out onto the northwest "arm" of the mesa, where you'll see the foundations of buildings from the mine camp, as well as old bottles, cans, and pieces of metal stoves. Also present, but less conspicuous, is evidence of past Indian activity: bits of chert (quartz rocks from which arrowheads were made) and old agave roasting pits. A pit toilet is available for campers in this area, who must camp in designated, posted sites.

Tonto Trail. 95 mi. from Red Canyon (east) to Garnet Canyon (west). Access: The Hance, Grandview, South Kaibab, Bright Angel, Hermit, Boucher, and South Bass trails all intersect the Tonto Trail. 3,600 ft. at Red Canyon; 2,800 ft. at Garnet Canyon. Water sources at Hance, Cottonwood (usually), Grapevine, Pipe, Monument, Hermit, and Boucher creeks, Indian Garden Spring, the Colorado River in several locations. Ask at the Backcountry Office about water sources before starting hike. Map: Depends on section hiked.

Highlights: Links many of the South Rim trails, creating some of the nicest loop hikes in the park.

Drawbacks: Long, shadeless, dry stretches make knowledge of water sources imperative.

This 95-mile trail traverses much of the lower canyon atop the Tonto Platform. Rather than hike all of it, most people include parts in shorter loop hikes linking trails from the South Rim. Hiking here is often more strenuous than expected. Distances that look short on the map sometimes take long periods to cover, as the trail contours around numerous drainages that cut partway into the Tonto Platform. Because the platform has little to no shade, and because many of its water sources are seasonal, long hikes here during summer are ill-advised. Especially dangerous are the stretches between the Grandview and South Kaibab trails and between Slate Canyon and the Bass Trail, both of which lack reliable water.

9 Wilderness Trails: North Rim

Clear Creek Trail. 8.7 mi. from Phantom Ranch to Clear Creek Drainage. Access: .3 mi. north of Phantom Ranch on the North Kaibab Trail. 2,600 ft. at Bright Angel Creek; 4,160 ft. at Tonto Plateau; 3,600 ft. at Clear Creek. Water source at Clear Creek. Maps: Phantom Ranch (7.5 min.) quadrangle.

Highlights: A scenic, relatively flat spur off the North Kaibab Trail, with views of Zoroaster Temple, Clear Creek, and the Colorado River.

Drawbacks: Dangerously hot and dry in summer.

After leaving the North Kaibab Trail, the Clear Creek Trail climbs in steep switchbacks east of Bright Angel Creek, eventually reaching an overlook of the Colorado River, sandwiched between the dark walls of the Granite Gorge. The trail then travels east above the river, gradually ascending to the Tonto Platform.

Before it reaches that level, however, watch for the interface between the black, 2-billion-year-old Vishnu Formation and the flat brown facade of the Tapeats Sandstone. You can touch the point of contact between these layers. This is as close as you'll get to "touching" the Great Unconformity, the gap of 1.2 billion years in the geological record caused by past erosion.

After reaching the Tonto Platform, the trail continues to the east (and then southeast), veering around the tops of numerous drainages, all beneath the imposing presence of Zoroaster Temple to the north. This long, shadeless stretch, where blackbrush and agave are among the tallest plants, makes the Clear Creek Trail a risky place for summer hiking. Eventually the trail crests a small rise, revealing a view of the confluence of the Colorado River Gorge and the drainage cut by Clear Creek. Turning northeast, the trail crosses Zoroaster Canyon and then traverses above Clear Creek before finally descending to the creek bed itself.

There are a number of nice campsites in the area just west of Clear Creek, all within easy walking distance of a pit toilet. From these campsites you can strike out on a number of excellent day hikes. Follow the creek 4 miles north to Cheyava Falls, a seasonal waterfall that, at 800 feet, is tallest in the canyon. Or walk (and down-climb) 6 miles south to the Colorado River. The narrows en route to the Colorado are subject to flash floods and should be avoided during wet weather and spring runoff.

Bill Hall Trail. 2.5 mi. to the Thunder River Trail. Access: Monument Point. To get here follow Hwy. 67 north from the park to FSR 422. Take FSR 422 west to FSR 292 to FSR 292A. After leaving Hwy. 67, roads are dirt Forest Service roads. (They're generally, but not always, passable for high-clearance 2-wheel-drive vehicles after the snow melts.) 7,200 ft. at Monument Point; 5,500 ft. at junction with Thunder River Trail. Maps: Tapeats Amphitheater (7.5 min.) and Fishtail Mesa (7.5 min.) quadrangles.

Highlights: Lops 4 miles off the length of the Thunder River Trail. Great place to spot wildflowers that thrive in disturbed areas.

Drawbacks: Adds 750 feet to the climb out, including very steep stretches that require scrambling.

Named for a former Grand Canyon ranger who died in the line of duty (at another park), the Bill Hall Trail is a steep shortcut in place of the upper Thunder River Trail. It lops 4 miles off the length of that trail while adding 750 feet to the elevation change.

From its trailhead at Monument Point, it follows an old Jeep trail for about a half mile along the rim, passing through an area charred by a recent forest fire. This area is now being reclaimed by wildflowers that thrive in disturbed areas, including coyote tobacco, prickle poppy, and globe mallow. The trail plummets below the rim in steep switchbacks through the Kaibab and Toroweap formations, then traverses to the west and northwest above the Coconino Sandstone until it reaches a break in the cliffs. Like the Tanner Trail, the upper section of this trail may force you to use your butt and hands in addition to your feet. The descent through the Coconino Sandstone involves one 15-foot down-climb that shouldn't pose a problem for most backpackers. Below the down-climb, 40 tight switchbacks will have you pivoting more often than a drum major. The trail intersects the Thunder River Trail on the Esplanade at the top of the Supai Formation.

10 Other Sports & Activities

CONDOR VIEWING

On the North Rim, between Jacob Lake and Lee's Ferry, a short side trip might result in your spotting the largest land bird in North America. Members of the vulture family, California condors will cruise up to 100 miles a day, at speeds approaching 50 m.p.h. They're grayish-black except on their heads, which are orange, and under each wing, where a triangular white patch is sometimes visible.

In December 1996, six of these birds, whose wings commonly span 10 feet, were released on the Vermilion Cliffs along Highway 89A near Lee's Ferry. Twenty-two more have been released in northern Arizona since then, and 20 survive in the area today. The releases were part of a larger project aimed at reintroducing the birds to the wild after they nearly went extinct in the 1980s.

In summer 1999, many of the birds frequented busy overlooks on the South Rim of Grand Canyon National Park. But don't count on seeing them there. By the time this book is in print, the condors are likely to have found a new haunt, says Chris Parish, condor coordinator/biologist for the Arizona Fish and Game Department.

If you'd like to see the condors, your best bet is to drive 14 miles east of Jacob Lake on Highway 89A to House Rock Valley Road (the first road to your left after you leave the National Forest). Turn left (north) and go 2 miles to a small ramada. In the cliffs above the ramada, nine additional condors were to be released in October 1999. If most of the condors are in the area, you'll probably meet scientists who are tracking them. They carry a spotting scope and binoculars and will help you sight the birds. When most of the birds leave, however, the scientists follow. If you're alone at the ramada, use your binoculars to scan the cliffs. You may spot birds that stayed behind.

Wherever you spot them, please don't approach, feed, or otherwise disturb the condors. If you see one who appears to be hurt or endangered, notify the **Arizona Game and Fish Department Region II Office** at ☎ **520/774-5045.** Be prepared to identify the time and location of the sighting and, if possible, the wing-tag number of the bird.

CROSS-COUNTRY SKIING

The crisp air, deep snow, and absolute silence make the **North Rim** a delightful place to ski. Unfortunately, Kaibab Lodge discontinued its Nordic ski program a few years ago. Now the closest skiing to the park starts south of Jacob Lake, at the gate that closes Highway 67; you can park your car here. From the gate, your safest option is to ski south on the snow-covered highway. Snowmobiles are banned from the highway at all times and on the land east of the highway. If you'd like to ski into the park and spend the night on the North Rim, you'll need to obtain a backcountry permit from the **Backcountry Office** (☎ **520/638-7875**).

When snow sticks on the **South Rim,** you can cross-country ski at the Grandview Nordic Center in the Kaibab National Forest near Grandview Point. To get there, drive east toward Desert View on Highway 64. About 1.7 miles past the Grandview Point turnoff, turn right on the road to the Arizona Trail. Park where the snow begins, then ski or walk down the road roughly a quarter mile to a bulletin board with instructions for the trails. The Forest Service has marked three loops in this area, each meandering through meadows and ponderosa pine forest: the intermediate 7.5-mile-long Twin Lakes Loop; the easy 1.1-mile Grandview Lookout Loop; and the easy 3.7-mile Boundary Loop. There's no charge. For more information call the **Kaibab National Forest Tusayan Ranger District Office** at ☎ **520/638-2443.** The South Rim's **General Store** (☎ **520/638-2262**) rents cross-country ski packages for $13.

FISHING

You're welcome to fish in the Colorado River, provided you have an Arizona Fishing Permit and trout stamp. One-day nonresident permits are available for $8.00 (or five days for $18.50) at the South Rim's **General Store** (☎ 520/638-2262) in Grand Canyon Village; at **Marble Canyon Lodge** (☎ 800/726-1789 or 520/355-2225), a quarter mile west of the Navajo Bridge on Highway 89A; and at **Lee's Ferry Anglers Guides and Fly Shop** (☎ 800/962-9755 or 520/355-2261), next to Lee's Ferry Lodge, four miles west of Navajo Bridge at Vermilion Cliffs. **The Marble Canyon/Vermilion Cliffs** area is about 45 miles southwest of Page and $2^1/_2$ hours north of Flagstaff.

Once you get your fishing permit, the next challenge is getting to the best fishing spots. To fish inside park boundaries, you either have to hike to the Colorado River or be on a river trip and fish during breaks from rafting (for information on river trips, see p. 93, later in this chapter).

The best trout fishing inside the park is at the eastern end of the canyon—upstream of Phantom Ranch. The river is clear and cold (48°F) year-round directly below the dam, making this a great trout hatchery (and a chilling place for the native species, which evolved to live in muddy water and extreme variations in temperature). Downstream, the river gradually warms and gathers sediment from its tributaries, causing the trout population to dwindle and enabling the bottom-feeders to survive. The five most abundant fish species in the park are carp, speckled dace, flannelmouth sucker, rainbow trout, and blue-head sucker.

Some of the best trout fishing in the Southwest is just upstream of the park's easternmost boundary, between Glen Canyon Dam and Lee's Ferry. Most of the hot spots in this 16-mile-long stretch of river can be reached only by boat, but anyone can walk up a mile of shoreline from the parking area at Lee's Ferry. And the fishing here sizzles at times. If you don't have your rod and waders with you, you can rent them, and boats too, from **Lee's Ferry Anglers** (☎ 800/962-9755 or 520/355-2261, www.leesferry.com, e-mail: anglers@leesferry.com). This shop, the best in the area, offers a complete guide service and carries a full line of fishing gear and tackle.

HORSEBACK RIDING
SOUTH RIM HORSEBACK RIDING

The only horseback riding near the South Rim is at **Apache Stables** (☎ 520/638-2891), which operates at Moqui Lodge, just outside the park's south entrance. Most of the horses at the stables are "dog friendly," as our guide put it. They're retired ranch horses that average 15 years in age. Because they're gentle and know the trails around the stables, you need only kick your steed periodically to ensure that it keeps going. The rest of the time, you can relax and enjoy your horse's swaying and the ponderosa pine forest.

The friendly horses make this a great family activity. Children as young as 6 (and 45 inches tall) are allowed on the 1-hour trail rides, which, like the 2-hour ones, loop through the Kaibab National Forest near the stables. Apache Stables also offers a 4-hour ride east through the forest, which goes close to Grandview Point. There, riders dismount and cross Highway 64 on foot to admire the canyon. This trip is closed to children under 14. Other options are a 1-hour evening trail ride and a wagon ride, both ending at a campfire where participants roast marshmallows and other food they've brought.

Prices for the rides, running mid-March to the end of November, are $65 for the 4-hour East Rim ride, $40 for the 2-hour ride, $25 for the 1-hour ride, $30 for the evening trail ride, and $8.50 for the wagon ride.

NORTH RIM HORSEBACK RIDING

On the North Rim, **Allen's Guided Tours** (☎ **435/644-8150**) offers horseback rides from 8am to 6pm Monday to Saturday. Departing from a corral a quarter mile south of Jacob Lake on Highway 67, the tours travel on gentle terrain in the Kaibab National Forest. One- and 2-hour rides cost $15 and $25, respectively. Half-day rides, which follow a stretch of the Arizona Trail, cost $45. Full-day rides, which cost $75, travel to and from an overlook of the eastern canyon and include a bag lunch. There is no weight or age limit.

CYCLING & MOUNTAIN BIKING

Inside the park, cyclists are required to stay on roads, many of them narrow and crowded. Routes such as Highway 64 and the Cape Royal Road are inherently risky for cyclists. But at least two good rides exist. Between mid-March and mid-October, the West Rim Drive is closed to most private cars, making it a haven for cyclists. Of course, you'll still have to watch out for tour buses, shuttles and a handful of private vehicles, and for people on foot, many of whom will be oblivious to your approach. On the North Rim, the entrance road is wide enough to accommodate cautious cyclists.

For **off-road cycling,** you'll need to go into the Kaibab National Forest just outside park boundaries. On the South Rim, you'll find excellent mountain biking on the Arizona Trail starting at Grandview Lookout Tower. To reach the lookout, take Highway 64 east from Grand Canyon Village. About 1.7 miles east of the Grandview

Point turnoff, turn right (south) onto the road for the Arizona Trail. Leaving the park, follow this dirt road 1.3 miles to Grandview Lookout and the trailhead. Beginning here, you'll find more than 20 miles of intermediate-level single-track (with a few short, technically demanding stretches thrown in), much of it along the Coconino Rim.

Another trail system, with loops of 3.7, 10.2, and 11.2 miles, is located near Tusayan. These loops follow old Jeep trails through rolling hills in the ponderosa pine forest. The trails have a few steep, rocky areas, but most of the terrain is only moderately difficult. To reach them, find the marked parking area .3 mile north of Tusayan on the west side of Highway 64. A single trail heads north from there, eventually crossing under the highway through a concrete tunnel and providing access to the loops. (*Note:* this is also a great place to run when you're staying in Tusayan.) For information on these trails and maps of the Tusayan Ranger District (☎ 520/638-2443), visit the **Forest Service Office** a half mile south of the park entrance on Highway 64.

The **mountain-biking** is even better on the North Rim, where the southwest edge of the North Kaibab Ranger District borders the rim of the canyon. Cyclists can use a combination of single-track, Jeep trails, and gravel roads to ride close to or alongside the rim in places. Visit the **Kaibab Plateau Visitor Center** in Jacob Lake (☎ 520/643-7298) for maps, road conditions, and trail descriptions. The visitor center is located on Highway 67, a few yards south of Jacob Lake Inn.

BIKE RENTALS

SOUTH RIM   The nearest bike rentals to the South Rim are at the following Flagstaff locations: **Absolute Bikes** (☎ 520/779-5969), 18 N. San Francisco St.; **Cosmic Cycles** (☎ 520/779-1092), 901 N. Beaver St.; and **Mountain Sports** (☎ 800/286-5156 or 520/779-5156), 1800 S. Milton Rd.

NORTH RIM   No bike rentals are available on the North Rim. However, **Kaibab Adventure Outfitters** (☎ 800/451-1133 or 801/259-7423) of Moab, Utah, offers van-supported 5-day mountain-bike tours (cost: $795) of the North Rim. They supply both bikes and camping gear.

MULE RIDES
SOUTH RIM MULE RIDES

Wearing floppy hats and clutching rain slickers, the day's mule riders gather at 8am (9am in winter) every morning at a corral west of

Bright Angel Lodge to prepare for their rides. You can almost hear the jangling nerves as they contemplate the prospect of descending narrow trails above steep cliffs on animals hardly famous for their intelligence. Although the mules walk close to the edges and have been known to *back* off the trails, accidents are rare, especially among riders who follow the wrangler's instructions. In fact, Fred Harvey has been guiding mule trips into the canyon for more than 90 years without a single fatality from a fall.

The rides, while usually safe, can nonetheless be grueling. Most people's legs aren't used to bending around a mule, and the saddles aren't soft. In addition to the pounding, the canyon can be scorching, and chances for breaks are few. Because the rides are strenuous for both riders and mules, the wranglers strictly adhere to the following requirements: You must weigh less than 200 pounds, be at least 4 feet 7 inches tall, speak fluent English, and not be pregnant. If the wranglers think you weigh too much, they won't hesitate to put you on the scale.

The most grueling of all is the ride to Plateau Point. It travels down the Bright Angel Trail to Indian Garden, then follows the Plateau Point Trail across the Tonto Platform to an overlook (Plateau Point) of the Colorado River. Having descended more than 3,000 vertical feet, the riders return on the same trails. This 12-mile, round-trip ride, which breaks for lunch at Indian Garden, doesn't reach the rim until mid- to late afternoon. Cost: $100.

The other rides are part of 1- or 2-night packages that include lodging and meals at Phantom Ranch. Going down, they follow the Bright Angel Trail to the river, then travel east on the River Trail before finally crossing the river via the Kaibab Suspension Bridge. Coming back they use the South Kaibab Trail. The 10.5-mile descent takes 5¹/₂ hours; the 8-mile-long climb out is an hour shorter. The Phantom Ranch overnight costs $278.70 for one person, $495.40 for two, and $227.20 for each additional person. The Phantom Ranch 2-night trip, which is offered only from mid-November through March 31, costs $385.95 for one, $647.90 for two, and $282.95 for each additional person. A livery service is also available. One-way transportation of a 30-pound duffel (or less) costs $43.60.

NORTH RIM MULE RIDES

Mule rides on the North Rim are through a small, family run outfit called **Grand Canyon Trail Rides.** Four types of rides are offered. Open to ages 6 and up, the easiest ride goes 1 mile along the rim on the Ken Patrick Trail before turning back. This 1-hour ride

Reserving a Mule Trip

Mule trips to Phantom Ranch fill up months in advance, so make your reservations early. Reservations for the next 23 months can be made beginning on the first of the month. For example, dates in December 2002 would first go on sale January 1, 2000. For **advance reservations** call ☎ **303/297-2757.** For reservations in the next 4 days, call the **Bright Angel Transportation Desk** at ☎ **520/638-2631,** ext. 6015. If you arrive without reservations, you can put your name on a waiting list by going to the desk in person.

The mule rides on the North Rim tend to fill up later than those on the South Rim. To sign up, visit the **Grand Canyon Trail Rides** desk (open daily 7am to 6pm) at Grand Canyon Lodge, or call ☎ **520/638-9875.** The off-season number is ☎ **801/679-8665,** and the Web address is www.onpages.com/canyonrides/.

costs $15 per person. Two half-day rides, each costing $40 per person, are offered. One stays on the rim, following the Ken Patrick and Uncle Jim trails to a canyon viewpoint; the other descends 2 miles into the canyon on the North Kaibab Trail, turning back at Supai Tunnel. The all-day ride, which includes lunch, travels 5 miles on the North Kaibab Trail to Roaring Springs before turning back. Cost for the all-day ride is $95. Riders must be at least 12 to go on the all-day ride. No one over 200 pounds is allowed on the canyon rides; for the rim rides, the limit is 220. All riders must speak English.

OVERFLIGHTS

Ten companies at Grand Canyon National Park Airport in Tusayan currently offer scenic airplane or helicopter rides over the canyon. With more than 250,000 people flying out of Tusayan alone every year, the flights, which generate a great deal of noise in parts of the park, have become a politically charged issue.

For many vacationers, however, the question is not whether overflights should be allowed, but whether to fly in an airplane or a helicopter. The airplane flights generally last longer, averaging about 45 minutes as opposed to 30 minutes for helicopters, and cost less—about $75 for a 50-minute ride, compared to about $95 for a half-hour chopper ride. The planes also cover more ground, crossing the canyon near Hermit's Rest and returning along the East Rim, near Desert View. The helicopter tours, meanwhile, usually fly out and back in the same corridor near Hermit's Rest. (Some do go for the full loop.) The helicopters cruise lower—just above the rim. And while they're not immune to an occasional bump, they tend to be smoother.

During my helicopter ride, cinematic scores played over headphones, setting an epic tone that didn't quite jibe with the canyon. The flight afforded stunning aerial views of the topography, but precluded smelling or touching it. It was also a bit stomach-churning. It didn't help that I was pinned in the helicopter's middle seat between two large, sweaty strangers. The IMAX movie often achieves similar effects—without disturbing the wilderness.

The following companies offer air tours originating from Tusayan: **Papillon Grand Canyon Helicopters** (☎ **800/528-2418** or 520/638-2419, www.papillon.com); **Air Grand Canyon** (☎ **520/638-2686**); **AirStar Airlines** (☎ **520/638-2139**); **Airstar Helicopters** (☎ **520/638-2622**); **Grand Canyon Airlines** (☎ **800/528-2413** or 520/638-2407, www.grandcanyonairlines. com); **Kenai Helicopters** (☎ **520/638-2764**).

RAFTING

White-water raft trips inside the park generally last from 3 to 14 days and must be booked well ahead of time. However, several companies offer shorter trips on the Colorado River near or inside Grand Canyon.

Aramark-Wilderness River Adventures, 50 S. Lake Powell Blvd., Page, AZ (☎ **800/528-6154** or 520/645-3279), offers half-day and full-day smooth-water raft trips from the base of Glen Canyon Dam to Lee's Ferry, where the companies floating into Grand Canyon *begin* their trips. You'll complete the motorized half-day trip, which travels below the sandstone walls of the Vermilion and Echo cliffs, in about 4 hours. Lunch is included. On the all-day trip, the boat drifts, engines off, for more of the time, and a buffet lunch is served on the beach. Aramark schedules two trips daily from May 15 to September 15, with a more limited schedule at other times. Cost for the half-day trip is $51 for adults, $44 for 11 and under. The full-day trip costs $71 for adults, $64 for 11 and under.

AMFAC offers the half-day trip, plus round-trip transportation (totaling 290 miles) from Moqui Lodge, just south of the Park's south entrance. Cost for this 12-hour tour is $96 ($48 for 12 and under). For advance reservations call ☎ **303/297-2757.** Within 4 days, call ☎ **520/638-2631,** ext. 6015.

One- and 2-day trips through the westernmost part of Grand Canyon are available through **Hualapai River Runners** (☎ **800/**

622-4409 or 520/769-2210), P.O. Box 246, Peach Springs, AZ 86434. These motorized trips begin with rapids in the lower Granite Gorge of Grand Canyon and end on Lake Mead. Costs range from $221 to $321 per person. A 15% family discount is also offered.

EXPLORING THE BACKCOUNTRY ON A RAFT

Taking a raft trip through the canyon allows you to see the canyon from a new perspective and gives hikers access to some of the prettiest spots anywhere.

All the companies operating in the Grand Canyon are experienced and run excellent trips, subject to the whims of the Colorado River and the storms that move through the canyon. For about $200 per day, all provide food, portable toilets, and some camping equipment, as well as access to parts of the inner canyon that are difficult, if not impossible, to reach on foot. Among them are some of the most beautiful places on earth.

While most trips begin at Lee's Ferry, the end points vary. Trips last anywhere from 3 to 14 days. Some companies allow for partial trips by picking up or dropping off passengers at various points in the canyon (most often at Phantom Ranch). The companies also differ on what makes a trip special. For example, some allow for plenty of day hiking; others don't. Because the trips do vary greatly, it's important to consider the following factors before planning yours.

MOTORIZED VERSUS NONMOTORIZED

MOTORIZED   Motorized trips are fastest, often covering the 277 miles from Lee's Ferry (above the canyon) to Pierce Ferry (in Lake Mead) in 6 days, compared to as many as 19 for nonmotorized trips. The motorized trips use wide pontoon boats that almost never capsize, making them slightly safer. Also, it's easier to move about on these solid-framed boats than on oar or paddle boats, a plus for people who lack mobility. Because of the speed of the trips, however, there's less time for hiking or resting in camp. If motorized trips are for you, consider using the companies **Aramark-Wilderness Adventures** (☎ **800/992-8022** or 520/645-3296) or **Western River Expeditions** (☎ **800/453-7450** or 801/942-6669).

NONMOTORIZED   For mobile people who want to bask in the canyon's beauty, I strongly recommend nonmotorized trips, even if it means seeing half the canyon instead of all of it. A motorless raft glides at close to the water's pace, giving passengers time to observe subtle, enticing patterns—swirls of water in eddies; the play of shadows and light as the sun moves across rock layers; the opening, unfolding, and gradual closing of each side canyon. Without motors running, the sounds of the water provide a dreamlike backdrop to the journey.

There are two types of nonmotorized boats: paddle boats and oar boats. **Oar boats** are wooden dories or rubber rafts, each of which holds six passengers and a guide who does most or all of the rowing. If the guides are highly skilled, the passengers on an oar-powered trip have an excellent chance of floating the entire river without taking a life-threatening swim in the rapids. (The latest statistics on river-related deaths show commercial river trips to be as dangerous as golf.)

In a **paddle boat,** six passengers paddle, assisted by a guide who instructs them and helps steer. This experience is ideal for fit people who want to be involved at all times. However, because of the inexperience of the participants, these trips may be more risky than others. And paddling can become burdensome during the long, slow-water stretches, especially when a head wind blows. **Canyon Explorations** (☎ **800/654-0723** or 520/774-4559) and **Outdoors Unlimited** (☎ **800/637-7238** or 520/526-4546) both have excellent reputations for paddle trips.

If an oar-powered company appeals to you, I recommend the company known as **Oars** (☎ **800/346-6277** or 209/736-4677, see listing below), which has some of the most experienced guides on the river. On my trip with Oars, the three guides had a combined 52 years on the Colorado. They were responsible, informative, and fun, sharing the joy they found in the canyon. During the busiest months, Oars assures quality service by sending six crew members out with each group of 16 passengers—providing one of the best crew-to-client ratios on the river.

Oars also offers paddle trips. However, in order to ensure that each group of paddlers meshes, the company accepts paddle boat reservations only by boatload (six).

Another factor to consider before scheduling your trip is the season. In **April,** the cacti bloom in the lower canyon, splashing bright colors across the hillsides, and the river is relatively uncrowded. However, cold weather—even snow—can occasionally make these trips a test of the spirit. In **May** the weather is usually splendid, but the river is at its most crowded. **June and July** can be oppressively hot. In **late July and August,** monsoons break the heat and generate waterfalls all along the river, but they also soak rafters. From **September 15 to the end of October,** no motorized rigs cruise the river, so the canyon is quiet, although cold weather can once again be a problem.

RIVER RAFTING COMPANIES

Aramark-Wilderness River Adventures. P.O. Box 717, Page, AZ 86040. ☎ **800/992-8022** or 520/645-3296. Fax 520/645-6113. www. riveradventures.com. E-mail: wilderness@aramark.com.

Aramark-Wilderness offers both motorized and oar-powered trips with trip lengths varying from 4 to 12 days; with 8-day motorized trips and 12-day oar trips.

Canyon Explorations. P.O. Box 310, Flagstaff, AZ 86002. ☎ **800/654-0723** or 520/774-4559. Fax 520/774-4655. www.canyonx.com. E-mail: canyonx@aol.com.

Canyon Explorations offers oar-powered and paddle trips with lengths varying from 6 to 16 days.

Oars/Grand Canyon Dories. P.O. Box 67, Angels Camp, CA 95222. ☎ **800/346-6277** or 209/736-4677. Fax 209/736-2902. www.oars.com. E-mail: reservations@oars.com.

Oars offers both oar-powered trips and paddle trips with trip lengths varying from 5 to 16 days.

Outdoors Unlimited. 6900 Townsend Winona Rd., Flagstaff, AZ 86004. ☎ **800/637-7238** or 520/526-2852. Fax 520/526-6185. www. outdoorsunlimited.com. E-mail: outdoor@ibm.net.

Outdoors Unlimited offers oar-powered and paddle trips with trip lengths ranging from 5 to 16 days.

Western River Expeditions. 7258 Racquet Club Dr., Salt Lake City, UT 84121. ☎ **800/453-7450** or 801/942-6669. Fax 801/942-8514. www. westernriver.com. E-mail: info@westernriver.com.

Western River Expeditions offers motorized and oar-powered trips with trip lengths varying from 3 to 12 days.

5

Where to Stay & Eat in Grand Canyon National Park

*T*his chapter lists accommodations and dining available inside Grand Canyon National Park, as well as campgrounds throughout the area. Many other hotels and restaurants exist in the nearby communities of Tusayan, Williams, and Flagstaff, Arizona, and in Kanab, Utah. Rooms in Flagstaff, Williams, and Kanab generally run at least $20 cheaper than comparable ones inside the park. (Tusayan, 1 mile from the park's south entrance, tends to be even more expensive than the park.)

If you're hoping to spend the night at or near the rim, be sure to reserve a room ahead of time (4 months ahead should usually be sufficient). The lodges inside the park and in Tusayan frequently fill up, forcing would-be lodgers to backtrack away from the park.

If you tire of new rooms with Southwestern motifs, a few historic hotels and lodges do remain. In the park, stay at **Grand Canyon Lodge** (on the North Rim), the **Bright Angel Lodge,** or the **El Tovar Hotel.** Protected by law, these historic structures cannot be gutted during renovation, so their rooms and cabins remain entertainingly quirky—unlike the other park lodging, which tends to be sterile.

See chapter 6, "Gateway Towns," for more information on where to stay and eat, and what to do outside of Grand Canyon National Park.

RESERVING A ROOM INSIDE THE PARK

Lodging inside the park is handled by **AMFAC Parks and Resorts,** 14001 E. Eliff, Aurora, CO 80014 (☎ **303/297-2757,** fax 303/297-3175). Beginning on the first of the month, you can reserve a room for the next 23 months. For example, on January 1, 2000, you could have reserved rooms through the end of December 2002. For reservations, only MasterCard and Visa are accepted. American Express, Diners Club, and Discover are acceptable upon arrival. AMFAC can take reservations up to the minute of your arrival. Pets are not allowed in accommodations inside the park.

The hotels themselves can be contacted through the same switchboard (☎ **520/638-2631,** fax 520/638-9247) and mailing address (P.O. Box 699, Grand Canyon, AZ 86023). The phone number for the **Grand Canyon Lodge** is ☎ **520/638-2611.** The hotels do not have specific street addresses. When you enter the park, you will receive a map locating all the hotels.

All the rooms in the park have relatively new furnishings, and all but a few have telephones and televisions. The only conspicuous difference in furnishings is at the El Tovar, where the furniture is more luxurious. The buildings themselves are what differs most within the park.

1 South Rim Lodges

EXPENSIVE

✪ **El Tovar Hotel.** ☎ **520/638-2631** (main switchboard) or 303/297-2757 (reservations only). Fax 303/297-3175. 75 units. A/C TV TEL. $114–$171 double; $194–$279 suite. AE, DC, DISC, MC, V. No pets.

The El Tovar, which was designed by Charles Whittlesey, is a cross between a Swiss chalet and a Norwegian villa. It's a dark, cool counterpoint to the warm, pueblo-style buildings of Mary Colter. Completed in 1905 to accommodate the influx of tourists on the Santa Fe Railroad, the El Tovar, situated a few yards from the rim, casts a long shadow over Grand Canyon Village. A pointed cupola sits like a witch's cap above its three stories of Oregon pine and stone, and spires rise above an upstairs deck. Nothing seems summery—from a distance, even its broad porches seem to recede into shadows.

The building's interior is as unforgettable as the outside. Moose and elk heads hang on varnished walls, dimly lit by copper chandeliers. Take away the modern-day tourists and the El Tovar probably looks much as it did at its inception, when it offered guests all manner of luxury, including a music room, art classes, a barber, and roof garden. The restaurant had its own greenhouse, dairy cows, and chickens.

While many of these amenities have gone the way of the Flagstaff-to-Grand Canyon stagecoach, the hotel is still the most luxurious at the canyon and the only one to offer room service and a nightly turndown. You'll still find a pleasant upstairs sitting area (reserved for guests) and rooms with classic American furnishings. At its inception, the rooms were larger, with shared baths at the end of each hall. When private bathrooms were added, new walls and floors were added to hide the plumbing. So the rooms became smaller and more

Grand Canyon Village

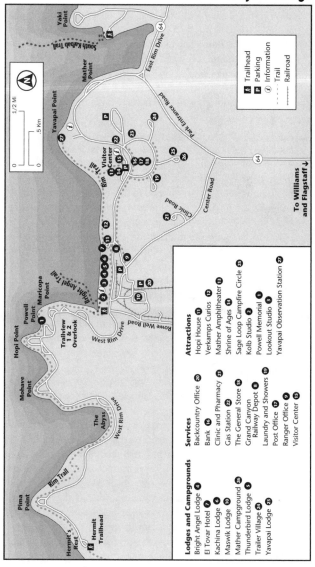

Lodges and Campgrounds
Bright Angel Lodge ④
El Tovar Hotel ⑦
Kachina Lodge ⑥
Maswik Lodge ⑩
Mather Campground ㉖
Thunderbird Lodge ⑤
Trailer Village ㉔
Yavapai Lodge ㉓

Services
Backcountry Office ⑳
Bank ⑯
Clinic and Pharmacy ㉑
Gas Station ㉒
The General Store ⑱
Grand Canyon Railway Depot ⑧
Laundry and Showers ⑲
Post Office ⑰
Ranger Office ⑨
Visitor Center ⑬

Attractions
Hopi House ⑪
Verkamps Curios ⑫
Mather Amphitheater ⑭
Shrine of Ages ⑮
Sage Loop Campfire Circle ㉕
Kolb Studio ②
Powell Memorial ①
Lookout Studio ③
Yavapai Observation Station ㉗

idiosyncratic. If the hotel isn't busy, ask to see a few before settling in.

Dining/Diversions: The El Tovar Dining Room is the best restaurant in the village and serves continental cuisine. Off the lobby is a cocktail lounge overlooking a broad lawn and a slice of the North Rim.

Amenities: Concierge, room service, tour desk.

MODERATE

Maswik Lodge. ☎ **520/638-2631** (main switchboard) or 303/297-2757 (reservations only). Fax 303/297-3175. 278 units. TV TEL. Maswik South $63–$73; Maswik North $63–$113. AE, DC, DISC, MC, V. No pets.

Built in the 1960s, Maswik Lodge is in a wooded area, a 10-minute walk from the rim. If you're not up to walking, the Maswik Transportation Center, the hub for the canyon shuttles, is opposite the lodge. The lodge has a restaurant, sports bar, and gift shop.

Most of the guest rooms are in the two-story wood-and-stone buildings known as Maswik North and South. The rooms in Maswik North have new carpeting, drapes, and bathroom tile—not to mention queen beds. The upstairs rooms in Building 12, all of which have private balconies and high ceilings, are among the nicest in the park. Rooms in Maswik South are 5 years older, a bit smaller, and have less pristine views. But during high season they cost $40 less. If you're staying at Maswik, bring a flashlight, as the area is dark at night.

Thunderbird and Kachina Lodges. ☎ **520/638-2631** (main switchboard) or 303/297-2757 (reservations only). Fax 303/297-3175. 55 units at Thunderbird, 49 at Kachina. A/C TV TEL. Park side $109; canyon side $119. AE, DC, DISC, MC, V. No pets.

The newest lodges inside the park, these are already slated for demolition in the new Grand Canyon master plan. It won't be any tragedy to see these buildings, which resemble 1960s-era college dormitories, get razed. Outside, they have flat roofs, decorative concrete panels, and metal staircases; inside are concrete steps, tile floors, and brick walls. The rooms are pleasant enough, with Southwestern-style furnishings and windows as wide as the rooms themselves. Although AMFAC refuses to guarantee a canyon view, most of the upstairs units on the more expensive "canyon side" have at least a partial view of the canyon. Check-in for the Thunderbird is at the Bright Angel Lodge; for the Kachina, it's at the El Tovar.

Yavapai Lodge. ☎ **520/638-2631** (main switchboard) or 303/297-2757 (reservations only). Fax 303/297-3175. 348 units. TV TEL. $63–$84 Yavapai West; $63–$99 Yavapai East. AE, DC, DISC, MC, V. No pets.

The largest lodge at the canyon, Yavapai is a mile from the historic district but close to Bank One, the South Rim's General Store, and the South Rim Visitor Center. Built between 1970 and 1972, the A-frame lodge has a large cafeteria and gift shop. The rooms are in 10 single-story buildings known as Yavapai West and 6 two-story wood buildings known as Yavapai East. Most rooms in Yavapai West have cinder-block walls, and all are compact. Because Yavapai West may eventually be razed under the park's master plan, little has been done to improve its rooms in recent years. Yavapai East's units are larger, and many have nice views of the forest. Most travelers would agree that they're worth the extra $15. There's more parking here than at the other lodges, since the lots were built to accommodate tour buses. The gravel paths connecting the buildings are very dark at night, so bring a flashlight.

INEXPENSIVE

Bright Angel Lodge & Cabins. ☎ **520/638-2631** (main switchboard) or 303/297-2757 (reservations only). Fax 303/297-3175. 34 units (10 with sink only, 10 with sink and toilet, 14 with bathroom); 55 cabin rms. $44 double (with sink only); $50 (with sink and toilet only); $60 (standard, with bathroom); $70 (historic cabins with queen beds); $96 (rim cabins); $225 (rim-side Bucky O'Neill Cabin, with fireplace). AE, DC, DISC, MC, V.

Guests of Bright Angel Lodge stay in tightly clustered buildings west of the main lodge. These buildings, which vary widely in both age and design, cover the site of the old Bright Angel Camp, whose tents and cabins served as lodging in the early 1900s. In the 1930s, Fred Harvey sought to provide affordable lodging for the new visitors coming by train and automobile to the canyon. At the company's request, Mary Colter designed both the lodge and the cabins alongside it. The cabins were built around several historic buildings, including the park's old post office and the Bucky O'Neill Cabin, the oldest continually standing structure on the rim.

Low-end accommodations start with dormitory-style rooms in two long buildings adjacent to Bright Angel Lodge. At $44 a night, the "hiker rooms" are the least expensive in the park. Each has a bed and desk but no television or private bathroom. Other rooms have double beds and toilets but no showers. Still others are appointed like standard motel rooms, only with showers instead of tubs.

Rooms in the historic cabins cost only $10 more than the nicest lodge rooms and are worth the extra money. These freestanding cabins, most of which house two guest rooms, recall a time when the canyon was a refuge from civilization. Most are bright inside, and the ones away from the rim are fairly quiet. At the high end of the price range are the four rim-side cabins, which have partial views of the canyon and cost $96. The luxurious Bucky O'Neill Cabin, one of the oldest structures in the park, boasts a fireplace and canyon views. It goes for $225. The rim-side cabins tend to fill up far in advance.

2 Lodging Inside the Canyon

✪ **Phantom Ranch.** Located at the bottom of the canyon, ¹/₂ mi. north of the Colorado River on the North Kaibab Trail. ☎ **520/638-2631** (main switchboard) or 303/297-2757 (reservations only). Fax 303/297-3175. Seven 4-person cabins, 2 cabins for up to 10 people, 4 dorms of 10 people each. $22.85 dorm bed; $65.95 cabins (for 2). $11.70 for each additional person. AE, DC, DISC, MC, V. No pets.

The only park lodging below the canyon rims, the cabins at Phantom Ranch often sell out on the first day of availability—more than 23 months ahead. To reserve a spot, call as early as possible. If you arrive at the canyon without a reservation, contact the **Bright Angel Transportation Desk** (☎ **520/638-2631,** ext. 6015) for information about openings in the next 4 days.

The reason for the booked slate? Clean sheets never felt better than at the bottom of the Grand Canyon, beer never tasted this good (not even close), and a hot shower never felt so, well, miraculous. Phantom Ranch is the only place below the rims inside the park that has these amenities.

The ranch's nine evaporatively cooled cabins are a simple pleasure. A famous Grand Canyon architect, Mary Colter, designed four of them—the ones with the most stone in the walls are hers—using rocks from the nearby Bright Angel Creek. Connected by dirt footpaths, they sit, natural and elegant, alongside picnic tables and under the shade of cottonwood trees. Inside each cabin, there's a desk, concrete floor, and 4 to 10 bunk beds, as well as a toilet and sink. A shower house for guests is nearby.

While most of Phantom Ranch was completed in the 1920s and '30s, four 10-person dorms, each with its own bathing facilities, were added in the early 1980s. Used mostly by hikers, these are ideal for individuals and small groups looking for a place to bed down; larger groups are better served by reserving cabins, which provide both privacy and a lower per-person price than the dorms.

During the day, some guests hike to Ribbon Falls or along the River Trail, while others relax, read, or write postcards that, if sent from here, will bear the unique stamp, "Mailed by mule from the bottom of the Grand Canyon." In the late afternoon, many guests and hikers from the nearby Bright Angel Campground gravitate to the canteen, which sells snacks when not serving meals. (For more on dining at Phantom Ranch, see p. 116.)

3 Lodging on the North Rim

✪ **Grand Canyon Lodge.** ☎ **520/638-2611** (main switchboard) or 303/297-2757 (reservations only). Fax 303/297-3175. 208 units. TEL. $74 Frontier Cabin; $80 motel rm.; $88 Pioneer Cabin; $94 Western Cabin; $104 Rim Cabin. AE, DC, DISC, MC, V. No pets.

Like the North Rim itself, Grand Canyon Lodge attracts little attention. Its architect, Gilbert Stanley Underwood, was best known for designing edifices such as train stations and post offices. Although Union Pacific Railroad built the lodge in 1928, the train never came closer than Cedar City, Utah. A few tourists came there on "triangle" bus tours that also stopped at Bryce and Zion canyons, but most went to the South Rim. Most still do.

After burning in 1932, the lodge reopened in 1937 and now seems to have grown into the landscape. Its roof of green shingles goes with the needles on the nearby trees, its log beams match their trunks, and its walls of Kaibab limestone blend with the rim rock itself. In its expansive lobby, a 50-foot-high ceiling absorbs sound like the forest floor. Beyond it, the octagonal "Sun Room" has three enormous picture windows opening onto the canyon. Two long decks with rocking chairs flank the sunroom, overlooking the canyon. The lodge also houses a saloon, a snack bar, a meeting room, and a full-service restaurant.

Made of the same materials as the lodge, 140 cabins have sprouted like saplings around it. There are four types, all with private bathrooms. With wicker furniture, bathtubs, and small vanity rooms, the Western Cabins and Rim Cabins are the most luxurious. The Western Cabins cost $10 less than the four Rim Cabins, which overlook the Bright Angel Canyon. The Rim Cabins generally fill up on their first day of availability, nearly 2 years in advance.

The two other types—Pioneer and Frontier—are more rustic. Tightly clustered along the rim of Transept Canyon, they have walls and ceilings of exposed logs, electric heaters, and showers instead of bathtubs. The Frontier Cabins each have one guest room with a double bed and a twin bed. The Pioneer Cabins, meanwhile, each have two guest rooms—one with a double bed and a twin bed, the other with two twins. For $95 ($21 more than the price of a Frontier Cabin), a family of five can stay in comfort in one of the Pioneer Cabins. If your reservations are for a Frontier or Pioneer cabin, ask at check-in for one that overlooks Transept Canyon. The lodge may be able to accommodate you, and there's no extra charge for the view.

A few motel rooms are also available. Although they're well maintained and were remodeled in 1999 (most now have queens instead of doubles), their atmosphere doesn't compare to the cabins.

4 Camping Near the South Rim

For maps and information on dispersed camping in the South Rim, stop by the **Tusayan Ranger District Office** (☎ **520/638-2443**).

INSIDE THE PARK

✪ **Desert View Campground.** 26 mi. east of Grand Canyon Village on Hwy. 64. No phone, no advance reservations. 50 sites. $10 per site. Open mid-May to mid-Oct.

At dusk, the yips of coyotes drift over this campground in piñon-juniper woodland at the eastern edge of the park. Elevated, cool, and breezy, the peaceful surroundings offer no clue that the bustling Desert View Overlook is within walking distance. The floor of the woodland makes for smooth tent sites, the most secluded being on the outside of the loop drive. The only drawback: The nearest showers are 26 miles away at Camper Services in Grand Canyon Village. During high season, this first-come, first-served campground usually fills up by noon. To secure a site, swing through in midmorning and see what's open.

Mather Campground. Near Grand Canyon Village on South Rim. ☎ **800/365-2267** (301/722-1257 outside the U.S.) for advance reservations, or 520/638-7851 (for campground-specific information). 319 sites, 4 group sites. No hookups. $15 Mar 1–May 31 and Sept 1–Nov 30; $12 June 1–Aug 31; $10 Dec 1–Mar 1. MC, V.

Despite having 319 campsites in a relatively small area, this remains a pleasant place. Piñon and juniper trees shade the sites, which are spaced far enough apart to afford privacy to most campers. The Aspen and Maple loops are especially roomy. Try to avoid sites 150 to 171 on the Juniper loop because they lie unpleasantly close to the entrance road. Also, it's good to be near, but not too near, the showers ($1 for 5 minutes), located in the Camper Services building next to the campground. If you're too close, hundreds of campers tramp past.

Because Mather is the only campground in Grand Canyon Village, it tends to fill up before the others. You can make reservations up to 5 months in advance by calling the 800 number, listed above.

For same-day reservations, check at the campground entrance. Even when the campground is booked, sites sometimes become available when campers leave early. Once everyone with reservations has a spot, additional spaces are offered. There's no waiting list, however, and no set time for the new spaces to be given away. All you can do is try your luck in person starting in late morning.

From December 1 to March 1, the campground is open on a first-come, first-served basis. Finding a site is usually no problem at this time. Out-of-state checks are accepted with social security number.

Trailer Village. Grand Canyon Village, P.O. Box 699, Grand Canyon, AZ 86023. ☎ **303/297-2757** (advance reservations) or 520/638-2631, ext. 6035 (same-day reservations, campground questions). Fax 520/638-9247. 84 full hookups. $20 per site plus $1.75 for each person after the first two. Open year-round.

The neighbors are close, the showers far (.4 miles) away, and the vegetation sparse. In surroundings like this, you might want to draw the curtains and stay in your RV. The beauty of a hookup is that it lets you do that. If, however, you'd like to venture outside during your stay, scout the property before taking a site. A few sites at the north end of the numbered drives have grass, shade trees, room for a tent, and one neighbor-free side. If you'd like to leave your RV altogether, you can catch a shuttle bus at a stop near the campground.

Like the lodges inside Grand Canyon National Park, Trailer Village is overseen by AMFAC—and therefore subject to the same rules as the lodges (except pets are allowed here). That means reservations can be made up to 21 months in advance. If you don't have reservations, check at the campground entrance even if the sign says no openings exist. A few spots open up in the late mornings when campers depart early. (Because reservations are guaranteed by credit card, few spots come open at night.)

OUTSIDE THE PARK

Flintstone Bedrock City. (In Valle at junctions of hwys. 180 and 64.) HCR 34 Box A, Williams, AZ 86046. ☎ **520/635-2600.** Unlimited tent sites, 27 hookups. $12 2-person tent; $14 electric hookup; $16 water/electric hookup; $1.50 each additional person. Open Feb–Nov.

Cartoon lovers will be curious about this Flintstones-themed campground, restaurant, and store, whose multihued, fake-stone buildings cling like putty to the windswept land at the intersection of highways 64 and 180. In addition to peddling the ubiquitous Grand Canyon T-shirts and dead-scorpion paperweights, the gift shop sells

Campgrounds in the Grand Canyon Area

Campground	Rim	Total Sites	RV Hookups	Dump Station	Toilets	Drinking Water	Showers	Fire Pits/ Grills	Laundry	Public Phones	Reserve	Fees	Open
Cameron Trading Post RV Park	South	48	48	yes	no	yes	no	no	no	yes	yes	$15	year-round
Demotte Park Campground	North	23	no	no	yes	yes	no	yes	no	no	no	$10	mid-May– mid-Oct
Desert View Campground	South	50	no	no	yes	no	yes	no	no	no	no	$12 per site	mid-May– mid-Oct
Diamond Creek Campground	South	open tent camping	no	no	yes	no	no	yes	no	no	no	$7 per person	Year-round
Flintstone Bedrock City	South	unlimited tent sites	27	yes	yes	yes	yes	no	yes	yes	yes	$12 two-person tent, $14 electric hookup, $16 water/electric, $1.50 each additional person	Feb–Nov
Grand Canyon Camper Village	South	300	250	yes	yes	yes	yes	yes	no	yes	yes	$23 full hookup, $21 water/electric, $19 electric, $15 tent sites, $19 teepees	year-round

Campgrounds in the Grand Canyon Area

Campground	Rim	Total Sites	RV Hookups	Dump Station	Toilets	Drinking Water	Showers	Fire Pits/ Grills	Laundry	Public Phones	Reserve	Fees	Open
Jacob Lake Campground	North	53	no	no	yes	yes	no	yes	no	no	no	$10	year-round
Kaibab Lake Campground	South	74	no	no	yes	yes	no	yes	no	no	no	$10	Apr–Oct
Kaibab Camper Village	North	130	70	yes	yes	yes	no	no	no	yes	yes	$22 hookups, $12 dry sites, $12 tent sites	May 15–Oct 15
Mather Campground	South	323	no	yes	yes	yes	yes	yes	yes	no	Mar–Nov	$12 March–May and Sept–Nov, $15 June–Aug	Mar–Nov
North Rim Campground	North	87	no	yes	yes	yes	nearby	yes	nearby	yes	yes	$15–$20 site, $4 tent only, no car	May 15–Oct 15
Ten X Campground	South	70	no	no	yes	yes	no	yes	no	no	no	$10	Apr–Oct
Trailer Village	South	84	84	nearby	yes	yes	nearby	yes	no	nearby	yes	$19	year-round
Tuweep	North	11	no	no	no	no	no	yes	no	no	no	No charge	when roads are passable

all manner of Flintstones paraphernalia, including earrings, T-shirts, key chains, and magnets. Fred's Diner serves up dishes such as the "Chickasaurus Sandwich" and the "Bronto Burger" for under $3. The Flintstones theme may seem tired by the time you finish seeing the park behind the gift shop. It features life-size re-creations of the settings from the cartoons, which, by the way, are shown all day in a viewing room. Only Flintstones fanatics will find the park to be worth its $5 admission fee.

One advantage to having a prehistoric theme is that no one can tell whether your campground is run-down. The buildings here seemed about as old as caves. So nothing looks out of character. One problem, however, is obvious: the proximity of some tent sites to Highway 64.

Grand Canyon Camper Village. In Tusayan (1 mi. south of the park on Hwy. 64), P.O. Box 490, Grand Canyon, AZ 86023-0490. ☎ **520/638-2887.** 50 tent sites, 250 hookups. $15 tent sites; $19 teepees; $19 electric; $21 water/electric; $23 full hookups. DISC, MC, V. Open year-round. Pets allowed.

This campground's advantage is its location: Just a mile south of the park entrance, it lies within easy walking distance of stores and restaurants on one side and of Kaibab National Forest on the other. Its disadvantages are its relatively narrow (average width: 27 feet) campsites and the noise from the nearby Grand Canyon National Park Airport, whose constant daytime helicopter takeoffs, together with the throngs of people at the campground itself, may bring back memories of Woodstock.

The tent sites are best. Shaded by ponderosa pines, they sit above the rest of the campground and border the national forest. The rest rooms are clean, the showers (25¢ for 2 min.) hot. There's also a playground and a gravel basketball court.

Kaibab Lake Campground. 4 mi. north of Williams on Hwy. 64. ☎ **520/635-8457.** 74 sites, no hookups. $10 per site. No credit cards. Open Apr–Oct.

The campsites at this Forest Service campground are on a forested hillside above the reddish waters of Williams Lake. There's no swimming in the lake, a reservoir for Williams, but the fishing for bottom-feeders isn't bad.

✪ **Ten X Campground.** 2 mi. south of Tusayan on Hwy. 64. ☎ **520/638-2443.** 70 sites, no hookups. $10 per site. No credit cards. Open Apr–Oct.

Large, wooded campsites make this Forest Service campground the nicest campground within 20 miles of the South Rim. With plenty of distance between you and your neighbors, this is a great place to linger over a fire. All sites have fire pits and grills, and the campground host sells wood. Later, you'll find the soft, needle-covered floor perfect for sleeping. This campground does sell out. If you're driving up from Flagstaff or Williams, consider snagging a site before going to the canyon for the day.

5 Camping Near the Eastern Entrance & the Western Canyon

Cameron Trading Post RV Park. U.S. 89 across from Cameron Trading Post (P.O. Box 339), Cameron, AZ 86020. ☎ **800/338-7385** or 520/679-2231. No tent sites, 48 full hookups. $15 per site. AE, DISC, MC, V. Open year-round.

This is no-frills RV camping near the eastern entrance of the park: Hookups are in a field, with no showers available and only a few cottonwood trees for shade. A few sites at the north end of the campground overlook the Little Colorado River—especially nice when the river is running. Although there's nothing in the way of recreation at the campground, the Cameron Trading Post, with its restaurant and shop of Native-American crafts, is across the street.

Diamond Creek Campground. Hualapai Indian Reservation (18.1 mi. from Peach Springs, 19 from Hwy. 66 on the Diamond Creek Rd.). ☎ **520/769-2210.** Open tent camping. $10 per person for camping; $5 for sightseeing. AE, DISC, MC, V. Open Mar–Oct. Pay and register before entering at the Hualapai River Trips Office, open daily 6am–6pm at Hualapai Lodge in Peach Springs. Closed in winter.

This primitive campground at the confluence of Diamond Creek and the Colorado River at the western end of the canyon is the only place where you can drive to the river inside the Grand Canyon. The gravel road, descending from 4,600 feet in Peach Springs to 1,350 feet at the campground, sometimes gets washed out, but high-clearance vehicles can negotiate it during dry weather. (Don't risk it during monsoon season.) Surrounded by cliffs of granite and schist, the campground is at a lovely spot. People who couldn't otherwise make it to the inner canyon will probably appreciate it most.

But there are some real drawbacks. You probably won't be alone; the beach serves as a popular pullout for raft trips, and the Hualapai River Runners begin their trips in the far western canyon here. If you don't commandeer one of the three metal ramadas, you could end up broiling in the midday sun. (Located just above the canyon's lowest point, this is one of its hottest places.) And, since there's no drinking water here, or a means of purifying the river water, you'll need to bring your own. You'll also have to pack out your own garbage. Seldom pumped, the lone portable toilet tests the will.

6 Camping Near the North Rim

INSIDE THE PARK

✪ **North Rim Campground.** 44 mi. south of Jacob Lake on Hwy. 67. ☎ **800/365-2267** advance reservations, or 520/638-2151 same-day reservations. 83 sites, 4 group sites. No hookups. $15–$20 per site; $4 for tent only (no car). MC, V. Open Oct 15–May 15.

Shaded by ponderosa pines and situated alongside Transept Canyon (part of Grand Canyon), this is a delightful place to pass a few days. The pines, which shade a soft, smooth, forest floor, are spaced just far enough apart to allow for a vigorous game of Wiffleball, among other activities.

But there's more here than a dream of fields. The 1^1/2-mile-long Transept Trail links the campground to Grand Canyon Lodge. The North Rim General Store, a Laundromat, and showers ($1.25 for 5 min.) are all within walking distance. The nicest sites are the rim sites, which open onto the canyon. These cost an extra $5 but are worth it, being some of the prettiest anywhere.

With only 83 sites, the North Rim Campground fills up for much of the summer. If you show up without a reservation only to find the "Sorry, campground full" sign on the entry booth, don't be afraid to ask what seems a stupid question. The gate-keepers often neglect to remove the sign after receiving cancellations, and you may just end up with a campsite. The best time to show up and ask about openings is at 8 a.m. That's when sites made available by the previous night's cancellations go up for sale.

The campground sometimes stays open on a limited basis after October 15, but few services are available in the park. Out-of-state checks are accepted with social security number.

CAMPGROUNDS NEAR THE PARK

DeMotte Park Campground. 5 miles north of the park boundary on Hwy. 67. ☎ **520/643-7298.** 23 sites, no hookups. $10 per site. Open mid-May to mid-Oct.

Bundle up for the nights at this Forest Service campground. It's 8,760 feet high (10 feet higher than Telluride, Colorado), in spruce-fir forest, so you're sure to be cool. The road through the campground curves sharply and some of the spaces are small, so this place may not work for large RVs.

✪ **Jacob Lake Campground.** U.S. 89A just north of Jacob Lake. ☎ **520/643-7298** or 520/643-7395. Fax 520/643-7770. 53 sites, no hookups. $10 per site. Open year-round, but water is seasonal and the road is not plowed.

Backcountry Camping

If you're thinking about hiking into the canyon and staying the night in the backcountry, flip to "Preparing for Your Backcountry Trip" and "Campgrounds" in chapter 4 for information about getting a backcountry permit, and for details about the best places to camp.

Nestled into rolling hills covered with ponderosa pine forest, this is a beauty of a Forest Service campground. Towering pines shade sites only a short drive from the services in Jacob Lake. This campground has regular naturalist programs. Although it is open year-round, water is seasonal, and during the winter the roads through the campground are unplowed.

○ **Kaibab Camper Village.** ¹/₂ mile west of Hwy. 67, just south of Jacob Lake. P.O. Box 3331, Flagstaff, AZ 86003. ☎ **520/643-7804** (when open); 800/525-0924 or 520/526-0924 (when closed). www.canyoneers.com. E-mail: answers@canyoneers.com. 50 tent sites, 80 RV sites (70 hookups, 10 dry sites). $22 for hookups (up to 4 people); $12 for dry sites (up to 4 people); $12 for tent sites (up to 2 people), plus $2 for each additional person.

Compared to most South Rim RV parks, where sagebrush is often the largest plant in sight, this is like a fairy tale. Everywhere inside the campground, ponderosa pines dust the sky like Jack's mythical beanstalk. Some campers even have a view past the trees to tiny Jacob Lake. While no Lake Tahoe (not even close), it still manages to attract deer and other animals. The setting makes this easily the prettiest RV park in the Grand Canyon area.

Tent campers will also be comfortable here, especially if they pay the extra $3 for one of the improved sites, which have sand rings and views of Jacob Lake. The use of generators is forbidden, so everyone can enjoy the quiet.

Only two things are missing: showers—the nearest public ones are inside the park—and flush toilets. Several signs stress the fact that the toilets are hooked up to a larger septic system. Still, they resemble portable toilets in every other conceivable way, including the fact that they're dark as caves at night. Personal checks (from U.S. banks) are accepted.

OUTSIDE THE PARK: DISPERSED CAMPING IN KAIBAB NATIONAL FOREST

Park visitors can camp for free simply by driving out of the park and into the Kaibab National Forest. The Forest Service's rules are simple: Camp at least a quarter mile from paved roads, camp-grounds, and water, but never in meadows. (No camping is allowed near Hull Cabin or Red Butte.) Pack out your garbage and remove any signs that you've been there. Bury human waste in holes 4 inches deep, 6 inches across, and at least 100 yards from water or creek beds. Completely douse campfires before leaving. (The ashes should be cool enough to handle.) If the forest seems dry, check with a local Forest Service office about burn restrictions.

The open camping in the National Forest on the North Rim is among the best anywhere. Here, a number of Forest Service roads lead to canyon overlooks where you're free to camp. The most ac-cessible of these used to be the East Rim Overlook, just 4.4 miles off of Highway 67 on FS Road 611. But the Forest Service, citing overuse and damage to the area's resources, recently closed the rim area to motorized vehicles. Visitors can still park nearby and walk to the overlook, which opens onto views of the Marble Platform and the eastern Grand Canyon. Other overlooks, such as Crazy Jug Point and Parissawampitts Point, remain open to vehicles and have lovely views of the central Grand Canyon, but they require long, bumpy drives. For maps and information on dispersed camping on the North Rim, visit the **Kaibab Plateau Visitor Center** (☎ **520/643-7298**) in Jacob Lake.

7 Where to Eat on the South Rim

Arizona Steakhouse. At Bright Angel Lodge. ☎ **520/638-2631.** Reserva-tions not accepted. Entrees $12.75–$20.70. AE, DC, DISC, MC, V. 5–10pm daily. AMERICAN.

Lining up before this restaurant's 5pm opening isn't a bad idea. In-stead of arriving after sunset to find an hour's wait, you can watch the sunset's colors through the long, canyon-facing windows. Or, when the days are longer, finish the meal in time to step outside for the evening's show of changing colors.

The service generally runs at a sluggish pace, which (ideally) cre-ates a relaxing atmosphere. You'll have plenty of time to choose from the restaurant's wine list or order an appetizer—the sautéed mush-room caps are one good choice. Entrees include hand-cut steaks and prime rib; marinated chicken breast, broiled halibut, grilled Atlan-tic salmon, and a daily vegetarian special. The food here tends to be inconsistent, but on a good night, meals are tasty.

Bright Angel Restaurant. Located in Bright Angel Lodge. ☎ **520/638-2631.** Reservations not accepted. Breakfast $1.95–$6.60; lunch

$6.10–$8.55; dinner $6.10–$17.55. AE, DC, DISC, MC, V. 6:30–10:45am and
11:15am–10pm daily. AMERICAN.

Although one longtime canyon resident described the food here as
"consistently terrible," it struck me as average American coffee shop
food. (Perhaps we're both right.) The burgers and patty melts are
tasty, as are some of the Southwestern dishes. At dinner the restaurant offers more expensive entrees such as New York steak and bone-
less rainbow trout, in addition to the lunchtime fare.

This is also a good place for families, who can dine here without
worrying much about the children's behavior. The games on the
kid's menu should distract the small fries until the french fries
arrive.

Still, this restaurant doesn't merit high marks. In addition to getting soiled by the throngs that tramp through it, it seems to serve
as a way station for new AMFAC employees destined either to be
fired or promoted to the fancy El Tovar Hotel. Besides, equally
good food is available for less money at the Maswik and Yavapai
cafeterias.

Desert View Trading Post Cafeteria. At Desert View, 25 mi. east of Grand
Canyon Village on Hwy. 64. ☎ **520/638-2360.** $2–$5. No credit cards. Summer 8am–6pm; rest of year 9am–5pm. CAFETERIA.

The sandwiches, pizza, and burgers here will sustain you until you
make it back to Grand Canyon Village. The breakfast offerings, including eggs and French toast, draw campers from nearby Desert
View Campground.

✪ **El Tovar Restaurant.** In the El Tovar Lodge. Reservations for dinner only.
☎ **520/638-2631,** ext. 6432. Breakfast $2.50–$9.70; lunch $5.95–$17.50;
dinner $15.75–$24.75. AE, DC, DISC, MC, V. 6:30–11am, 11:30am–2pm, and
5–10pm daily. CONTINENTAL.

More than 90 years after opening its doors, this restaurant remains
a pleasant dining experience. It starts with a lovely room—walls of
Oregon pine graced with murals depicting the ritual dances of four
Indian tribes and banks of windows at the north and south ends.
Atop the restaurant's linen tablecloths, fresh flowers catch light from
those windows, as do the clean white shirts of the wait staff, a group
professional enough to do justice to the room.

At dinner, a Southwestern influence spices the continental cuisine. A tasty appetizer is the baked portobello mushroom with arti-
choke, roasted peppers, and Jack cheese on smoked tomato coulis.
For an entree, meat eaters will enjoy the broiled filet mignon with
roasted garlic demi-glace, or the baked blue cornmeal-crusted

The Grand Canyon After Dark

Most people visiting the Grand Canyon aren't thinking about anything other than a campfire when they think of evening entertainment, but in fact there's quite a bit of nightlife. On the South Rim, **Maswik Lodge** has a spacious sports bar with a big-screen TV and a pool table. If your favorite team is on the tube at a time when you'd like to dine, grab a tray of food from Maswik Cafeteria, then consume it in the adjoining sports bar. Maswik is also the only bar inside the park where smoking is allowed. This, along with its unpretentious environment, makes it particularly popular with canyon locals.

The lounge at the **El Tovar Hotel** (11am to 11:30pm) is the most luxurious watering hole at the canyon, with copper lanterns, stained glass, and cushy furniture. Best of all, however, is its shaded porch, which overlooks an expanse of lush grass, the rim-side sidewalk, and a slice of the North Rim of the canyon. On a hot afternoon at Grand Canyon Village, cool off here over an iced tea, draft beer, or special cocktails such as the Sunset Surprise (vodka, peach Schnapps, and cranberry juice) or the Prickly Pear Margarita (a standard Margarita, but with the sweet juice from a prickly pear cactus). The interior of the lounge is smoke-free, but puffing is allowed on the porch.

During daytime, the ✪ **Bright Angel Lounge** (open 11am to 11:30pm daily) often feels more like a waiting room than a watering hole. People use this dark, air-conditioned bar room to kill time

Atlantic salmon. Meanwhile, vegetarians can munch on the blue corn tamales filled with black beans, guacamole, and fire-roasted corn salsa.

In 1999, some locals maintained that the food at the El Tovar had slipped, and my experiences seemed to validate this opinion. But the El Tovar seems likely to rebound, as it no doubt has in the past, and the atmosphere remains as enticing as ever.

The El Tovar accepts reservations for dinner only, but it's also open for breakfast and lunch. If you're traveling on a budget, consider dining here during nondinner hours, when you can get the same high-quality food for just a few dollars more than you'd spend at the other canyon restaurants. At breakfast, be sure to sample the coffee, the best inside the park, and order the quesadilla stuffed with when their traveling partners are dawdling on hikes or in the nearby shops. Yet the lounge has character in abundance, from its 1958 mural of Anglo tourists by the famous Hopi artist, Fred Kabotie, to the historic photos and postcards suspended in the clear coating on the bar top. At nighttime, when musicians sometimes play, an international crowd enjoys the sounds.

In addition, there are more traditional national park evening programs such as stargazing and lecture/slide shows on the Grand Canyon (see *The Guide* for information). From May through September most of these programs are held at Mather Amphitheater near the South Rim Visitor Center. For three weeks in September there's also the **Grand Canyon Chamber Music Festival** (☎ 520/638-9215).

On the North Rim, you'll find a full-service saloon at **Grand Canyon Lodge.** Inside the bar, cutouts of Kokopelli and other Native American rock art images hang alongside traditional western decor; mule wranglers swap stories with tourists; and when the night really starts hopping, someone usually ponies up for a round of "mule shots"—bourbon topped with Amaretto. Like the bar itself, this drink sweetens a Western tradition. If you'd like to take your beverage onto one of the lodge's patios, you're free to do so.

Evening ranger presentations are offered at both the Campground Amphitheater and inside Grand Canyon Lodge.

scrambled eggs, jalapeño Jack cheese, beef, and roasted red pepper cream.

The General Store Delicatessen. In the South Rim's General Store (at Mather Business Center). ☎ **520/638-2262.** Fax 520/638-9204. $2–$5. No credit cards. 8am–6pm daily. DELI.

Many Park Service employees duck into this delicatessen for lunch. Here you can sit in a corner booth, read the paper, and watch the tourists pass. The deli serves sandwiches, salads, and fried chicken, but the best offerings are often the specials.

Maswik and Yavapai Cafeterias. Located at Maswik and Yavapai lodges, respectively. ☎ **520/638-2631.** No reservations. Breakfast $1.40–$5.25; lunch and dinner $3.75–$6.75. AE, DC, DISC, MC, V. Maswik 6am–10pm daily; Yavapai 6:30am–10pm daily (may fluctuate seasonally). AMERICAN.

For the price of a burger, fries, and a soft drink at the Tusayan McDonald's, you can eat a full meal at either Maswik or Yavapai cafeterias. While the food at both usually tastes like college dormitory fare, there are some key differences between them. Maswik serves full-dinner plates that can be ordered at any of four stations. Its Mexican station serves up burritos and tostadas with beans and rice on the side. The best value in town may be the bean-and-cheese burrito, a filling meal even after a day of backpacking, which costs just $4.50. There's also a pasta station, a burger station, and another with fish and daily specials.

At Yavapai you can mix and match from a variety of stations, picking up a chicken leg from one, a slice of pizza from another, a dish of mashed potatoes from another. (A case of indigestion when you put it all together.) At the salad bar, you can assemble a dinner salad for under $2. Yavapai attracts more bus tours than Maswik, and when things slow down in the winter, Yavapai sometimes closes; Maswik doesn't.

8 Where to Eat Inside the Canyon

Phantom Ranch. Inside the canyon $1/2$ mi. north of the Colorado River on the North Kaibab Trail. To order meals more than 4 days in advance, call ☎ **303/297-2757**; to order meals within 4 days, contact the Bright Angel Transportation Desk at 520/638-2631, ext. 6015. Steak $26.75; stew $16.75; sack lunch $7.50; breakfast $12. AE, DC, DISC, MC, V (for advance reservations: MC, V only). AMERICAN.

At the bottom of the Grand Canyon, pretty much anything tastes good, so it's hard to say whether the food at Phantom Ranch would taste as great on the rim as alongside Bright Angel Creek. Whether you reach here by mule or on foot, the food almost always tastes exceptional.

If you want dinner served your way, however, bring a camp stove. Every evening two options are offered: a steak dinner at 5pm and a hearty beef stew at 6:30pm. The vegetarian plate consists of the side dishes to the steak dinner: vegetables, cornbread, and salad. With either dinner, the dessert is chocolate cake.

The family style, all-you-can-eat breakfasts are also excellent, as heaping platters of eggs, bacon, and pancakes are laid out on the long, blue tables. The only disappointment is the sack lunch, whose meager offerings (bagel, summer sausage, juice, apple, peanuts, raisins, and cookies) don't seem worth the price. Pack your own lunch and, if necessary, supplement it with snacks from the canteen.

Because the number of meals is fixed, hikers and mule riders must reserve them ahead of time through AMFAC (see number above) or at the Bright Angel Transportation Desk. As a last resort, inquire upon arrival at Phantom Ranch to see whether any meals remain. Up until 4pm this can be done in the canteen itself. After 4pm, ask at a side window behind the canteen. Between 8am and 4pm and from 8 to 10pm, anyone is allowed in the canteen, which has snacks, soda, beer (sold only after dinner), and wine.

9 Where to Eat on the North Rim

Grand Canyon Lodge Dining Room. At Grand Canyon Lodge. ☎ **520/ 638-2611,** ext. 160. Reservations required for dinner, not accepted for breakfast and lunch. Breakfast $1.85–$6.75; lunch $5.70–$7.45; dinner $12.25–$17.75. AE, DC, DISC, MC, V. 6:30–10am, 11:30am–2:30pm, and 4:45–9:30pm daily. CONTINENTAL.

Long banks of west- and south-facing windows afford views of Transept Canyon and help warm this room, where the high ceiling absorbs the clamor of diners. While it's unreasonable to expect gourmet dining in a place as remote as the North Rim, the food here is nearly as satisfying as the surroundings.

Served by waiters in black slacks, white shirts, and bolo ties, the broiled stuffed mushrooms are a delectable starter at dinnertime. One tasty main course is the Pasta Lydia—fresh asparagus and potatoes tossed in pesto sauce with bow-tie pasta. Also recommended is the New York strip steak with three-pepper glaze. Other choices include prime rib, steak, pork medallions, and dishes with fish or poultry. Lunch offerings include a variety of salads, sandwiches, and burgers. At breakfast, a full buffet costs under $8.

Grand Snack Shop. In the west wing of Grand Canyon Lodge. ☎ **520/ 638-2611.** Breakfast $1.95–$4.25; lunch and dinner $1.30–$3.80; 14-in. supreme pizza $15.50. 7am–9pm daily. AMERICAN.

The snack bar serves the best pizza on the North Rim, or so the joke goes. That speaks well for the pizza, which could just as easily—and no less truthfully—be called the worst. At $2.25 a slice, it's an economical alternative to firing up the camp stove. The snack bar also serves burgers, premade salads, and breakfasts. If all you desire is a cup of coffee and a muffin, stop by the saloon, where an espresso bar operates from 5 to 9:30am daily.

10 Picnic & Camping Supplies

If possible, stock up on your camping items at a large grocery store in a larger city such as Flagstaff. In general, prices are lowest in Flagstaff and rise steadily as you near the canyon, peaking at The South Rim's General Store inside the park.

SOUTH RIM

The General Store. In Grand Canyon Village. ☎ **520/638-2262.** Summer 8am–8pm; rest of year 8am–7pm.

Located in the business district of Grand Canyon Village, the General Store on the South Rim is the largest and most complete retailer in the canyon, selling groceries, canyon souvenirs, liquor, electronic and automotive goods, provisions for camping, and a full line of hiking and backpacking gear. Some of the camping equipment can be rented for overnight use.

Desert View Store. At Desert View (off Hwy. 64). ☎ **520/638-2393.** Summer 8am–7pm; rest of year 9am–5pm.

The smaller Desert View store has souvenirs, beer and wine, and a smaller selection of groceries.

NORTH RIM

North Rim General Store. Adjacent to North Rim Campground. ☎ **520/638-2611,** ext. 270. 8am–8pm daily (may vary).

The North Rim General Store is tiny but well supplied with groceries, beer and wine, and a very limited supply of camping equipment. Unlike the General Store on the South Rim, the North Rim general store can't outfit aspiring backpackers.

6

Gateway Towns

*T*he Grand Canyon isn't the only wonder in northern Arizona. The surrounding area on the Colorado Plateau is among the most stunning in the world, a sparsely populated landscape of 12,000-foot-high volcanoes and 3,000-foot-deep red-rock canyons—separated by the largest ponderosa pine forest on the planet. Lonely highways lace the countryside, inviting exploration. During your travels, you can track California condors, or watch elk wander the forests. You can walk the same paths and stand in rooms used for centuries by America's indigenous peoples, then learn about the cultures of their modern descendants. You can chat with cowboys in Williams or venture to Flagstaff's cultural attractions, including the Lowell Observatory and the Museum of Northern Arizona. The many diversions won't detract from your trip to the canyon; they'll simply enhance your appreciation of this area, with the canyon at its heart.

1 Flagstaff

150 miles N of Phoenix; 32 miles E of Williams; 78 miles S of Grand Canyon Village

Home to Northern Arizona University, the Museum of Northern Arizona, and the Hansen Planetarium, as well as dozens of excellent restaurants and clubs, Flagstaff lets you nurture your intellect, dine on gourmet food, and dance to live music without losing sight of the more important things—the 12,000-foot-high San Francisco Peaks, which rise just north of town. Its historic downtown, with its many shops and galleries, attracts a mix of students, locals, and tourists. Freight trains regularly clatter past, shaking cappuccinos and drowning out street musicians before continuing to points less desirable. Flanked by motels with colorful names such as the Pony Soldier, Geronimo, and El Pueblo, Route 66 parallels the tracks.

ESSENTIALS

GETTING THERE Flagstaff is on I-40, one of the main east-west interstates in the United States. I-17 also starts here and heads south to Phoenix. U.S. 89A connects Flagstaff to Sedona by way of

---

Buying Park Entrance Permits in Flagstaff

A vending machine located outside the Flagstaff Visitors Center sells entrance permits to the park. By using it, you can avoid waiting in line at the park entrance during peak hours.

Oak Creek Canyon. U.S. 180 connects Flagstaff with Grand Canyon Village, and U.S. 89 with Page.

Flagstaff's Pulliam Airport, which is located 3 miles south of town off I-17, is served by **America West Express** (☎ **800/235-9292**) from Phoenix.

Flagstaff is also served by **Amtrak** (☎ **800/872-7245** for reservations, or 520/774-8679 for station information only) from Chicago and Los Angeles. The train station is at 1 E. Rte. 66.

VISITOR INFORMATION   The **Flagstaff Visitors Center,** at 1 E. Rte. 66 (☎ **800/842-7293** or 520/774-9541, www.flagstaff.az.us), is open Monday to Saturday from 7am to 6pm and on Sunday from 7am to 5pm.

GETTING AROUND   Car rentals are available from **Avis** (☎ 800/831-2847 or 520/774-8421), **Budget** (☎ 800/527-0700 or 520/779-5255), **Enterprise** (☎ 800/325-8007 or 520/526-1377), **Hertz** (☎ 800/654-3131 or 520/774-4452), and **National** (☎ 800/227-7368 or 520/779-1975).

If you need a taxi, call **Friendly Cab** (☎ **520/774-4444**) or **Sun Taxi & Tours** (**800/483-4488** or 520/774-7400.

Pine Country Transit (☎ **520/779-6624**) provides public bus transit around the city. The fare is 75¢ for adults. **Nava-Hopi Tours** (☎ **520/774-5003**) offers trolley-bus tours of Flagstaff, costing $19.50 per adult; $9.50 for ages 5 to 15.

ORIENTATION   Downtown Flagstaff is located just north of I-40. Milton Road, which at its southern end becomes I-17 to Phoenix, leads past Northern Arizona University on its way into downtown where it merges with Route 66. Part of Route 66, Santa Fe Avenue, parallels the railroad tracks, linking the city's historic downtown with its east side. Downtown's main street is San Francisco Street, while Humphreys Street leads north out of town toward the San Francisco Peaks and the south rim of the Grand Canyon.

SUPERMARKETS & GENERAL STORES   If you want to stock up on food before you hit the road, here are several places to stop: **Albertson's,** 1416 E. Rte. 66 (☎ **520/773-7955**), open 24 hours;

Basha's, 2700 Woodlands Village Blvd. (☎ **520/774-3882**), open daily 5am to 1am; and **Fry's,** 201 N. Switzer Canyon Dr. (☎ **520/774-2719**), open 24 hours.

WHAT TO SEE & DO

✪ **Lowell Observatory.** 1400 W. Mars Hill Rd., Flagstaff. ☎ **520/774-2096.** www.lowell.edu/. Admission $3 adults, $1.50 ages 5–17. AE, MC, V. Visitor center open 9am–5pm Apr–Oct and noon–5pm Nov–March. Nighttime hours vary (call for specific program information).

Percival Lowell, an amateur astronomer, realized that Flagstaff's dry, thin air made the town a choice location for observing the heavens. Hoping to find life on Mars, the Boston aristocrat built an astronomical observatory atop a hill here in 1894, then used it to study the skies for the next 22 years. Though he never found life on Mars, the research done at his observatory has contributed greatly to our knowledge of the heavens. In the past century, Lowell Observatory helped discover Pluto, map out the moon, locate the rings of Uranus, and provide evidence of an expanding universe.

Today, in addition to conducting research, the 20 staff astronomers educate and entertain the public. It's most fun to come here on clear nights, when they'll help you peer through telescopes at stars far across the galaxy. (Call for a schedule of nighttime programs.) Yet stargazing isn't the only attraction. During daytime, tours of the observatory and historic rotunda library are offered. And the visitor center has exciting, state-of-the-art interactive displays, suitable for both adults and kids. They make a trip here worthwhile, any time.

✪ **Museum of Northern Arizona.** 3101 N. Fort Valley Rd. (U.S. Hwy 180), Flagstaff, AZ 86001. ☎ **520/774-5213.** Fax 520/774-5213. www.musnaz.org. E-mail: info@musnaz.org. Admission $5 adults, $4 seniors, $3 students, $2 kids ages 7–17. Daily 9am–5pm. AE, DISC, MC, V. No checks.

Bus Service to the Canyon

For those without cars, **Nava-Hopi Bus Lines** (☎ **800/892-8687** or 520/774-5003) provides regular bus service linking Grand Canyon National Park with Flagstaff. Buses from Flagstaff to Grand Canyon leave daily at 7:45am and 2:45pm, arriving at Maswik Transportation Center inside the park about two hours later. The one-way Flagstaff-to-Grand Canyon fare is $12.50 plus a $6 park entrance fee. If you'd like to charter a van from Flagstaff to the canyon, call **South Rim Travel** (☎ **888/291-9116** or 520/638-2748).

Flagstaff

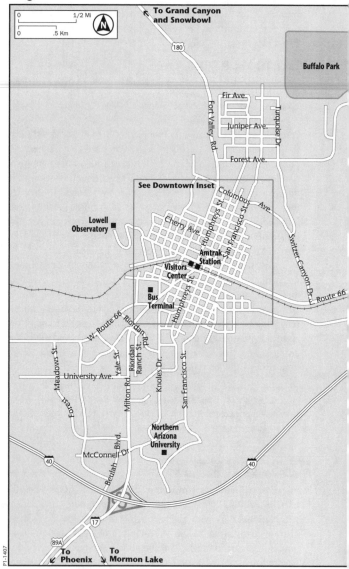

To Grand Canyon
and Snowbowl

180

Buffalo Park

Fir Ave.

Fort Valley Rd.

Juniper Ave.

Turquoise Dr.

Forest Ave.

See Downtown Inset

Columbus Ave.

Humphreys St.

Cherry Ave.

San Francisco St.

Lowell
Observatory

Amtrak
Station

Switzer Canyon Dr.

Visitors
Center

Humphreys St.

E. Route 66

Bus
Terminal

W. Route 66

Riordan Rd.

Riordan Ranch St.

Yale St.

Knoles Dr.

San Francisco St.

University Ave.

Meadows St.

Forest

Milton Rd.

40

Northern
Arizona
University

McConnell Dr.

Beulah Blvd.

40

17

89A

To
Phoenix

To
Mormon Lake

P1-1407

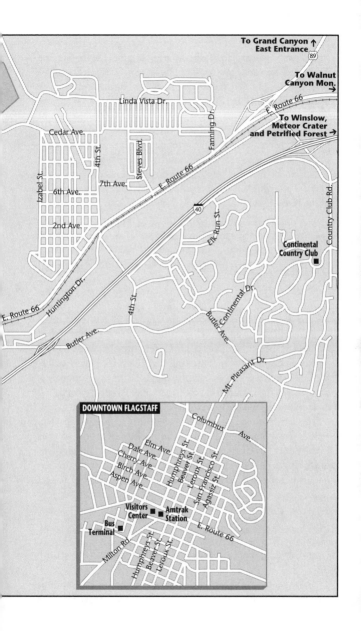

Founded in 1928 by a Flagstaff couple concerned about the widespread removal of artifacts from the area, this museum explores the history, science, and cultures of the Colorado Plateau. Its **Geology Room** has displays on the unique landforms in the area, and the **Special Exhibits Gallery** frequently shows art from the region. But the best attraction here—one of the best anywhere—is the anthropology exhibit, **"Native Peoples of the Colorado Plateau,"** which permanently occupies four galleries of the museum. Many of the finest Native American artifacts from the museum's five-million-piece collection are displayed. Always beautiful and occasionally moving, they are placed in a context that illuminates the history and spirit of the Native American peoples.

✪ **Sunset Crater Volcano National Monument.** 15 mi. north of Flagstaff on Hwy. 89. ☎ **520/526-0502.** Admission $3 per person, under 17 free. Fee also covers entrance to Wupatki National Monument. Summer 8am–6pm daily; rest of year 8am–5pm daily. Cash-only at entrance gate. DISC, MC, V at the store and the visitor center.

Sunset Crater formed in 1064 atop a weak spot in the earth's crust. An underground gas chamber exploded, spewing tons of cinders around the newly created vent in the earth. Within a few months of the explosion, cinders had piled up to form a 1,000-foot-tall pyramid-shaped crater. Lava poured intermittently from openings near the bottom of the crater for the next 200 years, snaking across the land before ossifying in choppy mounds that to this day look viscous. In one final flourish of activity, small eruptions deposited red and yellow ash atop the otherwise black cone.

The activity produced a landscape of eerie shapes and striking, subtle colors. During an expedition in the late 1800s, the explorer John Wesley Powell saw this colorful cone, perhaps in the low light in which it is most striking, and named it Sunset Crater. Today, the national monument has a picnic area, visitor center, and several walking trails. Try visiting here in early morning or late afternoon, when the colors are richest.

Walnut Canyon National Monument. Located 10 mi. east of Flagstaff off I-40 (exit 204). ☎ **520/526-3367.** Admission $3 adults, under 17 free. Summer 8am–6pm daily; rest of year 8am–5pm. Cash only at entrance gate. DISC, MC, V.

The Sinagua (a subgroup of the Ancestral Puebloans) occupied this wooded canyon for roughly 125 years from 1125 to 1250. They built hundreds of dwellings under natural rock overhangs on sunny east- and south-facing cliffs, and tucked granaries into the smallest openings. Atop the canyon rims, they dug out terraces and check

Using Flagstaff as a home base, one can easily visit Walnut Canyon, Sunset Crater, and Wupatki monuments in a long, rewarding day.

dams that would help keep their crops moist, and erected pit houses and pueblo-style dwellings.

Although most of the terraces and check dams have collapsed, 300 rooms remain. Twenty-five are on the **Island Trail**, a .9-mile-long loop that descends 185 feet (with over 100 steps) below the visitor center. Many others are visible from the trail, on the canyon walls. Another, relatively flat .7-mile trail travels along the rim of the canyon, affording views of the cliff dwellings in addition to skirting the rim-top ruins.

This is a pretty canyon and, with just 125,000 visitors annually, one of the quietest national monuments. By coming off-hours, you can sometimes find yourself alone here, and that's a great way to experience the world of the Ancestral Puebloans.

✪ **Wupatki National Monument.** 35 mi. north of Flagstaff on Hwy. 89. ☎ **520/679-2365.** Fax 520/679-2349. Admission $3 adults, under 16 free. Fee also good for Sunset Crater Volcano National Monument. Visitor center hours: June 1–Sept 30, 8am–6pm daily; Oct 1–May 31, 8am–5pm daily. Cash only at entrance gate. DISC, MC, V.

As their population grew in the 1100s, a large number of the Sinagua people moved onto the land north of Sunset Crater. Today, 800 ruins from this period are scattered across Wupatki National Monument. Some of the most remarkable are near the visitor center, including a mysterious ball court with walls 6 feet high, and pueblo ruins made from the same Moenkopi Sandstone atop which they're built. A blow hole, which releases air from underground caverns, may have had a special significance to the Indians who settled nearby. Other ruins are scattered along the road that loops through the monument, usually in elevated spots with expansive views of both the Painted Desert and San Francisco Peaks. Most of the Sinagua left in the 1200s and are believed to have become the modern-day Hopi (and perhaps Zuni). During summer, rangers regularly lead programs here.

WHERE TO STAY
EXPENSIVE TO MODERATE

Expensive chain hotels in Flagstaff include **AmeriSuites** (☎ 520/774-8042), 2455 S. Beulah (north of I-40 Exit 195B); **Flagstaff**

Hilton Garden Inn (☎ 520/526-5555), 350 W/ Forest Meadows; **Little America Hotel** (☎ 520/779-2741), 2515 E. Butler (off I-40 Exit 198); and **Residence Inn by Marriott** (☎ 520/526-5555), 3440 Country Club Dr.

Midprice chain hotels include: **Quality Inn Flagstaff** (☎ 520/774-8771), 2000 S. Milton (near I-40 Exit 195B); **Best Western Kings House Motel** (☎ 520/774-7186), 1560 E. Rte. 66; **Best Western Pony Soldier Motel** (☎ 520/526-2388), 3030 E. Rte. 66; **Comfort Inn** (☎ 520/774-7326), 914 S. Milton Rd. (near I-40 Exit 195B); **Days Inn Route 66** (☎ 520/774-5221), 1000 W. Rte. 66; **Days Inn East** (☎ 520/527-1477), 3601 E. Lockett (near I-40 Exit 201); **Days Inn I-40** (☎ 520/779-1575), 2735 S. Woodlands Village Blvd. (near I-40 Exit 195B); **Fairfield Inn by Marriott** (☎ 520/773-1300), 2005 S. Milton (near I-40 Exit 195B); **Holiday Inn Flagstaff Grand Canyon** (☎ 520/526-1150), 2320 E. Lucky Lane (off I-40 Exit 198); **Howard Johnson** (☎ 520/779-6944), 2200 E. Butler (off I-40 Exit 198); **Ramada Limited** (☎ 520/773-1111), 2755 S. Woodlands (near I-40 exit 195B).

✪ **Comfi Cottages.** 1612 N. Aztec St., Flagstaff, AZ 86001. ☎ 888/774-0731 or 520/774-0731. Fax 520/773-7286. www.comficottages.com. E-mail: pat@comficottages.com. TV TEL. 6 cottages in different locations in Flagstaff. $105–$210. Add $10 per person, per night, if more than 2 people. Rates include breakfast. AE, DISC, MC, V. Inquire about pets.

In the 1970s Pat Wiebe, a nurse at the local hospital, began purchasing and renovating small homes in Flagstaff. Today, she rents out six of these quaint cottages, all but one of which were built in the 1920s and '30s. They're old but not ancient, the type of places that have laundry chutes, flour bins, ironing boards that fold into the walls, see-through cupboard doors, and hardwood floors. Wiebe has modernized them somewhat, adding thermostat-controlled fireplaces, televisions, VCRs, and washer/dryers. And she goes out of her way to make them comfortable. In every unit you'll find fresh-cut flowers, antiques, cupboards stocked with breakfast foods, and rag dolls from her personal collection. Outside of each cottage is a picnic table and gas grill, and most have bicycles and sleds in the garage. These cottages, which sleep from two to six people, can make you feel as if you've acquired a new home, where kids are welcome. My favorite unit is the two-bedroom, one-bathroom cottage at 710 W. Birch Street. Like most of the others, it's just a short walk from the historic business district. And it's beautiful. Two of the cottages have air-conditioning. Out-of-state checks are accepted with ID.

✪ **The Inn At 410 Bed & Breakfast.** 410 N. Leroux St., Flagstaff, AZ 86001.
☎ **800/774-2008** or 520/774-0088. Fax 520/774-6354. www.inn410.com.
E-mail: info@inn410.com. 9 units. A/C. $125–$175. MC V. No pets.

Peering into each of the nine guest rooms at the Inn At 410 is like flipping the pages in an issue of *House And Garden*. Each expertly decorated room is daringly different, yet tasteful. Collectively, they make this 1894 home owned by Sally and Howard Krueger one of the most stunning B & Bs anywhere. One room, "Monet's Garden" is reminiscent of a French country garden. Sections of its walls have been painted to resemble broken plaster (far more appealing than the real thing, found in some Route 66 motels), while other areas have reproductions of Monet works brushed upon them. My favorite, "The Dakota Room," celebrates the cowboy way of life. It has barn wood on one wall, and wallpaper with a cowpoke motif on others. Atop the armoire sits a cowboy hat that once belonged to Sally Krueger's grandfather; her grandmother's old cowgirl boots rest on the mantle. All but one of the guest rooms here have gas fireplaces, and three of them have jetted tubs. Travelers who are willing to forego television will relish a night here. And when Sally, who recently shared her favorite recipes on a nationally televised cooking show, serves them breakfast, they may wish they could spend a lifetime.

Jeanette's Bed and Breakfast. 3380 E. Lockett Rd., Flagstaff, AZ 86004-4043. ☎ **800/752-1912** or 520/527-1912. Fax 520/527-1713. www.bbonline.com/az/jbb. E-mail: jbb@infomagic.com. A/C. 4 units, all with private bathroom. $95–$125 double. Rates include breakfast. AE, DISC, MC, V. No checks. No pets.

This B&B is as evocative, odd, and entertaining as the memories of a centenarian. Host Jeanette West (not a centenarian) has stashed small antiques and curios throughout the house, and she encourages guests to find and share them with her. The dresser in my room had an old Boy Scout's uniform in one drawer, a vintage Bible in another, and antique nail kits in a third. Collections of early electric typewriters, blow-dryers, and irons line the halls. Most of the rooms are named for relatives of either Jeanette or her husband, Ray, and reflect the lives of those people. With so many artifacts around, you could easily stay here without realizing that the house is new. Built in 1996, it's a replica of a 1912 Victorian, only with private bathrooms, each with an antique tub, in every room.

Radisson Woodlands Hotel Flagstaff. 1175 W. Rte. 66, Flagstaff, AZ 86001. ☎ **800/333-3333** (reservations only), or 520/773-8888. Fax 520/773-0597. 183 units. A/C TV TEL. $69–$119 double. AE, DC, DISC, MC, V. No pets.

Built in 1990, this four-story hotel has the look and feel of a luxury resort. A pianist often plays in the lobby, where crystal chandeliers hang above a polished marble floor. The decor in the common areas reflects Far Eastern influences. Asian-style vases sit alongside ornately carved teak doors, and one of the restaurants serves sushi. The rooms, with traditional European styling, are almost as opulent as the lobby, and they're quiet too.

Dining/Diversions: A good Japanese restaurant, **Sakura,** is on the premises, as well as a lounge and a coffee shop.

Amenities: Outdoor pool, two whirlpools, a sauna, a steam room, and a fitness center.

INEXPENSIVE

Inexpensive chain hotels include **Howard Johnson Inn** (☎ 520/526-1826), 3300 E. Rte. 66; **Motel 6** (☎ 520/774-1801), 2010 E. Butler (off I-40 Exit 198); **Motel 6** (☎ 520/774-8756), 2440 E. Lucky Lane (off I-40 Exit 198); **Motel 6** (☎ 520/779-6184), 2500 E. Lucky Lane (off I-40 Exit 198); **Motel 6** (☎ 520/779-3757), 2745 S. Woodlands Village Blvd. (near I-40 Exit 195B); **Ramada Limited** (☎ 520/779-3614), 2350 E. Lucky Lane (off I-40 Exit 198); **Econo Lodge Lucky Lane** (☎ 520/774-7701), 2480 E. Lucky Lane (off I-40 Exit 198); **Rodeway Inn East** (☎ 520/526-2200), 2650 E. Rte. 66; **Rodeway Inn West** (☎ 520/774-5038), 913 S. Milton (near I-40 Exit 195B); **Travelodge Flagstaff University Grand Canyon** (☎ 888/259-4404), 801 W. Rte. 66; **Travelodge Flagstaff** (☎ 520/526-1399), 2610 E. Route 66.

Hotel Weatherford. 23 N. Leroux. Flagstaff, AZ 86001. ☎ **520/779-1919.** www.weatherhotel.com. E-mail: weathtel@infomagic.com. 8 units (6 with shared bathrooms), 2 hostel rms. High-season rates: $45–$55; low-season $35–$45; hostel $16 per bed. AE, DC, DISC, MC, V. No pets.

Constructed in 1898, the hotel has some of the most intriguing common areas in town. An upstairs sitting room features quirky antiques such as a shoeshine stand and a rocking lounge chair, as well as panoramic photos of turn-of-the-century Flagstaff. The Zane Gray Room, on the hotel's third floor, has an ornately carved wood bar next to a fireplace and across from an original painting by the legendary 19th-century landscape artist Thomas Moran. Patrons of the Zane Gray Room can also enjoy the new wrap-around balcony, which overlooks the downtown streets.

The guest rooms, only two of which have private bathrooms, are small and quirky. Mine had a half-size bathtub, an antique metal bed (which was a bit too short), a wicker chair, and a bookcase holding a rocking horse and two Zane Gray books. A transom opened onto the hallway, helping create a draft. The only real drawback was the flow of loud partiers between the downstairs bar, where live music plays most nights, and the Zane Gray Room, which is situated just a few yards from the guest rooms. If you're planning to stay here, rest up in advance, then join the party, starting with a meal at the hotel's restaurant, Charly's.

Super 8 Motel. 3725 N. Kasper Ave. (on Rte. 66, 1 mi. west of I-40 Exit 201), Flagstaff, AZ 86004. ☎ **888/324-9131** or 520/526-0818. Fax 520/526-8786. www.travelweb.com. 90 units. A/C TV TEL. May–Sept $64 double; Oct–Apr $44. Rates include donuts. AE, DISC, MC, V. Pets encouraged.

This motel offers an inordinate number of cable TV channels. So kick off your shoes, flop on a bed, and flip through the many stations on the 19-inch color tube. The beds are comfortable and the rooms, all of which were repainted and redecorated in 1999, are relatively quiet. If the motel isn't full, ask for a place in the rear building. Slightly newer than the one in front, it has some of the largest rooms in the city and is farther from both the highway and the always-busy railroad tracks.

WHERE TO EAT
EXPENSIVE

Black Bart's Steak House, Saloon, and Musical Revue. 2760 E. Butler Ave., Flagstaff. ☎ **520/779-3142.** Reservations accepted. Dinner $10.95–$19.95. AE, DC, DISC, MC, V. Daily 5–9pm. AMERICAN.

Initially I was less than enthralled by the prospect of dining at a steak house and musical revue named for a legendary robber. Past experience had convinced me that people who sing near steaks sing badly, and that people who cook near singers cook badly, and that people who run steak houses offering bad singing and bad cooking were themselves legendary robbers. But this restaurant is a surprise. First, the music is nicely performed by music students from Northern Arizona University. They capably croon country, blues, and cabaret songs, then, before the audience finishes applauding, hurry back to the tables they're serving. Even more surprising is the fact that the food—an assortment of hand-cut steaks and prime rib, salmon, grilled tuna, ribs, and veggie kabobs—is actually pretty tasty. The highlight is the all-you-can-eat sourdough biscuits with honey butter, served with every meal.

✪ **Chez Marc Bistro.** 503 Humphreys St., Flagstaff, AZ 86001. ☎ **520/774-1343.** Fax 520/774-2557. Reservations recommended. www.

chezmarc.com. E-mail: dine@chezmarc.com. Lunch $11.95–$16.95; dinner $19.95–$29.95. AE, CB, DC, DISC, MC, V. Thurs–Sun 11:30am–2:30pm, 5–9pm; Mon–Wed 5–9pm. COUNTRY FRENCH.

Come to this country French restaurant if you'd like to splurge on a great meal. The talented chef, Marc Balocco, has cooked for luminaries such as Margaret Thatcher and Queen Elizabeth II, but he seems to take nearly as much pride in feeding everyday tourists and Flagstaff locals. Served by waiters in formal attire, you can dine in the bistro's brick-walled, wooden-floored interior, where magnums of champagne line the walls, or, during warm weather, on its outside terrace, surrounded by lovely gardens. You'll savor food that's superb not only taste-wise, but in texture and appearance. Start with the *crepe de saumon fume au caviar* (Norwegian smoked salmon rolled in a crepe with cucumber relish, sour cream, and topped with caviar), then, after the soup of the day, try *le thon aux epices* (seared Ahi tuna with spicy crust laid over a puree of butternut squash laced by a Pinot Noir sauce). For dessert, I recommend the soufflé glace (frozen Grand Marnier soufflé topped with candied citrus and fresh berry coulee). Cap it with French-pressed coffee and an after-dinner drink.

MODERATE

Beaver Street Brewery and Whistle Stop Cafe. 11 S. Beaver St., Flagstaff. ☎ 520/779-0079. Reservations not accepted. Lunch $6–$9; dinner $7–$15. AE, DISC, MC, V. Daily 11:30am–10pm. AMERICAN/ETHNIC.

The beers at this microbrewery in a 1938 supermarket run from heavy (a Guinness-like Oatmeal Stout) to light (a sweet, refreshing Hefe Weisen) to gravity-defying (the raspberry-flavored Bramble Berry Brew). So does the food. The menu includes everything from dense fondues and wood-fired pizzas to airy, sprout-filled salads. It even offers suggestions on which beer will go best with which food. My favorite beer is the aptly named Derail Pale Ale, whose taste lingers in your mouth. If you'd like to see how the beers are made, ask up front. If the restaurant isn't busy, owners Winnie and Evan Hanseth might take you on an impromptu brewery tour.

✪ **Charly's.** In the historic Hotel Weatherford, 23 N. Leroux, Flagstaff. ☎ 520/779-1919. Fax 520-773-8951. Reservations accepted. www. weatherford hotel.com. E-mail: weathtel@infomagic.com. Lunch $2.95–$8.95; dinner $6.50–$16.95. AE, DC, DISC, MC, V. Daily 11am–11pm (10pm in winter). SOUTHWESTERN/AMERICAN.

Charly's is spacious and cool, both inside, where the 12-foot-high ceilings of the Hotel Weatherford (built in 1897) provide breathing room, and on the sidewalk, a favorite place for summertime dining.

Besides steaks and burgers, the restaurant offers a number of vegetarian dishes and salads that make for perfect light dining. Start with the *crostini tapenade*—a dip of ripe olives, sun-dried tomatoes, capers, and garlic, served with toasted French bread. If you'd like to try Navajo fry bread but aren't up to eating a heavy meat stuffing, you can order it with sautéed vegetables instead. Or gorge on the Durango Tacos—soft tacos with avocado, cilantro, and onions, filled with your choice of beef, chicken, rock shrimp, or grilled vegetables. After dinner, you can dance at the hotel bar, which features live entertainment nightly and has 20 beers on tap.

Dara Thai. 14 S. San Francisco St., Flagstaff. ☎ **520/774-0047** or 520/774-8390. Reservations accepted for parties of 4 or more. Main courses $6.95–$14.95. AE, DISC, MC, V. Mon–Sat 11am–10pm. Closed Sun. THAI.

Among the 80-some entrees served at Dara Thai are many fine curry, vegetarian, and fish dishes. Your server will ask you to select the spiciness level for many sauces, and if you choose the highest level you may soon find your tongue hotter than Phantom Ranch in July. Fortunately, the restaurant provides Thai beer and white rice to cut the heat. Decorated with plants (some real, others painted on the cinder block walls), the dining area seems to have a psychological cooling effect, if not a physical one. Everything I've had here has been delectable.

Pasto. 19 E. Aspen Ave., Flagstaff. ☎ **520/779-1937.** Reservations recommended. Dinner $7.95–$15.95. AE, MC, V. Daily 5–9pm. ITALIAN.

This restaurant bills itself as "fun Italian dining," perhaps referring to the learn-to-speak-Italian tapes that sometimes play in the rest rooms, or maybe to the crayons on the tables. Still, the dining, including a few entrees priced under $10, is more delicious than fun. The Southwestern black-bean ravioli, which comes with a choice of sauces, is outstanding, as is the tortellini Florentine (garlic-lemon tortes under spinach and cream sauce).

The atmosphere is also pleasant. In the spacious and elegant dining room, there's a stamped tin ceiling, and old horns and trombones hang from a brick wall. The servers tend to be more formal than at most other Flagstaff restaurants. I watched one waiter precisely place a coffee cup next to a patron's hand, then rotate the cup so that the handle faced the customer's fingers. All this, for a man wearing river sandals.

INEXPENSIVE

✪ **The Black Bean Burrito Bar and Salsa Company.** 12 E. Rte. 66, Gateway Plaza Suite 104, Flagstaff. ☎ **520/779-9905.** $1–$6. No credit cards.

Summer hours Sun noon–8pm; Mon–Thurs 11am–10pm; Fri–Sat 11am–11pm.
Call for winter hours. MEXICAN.

The best burritos seem to turn up in the plainest environments. At
the Black Bean, you'll eat out of plastic drive-in baskets while sitting at a counter that opens onto a pedestrian walkway. Sure
enough, the burritos, which come with a choice of eight different
salsas, are delicious. A favorite among Northern Arizona University
students, the Black Bean offers 14 house specialty wraps (steamed
or stir-fried food wrapped in tortillas), including exotic flavors such
as peanut tofu and hummus, as well as traditional bean, chicken, and
steak burritos. Wrapped in aluminum foil, the burritos have the heft
of hand weights. But with most under $6, they won't burden you
financially.

✪ **Cafe Express.** 16 N. San Francisco St., Flagstaff. ☎ **520/774-0541.** Breakfast $2.50–$6.25; lunch and dinner $4.50–$8.95. MC, V. Daily 7am–9pm. NEW
AMERICAN.

Like Macy's (see review in this section), Cafe Express serves great
vegetarian fare and displays paintings by local artists. And, as at
Macy's, the help at Cafe Express tends to be casual, wearing the
shop's T-shirts and occasionally sitting down at tables to chat with
customers. But if the two restaurants were pastries, Macy's would be
a nut bran muffin, while Cafe Express would be a croissant. Cafe
Express's food is slightly more refined, in terms of both preparation
and ingredients. It may not be as healthful as the food at Macy's, but
it sure tastes good. The breakfast fare here features delicious
omelettes, huevos rancheros, and pancakes, with tofu available as a
substitute for eggs. The lunch and dinner menu includes soups,
sandwiches, enormous salads, and Southwestern fare. The most delectable items, however, are house specials like the tofu mushroom
stroganoff (a creamy blend of tofu, onions, mushrooms, sour cream,
and spices over rice) and spanakopita (Greek spinach pie). Don't
forget to order a slice of cheesecake or carrot cake, as the desserts
here are among the best in town.

Café Olé. 119 S. San Francisco St., Flagstaff. ☎ **520/774-8272.** No reservations. Lunch and dinner $3.75–$8.95. Mon–Tue 5–8pm; Wed–Fri 11am–3pm;
5–8pm; closed Sat–Sun. Cash only. MEXICAN.

Open only on weekdays, this small, family run restaurant takes its
sweet time preparing and serving fresh, lard-free Mexican food. The
menu features a limited selection of straightforward Mexican fare,
including enchiladas, tacos, tostadas, and burritos. Best of all, however, are the homemade tamales. Order them, then nurse a
margarita, nibble on the delicious chips and salsa, and admire the

painted table tops, hanging Christmas lights (shaped like little peppers), and the sombreros on the wall. Listen to the always-upbeat Spanish music. Observe the cat sidle past. If you're not driving, consider another margarita. After a half-hour or more of waiting, enjoy the food, the best Mexican fare in Flagstaff.

✪ **Macy's European Coffee House Bakery & Vegetarian Restaurante.** 14 S. Beaver St., Flagstaff. ☎ **520/774-2243.** Fax 520-774-4242. www. macyscoffee.com. Reservations not accepted. Main courses $3.50–$6.25. No credit cards. Mon–Wed 6am–8pm; Thurs–Sat 6am–9pm; Sun 6am–6pm. VEGETARIAN/BAKED GOODS.

A nice breeze always seems to blow through this restaurant, skimming the dust off the elaborately drawn menus on the chalkboards and stirring aromas of patchouli, spices, and coffee. Macy's may not be able to save the world, but its fine vegetarian food, fresh pastries, and great coffee encourage people to slow down and smell the latte. It's a place where vegans are welcomed, where bikes lean against the building, and where the bathroom graffiti is life-affirming. A cashier here earnestly told me that she loves everything on the menu. In addition to the standard menu items such as hummus sandwiches and breakfast couscous, Macy's serves daily specials, including a pasta of the day. It also shows the work of local artists.

2 Tusayan

1 mile S of Grand Canyon National Park; 60 miles N of Williams; 80 miles NE of Flagstaff; 340 miles N of Tucson

More a tourist outpost than a town, Tusayan has almost no houses. Most residents live in apartments or trailers behind the town's businesses. Employers pay a lot to house (or lure) workers, and to convince suppliers to lug their goods 60 miles off the interstate. So Tusayan isn't cheap. A cup of coffee costs about $1.50, and rooms generally go for about $20 more than in Williams or Flagstaff. Although most of the accommodations here are pleasant, the food is often bland, and the crowds can be annoying. Still, Tusayan's location makes it the next best thing to being inside the park.

ESSENTIALS

GETTING THERE By Car If you drive, make sure that you have plenty of gasoline in your car before setting out for Tusayan and the Grand Canyon; there are few service stations in this remote part of the state. Flagstaff, the nearest major city, is almost 80 miles away. From Flagstaff, it's possible to take U.S. 180 and 64 directly to Tusayan.

By Plane   The Grand Canyon Airport is located in Tusayan. It's served by two airlines flying out of Las Vegas: **Air Vegas** (☎ 800/255-7474 or 702/736-3599), which charges $200 round-trip; and **Scenic Airlines** (☎ 800/634-6801 or 702/638-3300), which charges $222 round-trip. Air Vegas departs from Henderson Executive Airport, and Scenic leaves from Tropicana Airport (part of McCarran International Airport). **Arizona Professional Air Travel** (☎ 800/933-7590, www.fly-in-america.com) offers commercial service between Flagstaff and Grand Canyon Airport. Costing about $200 (round-trip) per person, the flights are on tiny four- or six-passenger aircraft.

Other than these options, you'll have to fly into Flagstaff and then arrange another mode of transportation the rest of the way to Tusayan and the national park.

By Bus   Bus service between Phoenix, Flagstaff, Tusayan, and Grand Canyon Village is provided by **Nava-Hopi Tours** (☎ 800/892-8687 or 520/774-5003). **CASSI Tours** (☎ 520/638-0871 or 520/638-0821) operates a year-round shuttle between the Grand Canyon Airport in Tusayan and Grand Canyon Village. The shuttle stops hourly in Tusayan at the Best Western Grand Canyon Squire Inn, Moqui Lodge, the IMAX Theater, and Babbitt's Village Store, and in Grand Canyon Village at the Maswik Transportation Center. Cost for a one-way ticket is $4 for adults (16 and under ride free). The buses run from 9:15am to 7:25pm in high season and 9:15am to 6:05pm in low season.

GETTING AROUND   By Car   The nearest car rentals are in Flagstaff. On the South Rim, there's one **service station** in Tusayan; another at Moqui Lodge, $1/4$ mile outside the park's south entrance; and a third at Desert View inside the park's east entrance (this station is seasonal). Be forewarned that gas at these stations costs about 25¢ more per gallon than in Flagstaff, downtown Williams (away from I-40) or Cameron, so you may want to stop off in those places. No matter where you're heading, don't let the tank get too low. Covering the long distances within the park and to towns outside the park can burn a lot of gas.

By Taxi   Fred Harvey offers 24-hour **taxi service** to and from the airport, trailheads, and other destinations (☎ 520/638-2631).

A SUPERMARKET   Babbitt's Supermarket is located 1 mile south of the park entrance on Highway 180/64 (☎ 520/638-2854). It's open daily 7am to 10pm in summer, and 8am to

8pm during the slower times of the year. Or try the larger **General Store** inside the park's business district.

WHAT TO SEE & DO

Grand Canyon IMAX Theater. On Hwy. 64 in Tusayan. ☎ **520/638-2203.** Fax 520/638-2807. www.grandcanyonimaxtheatre.com. E-mail: imax@ thecanyon.com. $8 adults, $6 ages 3–11. Mar–Oct 8:30am–8:30pm, Nov–Feb 10:30am–6:30pm. Showings at half past the hour every hour.

If you quibble over facts, you'll detect flaws in the 34-minute IMAX presentation, *Grand Canyon—the Hidden Secrets,* which has been showing in Tusayan since 1984. For example, it shows the ill-fated members of General Powell's crew leaving the expedition by going down a side drainage that is clearly *not* Separation Canyon. But if you concentrate on the big picture—and the picture here is very, very big—you'll love the IMAX. Every inch of the six-story-high, 82-foot-wide screen is taken up by stunning footage of the canyon. Among the highlights: whitewater rafting that makes you feel as if you might drown, insects blown up to the size of buildings, and aerial footage from inside some of the canyon's rock narrows.

WHERE TO STAY
EXPENSIVE

✪ **Best Western Grand Canyon Squire Inn.** P.O. Box 130 (1¹/₂ mi. south of the park on Hwy. 64), Grand Canyon, AZ 86023-0130. ☎ **800/622-6966** or 520/638-2681. Fax 520/638-0162. 250 units. A/C TEL. Apr 1–Oct 17, $135 standard double; Oct 18–Mar 30, $85. AE, DC, DISC, MC, V.

There's a lot to do at this hotel, which prides itself on being the only full-service resort at Grand Canyon. You'll find two restaurants, two bars, tennis courts, a beauty shop, an exercise room, and an outdoor swimming pool. You can get a massage here or pause to consider the three-story-high mural and waterfall in the lobby. The kids will love the family recreation center, which features bowling and video games.

Costing $15 extra, the deluxe rooms are nearly spacious enough to justify their extra phones—found in the bathrooms, next to the oversized tubs. Thick-walled and quiet, they're among the nicest in town. The standard rooms, in two older buildings left from the Squire Motor Inn (1972), are no larger than the rooms at the other area motels, but they do offer amenities such as hair dryers and coffee makers. And with so much activity at this inn, you probably won't spend as much time in them as you might elsewhere.

Dining/Diversions: You'll find casual dining during breakfast and lunch in the hotel's coffee shop, the **Canyon Garden.** The more elegant **Coronado Room** (reviewed in the "Dining" section) dishes up regional fare, seafood, steaks, and chicken at dinnertime, after serving a large breakfast buffet in morning. A dimly lit lounge adjoins the Coronado Room, but the bar in the hotel basement is more fun. Officially named the **Saguaro Food and Spirits Sports Bar,** it's known as "the Squire" to the many locals who congregate there for pool, nightly drink specials, a large-screen television, and disco on Friday nights.

Amenities: Activities desk, meeting and banquet rooms, health spa, heated pool, tennis courts, game room, Laundromat, beauty salon.

✪ **Grand Canyon Quality Inn and Suites.** P.O. Box 520 (on Hwy. 64, 1 mi. south of the park entrance), Grand Canyon, AZ 86023. ☎ **800/221-2222** (reservations only) or 520/638-2673. Fax 520/638-9537. www. grandcanyonqualityinn.com. E-mail: gcqi@aol.com. 288 units. A/C TV TEL. High season $118 double; low season $68 double. AE, DC, DISC, MC, V. No pets.

In summer, guests here sun themselves around the large outdoor swimming pool and hot tub. In winter, they head for the hotel's atrium, where tropical plants and palm trees shade an 18-foot-long spa with a waterfall. As the area's hot tubs go, this one is the grandest. It's the perfect place to unwind after a long hike. When the guests finally finish soaking, they find themselves occupying some of the nicest accommodations in town, including a number of rooms with private decks and refrigerators.

Dining/Diversions: Open from 6am to 10pm daily, the family style restaurant offers three buffets as well as menu selections. The dinner fare is expensive, even by Tusayan standards, but the lunch buffet, costing only $8, is a good value if you're hungry. It's popular with tour groups. The Wintergarten lounge, open only during high season, is situated in the pleasant confines of the hotel's atrium.

Amenities: Heated pool, Jacuzzi.

Grand Hotel. P.O. Box 331 (on Hwy. 64, 1¹/₂ mi. south of the park entrance), Grand Canyon, AZ 86023. ☎ **888/634-7263** or 520/638-3333. Fax 520/638-3131. www.canyon.com. E-mail: thegrand@canyon.com. 122 units. A/C TV TEL. High season $138 standard, $148 balcony; low-season $89 standard, $99 balcony. AE, DISC, MC, V. No pets.

This newest hotel in Tusayan is also its most stylish. Modeled after a lodge of the old West, the hotel's lobby features an enormous fireplace, hand-woven carpets, and hand-oiled, hand-painted goatskin lanterns. Imitation ponderosa pine logs rise from the stone-tile floors to the high ceiling. The rooms are also pleasant, though perhaps not large enough to justify the high price charged for them. The nicest are the third-story rooms that have balconies facing away from the highway.

Dining/Diversions: The **Canyon Star Restaurant,** specializing in mesquite smoked barbecue and Southwestern cuisine, serves three meals daily and has nightly entertainment in summer. (See review in this chapter.) Among Tusayan's upscale bars, the most appealing by far is the **Canyon Star Saloon.** Below its stamped copper ceiling, patrons belly up to the bar; one of the stools is an old saddle.

Amenities: Native American workshops, heated pool and spa, meeting room.

MODERATE

A midpriced chain hotel in Tusayan is **Grand Canyon Rodeway Inn Red Feather Lodge** (☎ 800/538-2345 or 520/638-2414), on Highway 64, one mile south of the park.

Holiday Inn Express. P.O. Box 3245 (on Hwy. 64, 1¹/₂ mi. south of the park entrance), Grand Canyon, AZ 86023. ☎ **520/638-3000.** Fax 520/638-0123. www.gcanyon.com. 197 units. A/C TV TEL. Mar 15–May 30 $89–$109; June 1–Oct 15 $99–$139; Oct 15–Mar 14 $69–$89. Rates include continental breakfast. AE, DC, DISC, MC, V. No pets.

Decorated in a Southwestern motif, the rooms at this motel, which was built in 1995, feel crisp and new. Like the rooms at other Holiday Inn Expresses, each has an iron and ironing board, not to mention a 25-inch TV. In the morning, enjoy complimentary coffee, juice and pastries in the newly expanded breakfast area. The Holiday Inn Express also operates 32 suites, each with a different theme, in a building adjacent to the larger property. Each suite has one of eight different furniture packages, ranging from unpeeled hickory furniture from Indiana to polished furnishings hand-crafted by the Amish. My favorite, the Native American Room, showcases a number of historic photos of the Navajo, Havasupai, and Hopi. All have two telephones, two televisions, VCR, refrigerator, microwave, and a small living area, making them worth the extra $20 in cost over the standard Holiday Inn Express rooms.

Moqui Lodge. P.O. Box 369 (on Hwy. 64, ¹/₄ mi. south of the park), Grand Canyon, AZ 86023. ☎ **303/297-2757** (advance reservations) or 520/638-2424 (locally). Fax 520/638-2895. 136 units. TV TEL. $100 double. MC, V for reservations. AE, DC, DISC, MC, V all acceptable upon check-in. Closed Nov 1–Mar 31.

Situated just outside the south entrance gates, Moqui Lodge feels like part of the national park, only quieter. Built in the 1960s, the

A-frame lodge took the place of an old trading post that first opened for business in the 1920s. Inside the lobby, a chimney of flagstone and petrified wood climbs to a high ceiling supported by unpeeled logs.

Because I love old lodges, I wish I could recommend Moqui. However, the adjoining motel rooms now seem a little too dingy to merit approval. At least the guests here can still enjoy the Southwestern-style restaurant, which is popular with locals; the bar, which serves free chips and salsa all day long; and the nearby forest.

INEXPENSIVE

7-Mile Lodge. P.O. Box 56 (1¹/₂ mi. south of park entrance on Hwy. 64), Grand Canyon, AZ 86023. ☎ **520/638-2291.** Reservations not accepted. 20 units. A/C TV. High season, $80 double; low season, $48 double. AE, DISC, MC, V. No pets.

Instead of taking reservations, the owners of this motel start selling spaces at around 9am and usually sell out by early afternoon. If you need a place to stay, think about stopping here on your way into the park. Don't be put off by the motel's cramped office—surprisingly, the rooms are quite nice and large enough to hold two queen beds. Built in 1984, they have 2-inch doors and walls thick enough to muffle the noise of planes from the nearby airport.

WHERE TO EAT

Cafe Tusayan. Located next to the Rodeway Inn, 1¹/₂ mi. south of the park on Hwy.64, Tusayan. ☎ **520/638-2151.** Breakfast $1.95–$9.25; lunch $4.50–$8.95; dinner $4.50–$18.95. MC, V. Hours vary. AMERICAN/SOUTHWESTERN.

Since opening Cafe Tusayan in spring 1999 in a space formerly occupied by Denny's, the restaurant's owners have wisely kept the menu small. They serve a few varieties of salads; appetizers such as jalapeño poppers and sautéed mushrooms; and a handful of entrees, including salmon with herb butter, top sirloin steak, baked chicken, and stroganoff. Perhaps because the chefs are able to focus on just a few dishes, the food is some of the best in Tusayan.

Canyon Star Restaurant. In the Grand Hotel on Hwy. 64 (1¹/₂ mi. from the park's south entrance, Tusayan. ☎ **888/634-7263** or 520/ 638-3333. Reservations accepted. Breakfast $3.50–$7.50; lunch $7.95; dinner $14.95–$21.95. Summer hours 6:30am–10pm; winter hours 7am–9:30pm. AE, DISC, MC, V. REGIONAL.

The entertainment at this sprawling restaurant seems designed to give tourists exactly what they hope to find in the American West. Each night during summer, lonesome cowboy balladeers and spiritual Native American drummers take turns performing for the visitors. In case anyone gets bored with this sanitized western show, video clips of the canyon play constantly on monitors above the dance floor. The distractions are more than enough to make a person forget the food, including the mesquite smoked barbecue.

✪ **Coronado Dining Room.** In the Best Western Grand Canyon Squire Inn (1¹/₂ mi. south of the park on Hwy. 64), Tusayan. ☎ **520/638-2681,** ext. 4419. Reservations not accepted. Breakfast buffet $8.95; dinner $10.95–$19.95. AE, DISC, MC, V. 6:30–11am (high season only) and 5–10pm (year-round). SOUTHWESTERN.

During my stay, the best-dressed people in town were the waiters (there were no waitresses) in this restaurant. Besides dressing sharply, they worked hard too. The busboy kept my water full all night, touching my glass with a clean cloth napkin. There were other nice touches: table-top candle holders that looked like small electric lamps; ample room between tables; and moist, delicious dark bread. The service, combined with the high-backed wooden chairs and the dimly lighted metal chandeliers, made the room seem far more formal than anywhere else in town.

This restaurant, which is the best in Tusayan, serves the usual mix of Southwestern and American food. The difference is that everything here is prepared with more expertise than in other area restaurants. Of the Southwestern dishes, the *pollo asada* (charbroiled chicken breast with tomatoes and scallions) scores high marks. Also great is the chicken marsala.

On summer nights, the most opportune time to eat here is between 5 and 7pm, when some entrees are discounted by $2 or more. The adjoining, family oriented Canyon Room serves less expensive fare for breakfast and lunch, but offers the same menu as the Coronado Room at dinnertime.

Moqui Lodge Dining Room. At Moqui Lodge on Hwy. 64 (¹/₄ mi. from the park's south entrance), Tusayan. ☎ **520/638-2424.** Reservations not accepted. Breakfast $6.35; dinner $4.95–$18. Daily 6–10am and 5–10pm. AE, DC, DISC, MC, V. Lodge closed Nov 1–Apr 1. MEXICAN.

Occupying a wide wood-paneled room with a ceiling that's high but humble, this restaurant calls to mind a country church. Electric candles and metal chandeliers flush the darkness from every corner, giving the room an open, inviting feel. When crowded, voices sometimes resound off the woodwork like the din when a church lets out.

Moqui attracts diners of both denominations (local and tourist), most of whom enjoy the appetizing, albeit cheese-heavy Mexican fare, including tostadas, enchiladas, and tacos. The fajitas—chicken or beef served with peppers and onions, with warm flour tortilla—make a trip here worthwhile. For dessert, try the "world-famous" Derby Pie. At breakfast, Moqui offers a large buffet for $6.35.

We Cook Pizza and Pasta. On Hwy. 64, 1 mi. south of the park entrance, Tusayan. ☎ **520/638-2274.** Reservations not accepted. Dinner $10–$20; lunch $7–$12. Credit cards not accepted. Summer 10:30am–9:30pm, winter 11am–9pm. ITALIAN.

In this restaurant's lengthy name, the owners forgot to mention how much they charge. The prices here are high even by Grand Canyon standards, especially for a place without table service. A large four-item pizza runs $20.50, and some pasta dishes cost over $10. After paying dearly for your food, you'll have to sit at one of the long picnic tables and wait for your number to be called. Since you can't reserve tables here, the only way to shorten your wait is by ordering your pizza by telephone ahead of time.

At least the food is palatable. Pasta dishes such as the spicy shrimp linguine and the Cajun chicken fettuccini taste especially delicious to people who are salt-deprived, and the pizza pleases most diners. If you're on a budget, however, you can find less-expensive, carry-out pizza at **Piccadilly Circus** (☎ **520/638-2608**), inside the Shell station across from the IMAX Theater.

3 Williams

59 miles S of Grand Canyon; 32 miles W of Flagstaff; 220 miles E of Las Vegas

With timber above it, ranches below it, and railroads running through it, this town of 2,700 attracted one of the most raucous crowds in the West after being incorporated in 1892. Cowboys, loggers, prospectors, trappers, and railroad workers all frequented the brothels, gambling houses, bars, and opium dens on the town's infamous Saloon Row. Although quieter now, Williams has done an especially good job of packaging its lively past. Much of Saloon Row and many other 19th-century buildings have been restored. The town's newly renovated train depot now serves as the start and finish for the daily runs of the Historic Grand Canyon Railroad. And Route 66, which splits the town's business district, has been enshrined in the T-shirts and caps sold by local businesses. To entertain the tourists, gun-slinging cowboys stage raucous shoot-outs in the streets every summer night.

ESSENTIALS

GETTING THERE   Williams is on I-40 just west of the junction with Highway 64, which leads north to the South Rim of the Grand Canyon.

Amtrak (☎ **800/872-7245**) recently established a new, unstaffed stop in Williams. A free shuttle bus brings departing passengers from the drop-off into town, to the station for the **Grand Canyon Railway.** The **Historic Grand Canyon Railway** (☎ **800/843-8724**) offers daily service linking Williams and Grand Canyon Village. (See "What to See & Do" below.) The train leaves Williams in the morning and returns in late afternoon. Round-trip coach tickets cost $49.95 for adults and $24.95 for children under 17; upgrades are $20 to $70 extra. Tickets include the entry fee to the park.

Nava-Hopi Tours (☎ **800/892-8687** or 520/774-5003) has daily bus service connecting Williams with the Grand Canyon ($18 round-trip), Flagstaff ($14 round-trip), and connections to Phoenix.

VISITOR INFORMATION   For more information on the Williams area, contact the **Williams–Grand Canyon Chamber of Commerce,** 200 W. Railroad Ave., Williams, AZ 86046-2556 (☎ **800/863-0546** or 520/635-4061; www.thegrandcanyon.com; e-mail: williams@thegrandcanyon.com). The visitor center here is open 8am to 5pm daily. A vending machine located outside the building sells entrance permits to the park.

GETTING AROUND   There are no longer any car rental agencies in Williams. Taxi service is available through **Smitty's Taxi** (☎ **520/635-9825**).

SUPERMARKET   **Safeway** is located at 637 W. Rte. 66 (☎ **520/ 635-0500**); it's open daily from 6am to 11pm (hours may vary in winter).

WHAT TO SEE & DO

✪ **Grand Canyon Railroad.** Williams Depot, 235 N. Grand Canyon Blvd. (take I-40 Exit 163, go $1/2$ mi. south), Williams. ☎ **800/843-8724.** Fax 520/ 773-1610. www.thetrain.com. Round-trip coach tickets are $49.95 adult, $24.95 children under 17 (plus tax and $6 National Park Service entry fees for ages 17–61); upgrades cost $20–$70 per person. AE, DC, DISC, MC, V. Train departs daily at 9:30am and arrives at Grand Canyon at 11:45am. Leaves Grand Canyon at 3:15pm, arriving in Williams at 5:30pm.

In 1968, the automobile helped end the Santa Fe Railway's service between Williams and Grand Canyon. By 1989, when service resumed on the 65-mile-long line, automobiles were clogging the park's narrow roads. Thousands of visitors discovered that the historic train not only spared them the headache of driving, but was fun. Today, the railroad carries more than 100,000 passengers annually, many of whom buy package tours that include transportation to Williams. (Call the Grand Canyon Railway for more information.)

The trip starts at the historic Williams Depot and the original Fray Marcos Hotel. Built in 1908, this concrete building, on the National Register of Historic Places, survives today only because the railroad realized in the 1970s that to demolish it would cost more than to leave it standing. It now houses a gift shop and a free museum tracing the history of the Grand Canyon Railway.

At 9:30 every morning, after local cowboys stage a Wild West gunfight outside the depot, conductors help passengers board the train. Coach passengers sit in restored 1923 Harriman coaches with Pullman windows, art deco–style lamps, and tiny ceiling fans. For $20 more, you can purchase an upgrade to the Club Car, with a fully stocked mahogany bar. For $50 more than coach fare, you can enjoy first class treatment, including continental breakfast in the morning and champagne and appetizers on the trip home—all while sitting in comfortable recliner chairs. If you really want to savor the ride, however, I recommend parting with another $20 above the first class fare in order to purchase a seat either in the chief class, which occupies a parlor car with elegant furnishings and an open-air platform; or, better still, in the deluxe observation class, whose seats are in a glass dome atop the car.

In summer, a rare steam engine pulls the train at speeds up to 30 miles per hour. (Steam-engine purists should be forewarned that a vintage diesel locomotive often helps pull the train. In winter, only the diesel is used.) While the train chugs across the high desert, U.S. Forest Service employees discuss the land on the canyon rim, and musicians play folk and country standards. The trip ends at the historic Grand Canyon Depot in Grand Canyon Village. From here, passengers can lunch at the historic El Tovar Hotel or take Fred Harvey bus tours of the rim. You can sign up for bus tours while reserving train tickets.

Jeff Gordon Museum and Fan Club Headquarters. 117 E. Rte. 66, Williams, AZ 86046. ☎ **520/635-5333.** www.jeffgordonfanclub.com. E-mail: jgfan@primenet.com. Open Mon–Fri 7am–5pm, Sat–Sun 8am–4pm. Free.

Highbrows may wonder whether a 28-year-old stock-car racer really merits a museum chronicling his life. But Jeff Gordon isn't just any stock-car racer; as two-time-defending Winston Cup champion, he's *the man*—and a nice guy too. In this small museum on Route 66, you'll find everything from Gordon's first go-cart racing suit to a tall-boy Busch beer can commemorating a recent Busch Grand Nationals race. The biggest highlight may be the museum's collection

Western-Style Gun Fights

The same bad guys, sheriffs, and deputies who battle every morning near the Grand Canyon Railway Depot shoot at one another all over again at 7pm summer nights in downtown Williams. The free show, which moves to a different block of Route 66 each night, entertains thousands of visitors every year. If you're in town, don't miss it. To find out where the show will be on a given night, consult one of the schedules available at the **Williams–Grand Canyon Chamber of Commerce** (☎ **800/863-0546** or 520/635-4061) or at businesses throughout town.

of the many, many Kellogg's cereal boxes graced by Gordon's boyish face.

WHERE TO STAY
EXPENSIVE

Best Western Inn of Williams. 2600 Rte. 66, Williams, AZ 86046. ☎ **520/635-4400.** Fax 520/635-4488. 79 units. A/C TV TEL. $79–$135 double. Rates include continental breakfast. AE, DC, DISC, MC, V. No checks. No pets.

Some of the nicest rooms in Williams are at this hotel, atop a forested hill west of town. In addition to sofas, glass-topped coffee tables, and classic American furniture, the rooms offer smaller amenities such as coffeemakers and hair dryers. Outside, the pines grow to near the edge of the swimming pool.

Dining/Diversions: A free hot breakfast is served in a small dining area. No other meals are available. The hotel also has a lounge. A nearby Denny's delivers room-service meals.

Amenities: Heated pool, Laundromat.

Fray Marcos Hotel. 235 N. Grand Canyon Blvd., Williams, AZ 86046. ☎ **800/843-8724** or 520/635-4010. Fax 520/635-2180. 89 units. A/C TV TEL. Apr 1–Sept 1, $119 double; Sept 2–Oct 31, Nov 26–29, Dec 19–Jan 3, and Mar, $99 double; Nov 1–Feb 28, $69 double. AE, DISC, MC, V. No pets.

Named for a Franciscan monk believed to have been the first white person in the region, this sprawling, luxurious hotel replaces the original Fray Marcos Hotel. (Located next door, the original hotel now houses a gift shop and the museum for the Grand Canyon Railway.) In the lobby of the new hotel, oil paintings of the Grand Canyon adorn the walls, and cushy chairs surround a large flagstone fireplace. Bellhops carry luggage to the spacious, comfortable, Southwestern-style rooms.

The Grand Canyon Railway, which starts and ends its daily runs next to the hotel, has become hugely popular with tour groups, many of whom stay at the Fray Marcos. Its success has translated into rapid growth for the hotel. In late 1999, the Fray Marcos was in the process of adding a new wing that would more than double its size, to 199 rooms. A pool and exercise room were also in the works. Although this is a nice hotel providing good service, it inevitably feels less intimate and more commercial than other area lodges.

Dining/Diversions: Max and Thelma's, a new 300-seat restaurant located next to the hotel, combines buffet-style dining and table service. **Spenser's Lounge,** which features a beautiful 100-year-old bar imported from Scotland, offers simple dining and top-shelf liquor.

✪ **Sheridan House Inn.** 460 E. Sheridan Ave., Williams, AZ 86046. ☎ **888/ 635-9345** or 520/635-9441. Fax 520/635-1005. www.thegrandcanyon.com/ sheridan/. E-mail: egardner@primenet.com. 12 units. A/C TV TEL. $110–$225 double. AE, DISC, MC, V. Ask about pets in advance. Kids OK.

A display case just inside the front door of this inn holds ancient clay figurines from China and Central America, as well as tiny oil lamps from the Middle East. Beyond that, the home's interior bristles with bronze sculptures (including replicas of Remingtons) and shimmers with original paintings. Guest rooms are ultraluxurious, with brass beds, glass-topped coffee tables, TVs, stereos, VCRs, and refrigerators stocked with cold drinks. Outside, under the ponderosa pines at the end of this quiet, dead-end street (a short walk from downtown Williams), the hot tub awaits. Making this setting all the more enjoyable are the innkeepers, Steve and Evelyn Gardner. Unassuming and down-home friendly, they wouldn't seem the least bit out of place at the nearby Jeff Gordon Museum, even though their home more closely resembles the Louvre.

Dining/Diversions: Breakfast and nightly cocktail hour with hors d'oeuvres (barbecue and salad—don't plan on eating afterward).

Amenities: Slate pool table; hot tub; refrigerators, VCRs, and stereos in the units. Some units have washer/dryers.

MODERATE

Midprice chain hotels in Williams include **Days Inn** (☎ 520/635-4051), 2488 W. Rte. 66; and **Fairfield Inn by Marriott** (☎ 520/ 635-9888), 1029 N. Grand Canyon Blvd., off I-40 exit 163.

Holiday Inn Williams. 950 N. Grand Canyon Blvd. (off I-40 exit 163), Williams, AZ 86046. ☎ **520/635-4114.** Fax 520/635-2700. www.hionline.com. 120 units. A/C TV. $49–$159 double. AE, CB, DC, DISC, MC, V. Pets welcome.

Convenient to both I-40 and downtown Williams, this family friendly hotel is a great place to regroup during an extended trip with kids. For recreation, it has an indoor pool, sauna, and oversized spa. The restaurant delivers food to the rooms, which are clean and comfortable.

Quality Inn Mountain Ranch Resort. 6701 E. Mountain Ranch Rd. (5 mi. east of Williams on I-40, Pittman Valley Rd. exit), Williams, AZ 86046. ☎ **520/635-2693.** Fax 520/635-4188. www.mountainranchresort.com. E-mail: mrllama35@aol.com. 72 units. A/C TV TEL. $69–$109 double. AE, DC, DISC, MC, V. Closed Nov 1–May 1. Pets $20 extra on the first night.

Like friendly gym teachers, the front desk employees at this resort loan out sporting goods to guests, asking only that they do their best to return them intact. The guests enthusiastically (and sometimes erratically) serve tennis balls on the motel's two tennis courts, spike volleyballs on the volleyball court, kick soccer balls on the expansive lawn, and putt golf balls on the putting-practice area. Sometimes they jostle their own, um, selves by taking horseback rides (cost: $22 for 1 hour) at the nearby stables. On November 1, when cold weather might otherwise force guests into their rooms, the resort shuts down until March.

There's also a swimming pool, coffee shop, and a tiny lounge that serves some of the cheapest cocktails around, including $2 well drinks. All the rooms are pleasant, but the downstairs ones conveniently have two doors—one facing the parking lot and forest, the other opening onto the lawn and playing courts.

✪ **Red Garter Bed and Bakery.** 137 W. Railroad Ave. (P.O. Box 95), Williams, AZ 86046. ☎ **800/328-1484** or 520/635-1484. www.redgarter.com. E-mail: redgarter@the grandcanyon.com. 4 units, all with bathroom. A/C TV. $65–$105. Rates include continental breakfast. AE, DISC, MC, V. Closed Dec–Jan. No pets.

In the early 1900s, this Victorian Romanesque building had a brothel upstairs, a saloon downstairs, and an opium den in the back. The innkeeper, John Holst, has worked hard to preserve both the building, built in 1897, and its colorful history. A general contractor specializing in restoration work, he fully refurbished the structure, which served as a tire storage in the early 1970s. Using early county and city records, he also fleshed out the building's history, which he gladly shares with visitors.

Each of the four guest rooms has custom-made (by Holst himself) moldings, a 12-foot-high ceiling, a ceiling fan, and antique furnishings. My favorite guest room, **The Best Gals' Room,** overlooks Route 66 and is the largest and most luxurious of the four. Its two adjoining rooms were once reserved for the brothel's "best gals," who would lean out of the Pullman windows to flag down customers. Standing in this room today, you can read the historic graffiti on the wall, then pull back the velvet drapery to gaze down at the modern-day cowboys on Route 66.

INEXPENSIVE

Inexpensive chain hotels include the **Travelodge** (☎ **520/635-2651**), 430 E. Rte. 66; **Motel 6** (☎ **520/635-9000**), 831 W. Rte. 66; **Howard Johnson Express** (☎ **800/720-6614** or 520/635-9561), 511 N. Grand Canyon Blvd., off I-40 exit 163; and **Super 8 West** (☎ **520/635-4045**), 911 W. Rte. 66.

Norris Motel. 1001 W. Rte. 66 (P.O. Box 388), Williams, AZ 86046. ☎ **800/341-8000** reservations only, or 520/635-2202. Fax 520/635-9202. 33 units. www.thegrandcanyon.com/norris. E-mail: ukgolf@primenet.com. A/C TV TEL. June–Aug, $59 double; Sept–Oct and Apr–May, $48 double; Nov–Mar, $30 double. AE, DISC, MC, V. No pets.

In an era when many hotels regrettably advertise being "American owned," the sign at the Norris Motel heralds "British Hospitality." Brian and Kathleen James, the British-born managers, do everything possible to make guests feel at home, even letting them walk their golden retriever, Sophie. While all three buildings are pleasant, the newest, built in 1990, has the best view of the surrounding hills and is closest to the outdoor pool and spa. The oversized rooms in the new building easily house two double beds (or one queen), a desk, table, and refrigerator, all for a price lower than at most chains.

WHERE TO EAT

Cruisers Cafe 66. 233 W. Rte. 66, Williams. ☎ **520/635-2445.** www.thegrandcanyon.com/cruisers. Lunch/dinner $4.25–$14.95. AE, MC, V. Summer, daily noon–10pm; winter, usually 3–10pm. AMERICAN.

Built in an old Route 66 gas station, this restaurant, (formerly Tiffany's) is jammed with gas-station memorabilia, including stamped glass, filling-station signs, "Sky Chief" gas pumps, and photos of classic stations. Served up with plenty of napkins as well as drinks in unbreakable plastic mugs, the roadhouse-style food will fuel you for days to come. Start with the sampler of appetizers—wings, chicken strips, mozzarella sticks, and fried mushrooms—

served on a real automobile hubcap. The burgers are tasty, but the best choice, if you really want to fill up, is the baby back ribs. The daily specials in the bar attract the locals.

Grand Canyon Coffee and Cafe. 125 W. Rte. 66, Williams. ☎ **520/ 635-1255.** Reservations not accepted. $3.50–$4.50. AE, MC, V. Summer, Mon– Sat 7am–4:30pm, 7–8:30pm. SANDWICHES.

For lunch, try this restaurant, which prominently displays Harley-Davidson T-shirts but traffics in food and drink that most bikers wouldn't touch, including Mocha Espresso Frappes, fruit smoothies, bottled water, and panini sandwiches served on focaccia bread. Cooked on a cast-iron grill imported from Switzerland, the panini sandwiches are delicious—and they're relatively inexpensive. One great choice is the "Chunky Cheese"—cheddar, mozzarella, and Swiss cheeses with tomato, grilled onion, and mayo.

✪ Old Smoky's Restaurant. 624 W. Route 66. ☎ **520/635-2091.** Reservations not accepted. Breakfast $2–$6; lunch $3–$7. AE, DISC, MC, V. Daily 6am–1:30pm. AMERICAN.

Built in 1946, this tiny Route 66 restaurant pays homage to the mountain-man lifestyle of the town's namesake, Bill Williams. On its walls of varnished wood hang logging saws, a muzzle loader gun, and coonskin caps. The breakfasts, which are the best in town, could easily satisfy a hungry logger. Try the Old Smoky's Special (one egg, potatoes, two bacon or sausage links, and four dollar-size hotcakes) or the Billy Hatcher Omelette (homemade red chile and beans topped with melted cheddar and onion). Lunches include burgers, sandwiches, and chili.

Pancho McGillicuddy's Mexican Cantina. 141 Railroad Ave., Williams. ☎ **520/635-4150.** Reservations accepted. $3.75–$13.50. AE, DISC, MC, V. Summer daily noon–10pm. Hours vary in winter. MEXICAN/AMERICAN.

The first tough decision at this restaurant is where to eat. Your choices are the outside deck, which receives some nice late-afternoon sun and features live entertainment in summer; the main dining room, done up like a courtyard in a Mexican villa; and the historic barroom, site of the (1893) Cabinet Saloon. The next tough choice is which of the heavy but zesty Mexican dishes to order. The chicken *mole* (chicken breast served with a sweetened red chile sauce) is one good option. Others include a *carne asada* (rib-eye steak broiled over a flame and topped with green chiles, tomatoes, onion, and cheese) and red snapper in tomato and olive sauce. If, by chance, the food doesn't melt in your mouth, you can wash it down with a Dos Equis.

Red Garter Bakery. 137 W. Railroad Ave., Williams. ☎ **520/635-1484.** Reservations not accepted. $2–$5. AE, DISC, MC, V. Daily 6–11am and 4–8pm. Closed Dec–Jan. BAKERY.

John Holst, innkeeper at the Red Garter Bed & Breakfast, cooks up mouthwatering scones, strudels, cinnamon rolls, and European-style bread for his guests—and anyone else who stops by his bakery. The pastries alone make a visit here worthwhile, but there's more. The fresh-ground coffee is rich and strong, and the bakery is in a historic building graced with its original wood floor, on which sits an enormous antique coffee grinder. It's conveniently located right across the tracks from the Williams Depot.

✪ **Rod's Steak House.** 301 E. Rte. 66, Williams. ☎ **520/635-2671.** $7–$24. MC, V. Daily 11:30am–9:30pm. STEAKS.

If you're a steak lover, brake for the cow-shaped sign on Route 66 as you would for real livestock. This landmark restaurant, sprawling across a city block between the highway's east- and westbound lanes, has hardly changed since Rodney Graves, an early member of the U.S. Geological Survey, opened it in 1946. Printed on a paper cut-out of a cow, the menu is still only about 6 inches across—more than enough space for its laconic descriptions of the restaurant's offerings. You can choose nonsteak items such as "beef liver grilled onions and bacon" and "jumbo fantail shrimp tempura battered"; or prime rib in three sizes, from the 9-ounce "ladies lite cut" to the 16-ounce "cattleman's hefty cut." The corn-fed mesquite-broiled steaks have kept this place in business for a half-century. No matter what meat you choose, you'll have a choice of a dinner salad or soup. Better still, you'll receive a steady supply of yeast rolls with mesquite honey (a real delight).

4 Cameron

51 miles N of Flagstaff on U.S. 89, and 30 minutes from Desert View and the eastern entrance to the park

Cameron is a convenient place to stay if you plan on exploring the eastern end of the park.

SUPERMARKET   Simpson's Market (☎ 520/679-2340) is located at the junctions of highways 89 and 64, next to the Chevron. It's open daily from 6am to 9pm (7am to 9pm in winter).

WHAT TO SEE & DO

The **Cameron Trading Post** (☎ **800/338-7385** or 520/679-2231), at the crossroads of Cameron where Highway 64 to

Grand Canyon Village branches off U.S. 89, should not be missed. The original stone trading post, a historic building, now houses a gallery of old and antique Indian artifacts, clothing, and jewelry. This gallery offers museum-quality pieces, and even if you don't have $10,000 or $15,000 to drop on an old rug or basket, you can still look around. The main trading post is a more modern building and is the largest trading post in northern Arizona.

WHERE TO STAY

✪ Cameron Trading Post Motel. On Hwy. 89 (P.O. Box 339), Cameron, AZ 86020. ☎ **800/338-7385** or 520/679-2231. Fax 520/679-2350. 66 units. A/C TV TEL. May 1–Oct 31, $74 double; Nov 1–Feb 28, $59; Mar 1–Apr 30, $69. AE, DC, MC, V. Pets OK.

Renovated in the early 1990s, the rooms in this motel are some of the nicest in the Grand Canyon area. Each features its own unique Southwestern-style furnishings, many of them handmade by the motel's staff. The motel's Hopi building borders a terraced garden with stone picnic tables, a fountain, and a large grill. The campground opposite the motel offers full hookups for $15 per night.

WHERE TO EAT

Cameron Trading Post Dining Room. On U.S. 89 in Cameron. ☎ **800/338-7385** or 520/679-2231. Breakfast $3.95–$6.95; lunch $4.50–$8.95; dinner $6–$15. AE, DC, MC, V. Summer 6am–10pm daily; winter 7am–9pm. NAVAJO/SOUTHWESTERN/AMERICAN.

The menu at this restaurant draws upon a variety of cultures. As you might guess from the location, the Navajo dishes are the tastiest— particularly the hot beef, available only at lunch. A taste of the seafood, meanwhile, might remind you the ocean is a long way away.

5 Towns & Outposts Near the North Rim

The area surrounding Grand Canyon north of the Colorado River is some of the most sparsely populated—and scenic—in the continental United States. Highway 89A crosses the Colorado River at the northeastern tip of Grand Canyon—just 5 miles downstream of **Lee's Ferry,** where most river trips in the canyon begin. Continuing west from the bridge on Highway 89A, you'll pass three lonely lodges—**Marble Canyon Lodge, Lee's Ferry Lodge,** and **Cliff Dweller's Lodge**—each a few miles apart, at the base of the aptly named Vermillion Cliffs. This eerie desert landscape, which features balancing rocks and other striking landforms, gives way to forest when you begin the 4,800-vertical-foot climb from the Marble

Platform to the Kaibab Plateau. Because the area surrounding the park's North Rim is largely National Forest, you may have to travel a ways if you fail to find a room inside the park. The closest lodging to the park's northern entrance is at **Kaibab Lodge,** 18 miles north of the North Rim on Highway 67, and at **Jacob Lake,** 44 miles north of the North Rim. If those two lodges are full, you may have to drive as far north as Fredonia, Arizona or Kanab, Utah to find a room.

WHERE TO STAY & EAT
NEAR THE PARK

Jacob Lake Inn. (Junction of hwys. 67 and 89A.) Jacob Lake, AZ 86022. ☎ **520/643-7232.** Fax 520/643-7235. E-mail: jacob@jacoblake.com. 12 motel units, 27 cabins. May 14–Nov 31, $69 double; Dec 1–May 13, $49 double. AE, DC, DISC, MC, V. No checks. Small pets $5 extra; large pets not allowed.

In 1922, Harold and Nina Bowman bought a barrel of gas and opened a gas "stand" near the present-day site of the Jacob Lake Inn. Seven years later they built this inn at the junction of highways 67 and 89A. Today, Jacob Lake Inn is the main hub of activity between the North Rim and Kanab, Utah. To serve the growing summer crowds, the Bowmans' descendants and their friends travel south from their homes in Utah. They run the bakery, churning out excellent fresh-baked cookies; the soda fountain, which serves milkshakes made from hard ice cream; the gift shop, which features museum-quality pieces by Native American artists; not to mention the restaurant, the motel, and the full-service gas station. *Note:* The inn now has an ATM. It's the nearest one to the North Rim.

Lodgers can choose between motel units and cabins. The rooms in the front building are not nearly as peaceful as the rooms and cabins behind the lodge. Built in 1958, the motel rooms in back are solid and clean, if a bit threadbare in spots. The bathrooms have showers but no tubs, and many of them drain onto the same tile floor as the bathroom itself—a curious design. Most people prefer the rustic cabins, even though they cost more than the motel rooms. The cabin floors creak, the guest rooms (from one to three per cabin) are cramped, and most smell like soggy pine needles. In other words, they're exactly how cabins should be. (Unfortunately, two have been nicely restored and therefore ruined.) Another advantage to the cabins is that each has its own private porch, either attached to the building or standing alone in the Ponderosa pine forest.

Dining: The restaurant here, with both a U-shaped counter and a dining room, serves tasty burgers, sandwiches, and steaks, but the most delicious entree may be the trout. Also popular is the cranberry chicken sandwich. Even if you don't need a meal, it's worth stopping here to buy a few home-baked cookies or a real milkshake.

Kaibab Lodge. HC 64, Box 30 (26 mi. south of Jacob Lake on Hwy. 67), Fredonia, AZ 86022. ☎ **520/638-2389** (May 15–Oct 30); 800/525-0924 or 520-526-0924 (rest of year). Fax 520/527-9398. www.canyoneers.com. E-mail: answers@canyoneers.com. 29 units. $70 double. DISC, MC, V. Leashed pets allowed.

The main lodge here feels as warm and comfortable as a beloved summer camp. It has an upright piano, plastic trees, Christmas lights, wagon wheels, Indian rugs, watercolor paintings, board games, and portable heaters, all under an open-framed ceiling and enormous pine beams that date from its construction in the 1920s. Perhaps because the guest rooms lack phones and all but two lack televisions, guests tend to congregate in the Adirondack-style chairs in front of the 5-foot-wide fireplace, in the small television room, or at the tables across from the counter that doubles as front desk and beer bar. There's also a small gift shop and a restaurant that serves breakfast and dinner.

Each cabinlike building houses two to four of the 24 guest rooms, which sleep from two to five people. The rooms are spare but clean, with paneling of rough-hewn pine. Most have showers but not tubs. One luxury room, added in 1999, has a queen bed, microwave, refrigerator, and coffeemaker. Because the walls of the older units are thin, it's best to share a cabin with friends. Located roughly a quarter mile from the highway, the rooms open onto the broad expanse of DeMotte Park, one of the large, naturally occurring meadows on the Kaibab Plateau.

NEAR LEE'S FERRY

Cliff Dweller's Lodge. 9 mi. west of Navajo Bridge on Hwy. 89A (HC 67-30), Marble Canyon, AZ 86036. ☎ **800/433-2543** or 520/355-2228. 20 units. A/C. May 1–Oct 15 $60–$70 double; Oct 16–Apr 31 $40–$53. Often closed in mid-winter. DISC, MC, V. No pets.

Cliff Dweller's Lodge sits in the most spectacular setting in the Marble Canyon area. It's just a few hundred yards from an eye-catching area of balancing rocks (formed when boulders, having toppled off the nearby Vermilion Cliffs, "capped" the softer soil directly underneath them, thereby slowing its erosion). Against the side of one of these boulders, two former New Yorkers built a house in the 1920s and began serving dinner and drinks to the occasional passer-by. Known simply as "Old Cliff Dweller's," the house still stands today.

The "new" Cliff Dweller's, which dates from the '50s, is set back 50 yards or so from the highway, so the rooms are very quiet. Unless you strongly prefer queen beds to doubles, ask for a room in one of the older buildings, some of which have carports and recessed patios. Located in the oldest building, my favorite rooms have wood paneling even on the ceilings and in the windowless bathrooms, which look a bit like saunas. In addition to having more character, these rooms cost about $10 less. If you want a bathtub, be sure and ask for one, as eight rooms have only showers. There's a package liquor store on the premises, and the restaurant, Canyon Dreamers Cafe, serves great chili.

Lee's Ferry Lodge. 4 mi. west of Navajo Bridge on Hwy. 89A (HC 67-Box 1), Marble Canyon, AZ 86036. (Located in the tiny "Arizona designated place" of Vermilion Cliffs.) ☎ **520/355-2230** or 520/355-2231. Fax 520/355-2301. 11 units. A/C. $53 double. MC, V.

This sleepy roadside lodge, built in 1929, is one of my favorite places anywhere for relaxing. Some of the world's best porch-sitting can be enjoyed outside the low sandstone buildings, a popular stopping place for trout fishers trying their luck above Lee's Ferry. The porches afford stunning views south across the highway toward greenish pink Marble Platform or north to the Vermilion Cliffs. Although the motel sits close to the road, traffic is slow at night.

Some of the older rooms, which tend to be small and rustic, have been redecorated in themes ranging from cowboy to—yes—fish. Double rooms in newer, prefab style buildings are available for groups. When you tire of porch-sitting, head for the adjacent bar and grill, which serves 150 bottled beers and the best food near the North Rim.

The only thing not restful are the showers, which erupt like Old Faithful, only less faithfully.

Dining: After rigging boats for trips down the Colorado, many river guides come to the restaurant here, and not just because it stocks 150 types of bottled beer. They also come for nicely prepared steaks, chicken, and fish, and for imaginative sandwiches such as the "Turkey in a Straw"—sliced turkey breast, sauerkraut, and Swiss cheese grilled on sourdough bread and served with Thousand Island dressing. It's easily the best food near Lee's Ferry and arguably the best within 2 hours of the North Rim. The staff provides low-key, friendly service, in a dining room whose wood walls, tables, chairs, and bar seem to all have been sawed from the same tree. The restaurant can be very crowded at dinnertime during peak fishing periods (generally fall and spring).

Marble Canyon Lodge. P.O. Box 6001 (^{1}/4 mi. west of Navajo Bridge on Hwy. 89A), Marble Canyon, AZ 86036. ☎ **800/726-1789** or 520-355-2225. Fax 520-355-2227. 60 units. A/C TV. $60 double. DISC, MC, V.

The closest to Lee's Ferry, this lodge frequently fills up with rafters eagerly awaiting the journey into the canyon. The lodge, a historic 1927 building, steadily attracts visitors stocking up for one excursion or another. The traffic gives the place a busier, less personal feel than at the nearby Cliff Dweller's and Lee's Ferry lodges. The rooms here vary, but the ones in building no. 3 are brightest and most pleasant. Although restaurant and lounge are on the premises, my favorite attraction here is the book store, which stocks a number of rare and out-of-print titles on the region.

6 Kanab, Utah & Fredonia, Arizona

78 miles NW of Grand Canyon National Park; 80 miles S of Bryce Canyon National Park; 42 miles E of Zion National Park; 303 miles S of Salt Lake City

The first Mormon settlers in this area were run off by the Navajo. The second group, who arrived in the 1870s, managed to hold on. Brigham Young himself surveyed the land in Kanab and helped lay out the downtown, which remains largely unchanged today. For years Kanab survived on ranching. Later, in the 1960s, uranium mining boosted the economy. So did film crews who shot Westerns in the spectacular red-rock canyons that surround the town. Today tourism drives the economy, as throngs of travelers stay here while visiting Grand Canyon, Bryce, and Zion parks, not to mention the new Grand Staircase/Escalante National Monument. The town doesn't even have a bar that serves liquor, but the people are friendly, the food wholesome, and the nights serene. Seven miles south of Kanab is the smaller town of Fredonia, Arizona.

ESSENTIALS

GETTING THERE By Car Kanab is located on U.S. 89 at the junction of U.S. 89A, which crosses into Arizona just 7 miles south of town. To reach Fredonia from the North Rim, take Highway 67, 44 miles north to Jacob Lake, then take Highway 89A, 29 miles northwest to Fredonia.

VISITOR INFORMATION The **Kane County Travel Council and Film Commission** is located at 78 S. 100 E., Kanab, UT 84741 (☎ **800/SEE-KANE** or 801/644-5033).

GETTING AROUND The only way to reach Kanab (easily) is by automobile. The nearest car rental agencies are in St. George, Utah, and Cedar City, Utah. Ground zero in Kanab is where Center and

Main streets intersect. U.S. 89 comes in from the north on 300 West Street, turns east onto Center Street, south again on 100 East Street, and finally east again on 300 South. U.S. 89A follows 100 East Street south to the airport and, after about 7 miles, the smaller town of Fredonia, Arizona.

FAST FACTS The **Kane County Hospital & Skilled Nursing Facility** is at 220 W. 300 North St. (☎ **435/644-5811**). In an **emergency,** dial ☎ **911.** The **post office** is at 39 S. Main St. (☎ **435/644-2760**). **Glazier's Food Town** is located at 264 S. 100 E. (☎ **435/644-5029**), open daily 7am to 10pm. A slightly larger store, **Honey's IGA Food and Drug,** is at 260 E. 300 South (☎ **435/644-5877**). It's open daily 7am to 10:30pm.

WHAT TO SEE & DO

The citizens of Kanab barely acknowledge the existence of the sprawling, 1.9-million acre **Grand Staircase-Escalante National Monument,** even though its southwest boundary stretches to within just a few miles of town. Many Kanab residents believe it will interfere with the area's economic development. So far, there are few developed areas for visitors to this rugged desert landscape, where erosion has carved out narrow canyons, broad mesas, amphitheaters, spires and arches. There are, however, a few bumpy, beautiful roads through the area and many tantalizing places to hike. Before venturing into this mazelike country, the best thing to do is gather maps and advice from locals. **The Bureau of Land Management Kanab Field Office** (☎ **435/644-2672**), 318 N. 100 East in Kanab, sells USGS maps of the area and can help you plan your excursion. If you're considering hiking, stop at **Willow Creek Books** (☎ **435/ 644-8884**), 263 S. 100 East in Kanab. The shop's friendly proprietor, Charlie Neumann, happily dispenses advice, maps, outdoor gear, books (including guidebooks of the area), and—in case you lack incentive—espresso.

GETTING THERE Highway 12 between Boulder, Utah, and Tropic, Utah, crosses the north end of the monument, and Highway 89 between Kanab, Utah, and Page, Arizona, clips the monument's southernmost tip. Linking these highways are a number of gravel roads, which travel through the heart of the monument. If your aim is simply to cross the monument's boundary, drive 12 miles east of Kanab on Highway 89. To really experience it, however, obtain some information from locals about the roads and trails going into its heart (see above).

Paria Movie Set. 29 mi. east of Kanab on Hwy. 89, then 5 mi. east on a dirt road (passable during dry weather) marked with signs for the Paria Movie Set. No phone. Free admission. 8am–5pm Mon–Fri.

A number of sets still stand today from the many films, television shows, and commercials shot in the desert canyons in Kane County, Utah. The Paria Movie Set is one of the most interesting of them. Here, a well-preserved town from *The Outlaw Josey Wales* sits in a section of the upper Paria Canyon that in itself is worth the trip. Streaked with the rainbowlike colors of the Chinle formation, this is some of the most glorious land in the Southwest. Another mile or so past the movie set is a *real* ghost town, old Pahreah, on the banks of the Paria river. Several rock buildings and a cemetery remain from the town, which in the 1870s was home to more than 100 people. To extend your stay, bring a lunch to eat on the picnic tables of the four-site primitive campground, located a short walk from the movie set. The **Kane County Travel Council and Film Commission** (☎ **800/733-5263**), 78 S. 100 E., Kanab, Utah 84741, has more information on the movie sets around Kanab.

Pipe Spring National Monument. On AZ 389, 14 mi. southwest of Fredonia. ☎ **520/643-7105.** Fax 520/ 643-7583. E-mail: pisp_interpretation@nps.gov. Admission $2 adults, 16 and under free. Personal checks (from U.S. banks) accepted. Summer daily 7:30am–5:30pm; rest of year daily 8am–5pm.

The perennial spring here—a rarity on the Arizona Strip—was treasured first by generations of Native Americans and later by Mormons, who found it in 1858 and settled alongside it a few years later. After the first settlers were killed by Navajo in 1866, the next ones took no chances. Directly atop the spring, they built two two-story houses with high stone walls from one to the other. Each wall had a large wooden door that could be opened to allow wagons into the courtyard or closed to form a barricade. With stockpiled food and a constant supply of water, the settlers were prepared for prolonged conflict.

Fortunately, Winsor Castle, as the fortress was known, never saw another battle, as the Navajo and settlers signed a treaty in 1870. Pipe Spring became a prosperous Mormon settlement, with more than 2,000 cattle in its heyday. Today, Winsor Castle has been fully restored and is filled with antiques from the 19th century. Several outbuildings are also open, and the visitor center displays tools used by the Mormon settlers as well as Native American artifacts. Guided tours depart every half hour from the visitor center.

WHERE TO STAY
EXPENSIVE

Nine Gables Inn Bed & Breakfast. 106 W. 100 North, Kanab, UT 84741. ☎ **435/644-5079.** 3 units (showers only). A/C. $80–$110 double. Apr 1–Oct 30. May be open at other times (call to check). MC, V. No pets. Older kids acceptable.

This B&B occupies a home built in 1872 by the town's first Mormon bishop, Levi Stewart. The oldest building in Kanab, the home has always had an extra room for guests, and famous travelers such as Buffalo Bill Cody, Zane Gray, and Brigham Young all used it to take refuge from the rugged landscape around town. Today, guests take refuge in three upstairs guests rooms, two of which still have decks where people slept outside on hot nights before air conditioning existed. All have pedestal sinks in the bathrooms and are decorated with the heirlooms of the owners, Jeanne and Frank Bantlin. These furnishings make the place resemble a home, and the amiable hosts make it feel like one.

MODERATE

Kanab has two pleasant, moderately priced chain hotels: **Holiday Inn Express** (☎ **801/644-8888**), 815 E. Hwy. 89, and **Best Western Red Hills** (☎ **435/644-2675**), 125 W. Center St.

Best Western Thunderbird Resort. Located at junction of Hwys. 89 and 9 (P.O. Box 5536), Mt. Carmel Junction, Utah 84755. ☎ **888/848-6358** or 435/648-2203. Fax 435/648-2239. www.bwthunderbird.com. 61 units. A/C TV TEL. High season $79 double; low season $46. AE, DC, DISC, MC, V. Small pets allowed.

Located 19 miles north of Kanab on Hwy. 89, this resort, built in 1969 on the site of an old homestead, is worth the drive from town even if you're not en route to Zion or Bryce parks, which are located north of here. My favorite rooms are in the low cinderblock building between fairways on the golf course. Ugly as maintenance shacks on the outside, these rooms have pleasingly contemporary designs within. The quietest room in the hotel may be no. 11, the unit farthest away from the road and farthest into the nine-hole, par-31 golf course. Other rooms are located in a two-story, faux-adobe building bordering the outdoor pool and hot tub. Like the rooms on the golf course, these have private patios with views of the lovely surroundings. As for golf, greens fees are just $8, and guests can borrow clubs for free. There's a restaurant on the premises, but better dining is available across the street at the Golden Hills Restaurant.

Parry Lodge. 89 E. Center St., Kanab, UT 84741. ☎ **800/748-4104** or 801/
644-2601. Fax 801/644-2605. www.infowest.com/parry/index.html. E-mail:
bpalmer@xpressweb.com. 89 units. A/C TV TEL. High season $67 double; low
season $30. AE, DISC, MC, V. Pets $5.

Many of the older rooms in this 1929 Colonial-style lodge display
plaques bearing the names of stars who stayed here while filming
Westerns. Room 131, for example, was built to house Frank
Sinatra's mother-in-law while the famed crooner starred in *Sergeants
Three.* (Sinatra stayed in an adjoining room.) Maple trees shade the
older one-story buildings, making them look as if they really were
in the original colonies. If you want to spread out, though, bypass
these historic buildings in favor of the two-story building. Completed in 1985, it has expansive (if somewhat drab) rooms. Open for
all three meals, the lodge's restaurant serves good breakfasts.

INEXPENSIVE

Clean, inexpensive rooms can also be found at **Crazy Jug Motel**
(☎ **520/643-7752**), 465 S. Main St. (Highway 89A), Fredonia,
and at the **Blue Sage Motel and RV Park,** (☎ **520/643-7125**),
330 S. Main St. (Highway 89A), Fredonia.

Aiken's Lodge. 79 W. Center St., Kanab, UT 84171. ☎ **800/524-9999** reservations, or 435/644-2625. Fax 435/644-8827. 31 units. A/C TV TEL. $29–$36
double Nov 1–Apr 30; $49–$54 May 1–Oct 31; family units $59–$69. AE, DISC,
MC, V. Pets $10. Limit one pet per room.

This motor lodge has aged nicely during its 50 years. Its large, clean
rooms have huge windows, solid walls, and showers instead of baths.
My favorite ones, upstairs in the two-story section of the motel, have
views over the shade trees to the surrounding red-rock cliffs as well
as down to the small outdoor swimming pool. The quietest rooms,
however, are in the single-story building farthest from Center Street.
Large families can stay in the motel's two-bedroom, two-bathroom
or three-bedroom, three-bathroom units for a fraction of what they'd
pay for separate rooms.

Grand Canyon Motel and Old Travelers Inn. 175 Main St. (Box 456),
Fredonia, AZ 86022-0456. ☎ **520/643-7646.** Fax 520-643-7287. E-mail:
gcmotel@xpressweb.com. 15 units, six with kitchenettes, all with refrigerators,
8 with showers only. A/C TV. Grand Canyon Motel, $32.50 May 15–Oct 31, $27
Nov 1–May 14. Old Travelers Inn, $30 year-round. AE, MC, V. Small pets
accepted.

Low prices make this hotel popular even during winter, when its
occupancy still averages 80%. Four rooms are in the historic Old

Travelers Inn, built in 1886. With high ceilings, original trim, and ceiling fans, they resemble B&B rooms, only without an innkeeper around. The other units are in cabin-type buildings, built between 1936 and 1948. Six of the units have kitchenettes, all have refrigerators. The cabin rooms, each with cable television, refrigerator, and pine furniture, are a tad dark, but they surround a grassy courtyard shaded by elm and spruce trees. You can cook on the barbecue grills or simply relax on the grass—a rarity on the Arizona strip. Some of these rooms also have kitchenettes.

WHERE TO EAT

Houston's Trails End Restaurant. 32 E. Center St., Kanab. ☎ **435/644-2488.** Fax 435/644-8148. Breakfast $3–$7; lunch $4–$7.75; dinner $5.25–$17.25. AE, DISC, MC, V. 6am–10:30pm daily. Closed Dec 1–Mar 1. STEAK/SEAFOOD/MEXICAN.

For a taste of Kanab's traditional fare, head for Houston's. While country music plays over the stereo, waitresses wearing toy sidearms serve up meaty courses. The house special is a chicken-fried steak. Other specialties include a chicken breast slathered in barbecue sauce and baby back ribs baked all day. The soup is made fresh daily, as are the enormous yeast rolls that come with each dinner. Breakfast includes a choice of omelettes, and lunch consists primarily of burgers and sandwiches.

Nedra's Cafe. Hwy. 89A, Fredonia. ☎ **520/643-7591.** $2.75–$15.95. AE, DC, MC, V. May 15–Oct 31, 7am–10pm daily; Nov 1–May 14, 11am–8pm Thurs–Sun. MEXICAN.

Because this restaurant serves tasty Mexican food at a moderate price, it's a great place to fill up after completing a North Rim backpacking trip. In addition to enchiladas, tostadas, burritos, and tacos, Nedra's serves less-common Mexican dishes such as *carnitas* (seasoned roast pork topped with fresh cilantro and green onions) and *machaca* (shredded beef cooked with tomatoes, onion, green chilies, cilantro, and egg). A few American courses are on the menu, including hamburgers, sandwiches, and steaks. In Kanab you'll find a similar restaurant, **Nedra's Too.** But the tastiest Mexican fare in that community is at **Escobar's Mexican Restaurant** (☎ **435/644-3739**), 373 E. 300 South.

✪ **Wildflower Health Food.** 18 E. Center St., Kanab. ☎ **435/644-3200.** Sandwiches $2.99–$3.95. MC, V. Mon–Sat 10am–6pm. HEALTH FOOD.

When you absolutely cannot eat another bite of red meat or white flour, head to this tiny eight-table restaurant and store for a light lunch. Offerings include sandwiches made with fresh vegetables and a choice of tempeh, tofu, hummus, turkey or pastrami; fresh salads; daily soup specials (served with fresh baked bread); and baked goods. The restaurant also has smoothies injected with enough supplements and pick-me-ups to cleanse you of that maple roll you had for breakfast.

Wok Inn. 86 South 200 West, Kanab (next to Super 8 Motel). ☎ **435/ 644-5400.** Reservations accepted. Lunch $4.50; dinner $6.95–$15.95. AE, DISC, MC, V. 11:30am–10pm Mon–Fri; 1–10pm Sat; 5–10pm Sun. Closed in winter. HUNAN/SZECHUAN.

For the past 7 years this Chinese restaurant has occupied a historic building that in the 1920s served as a rest station for bus passengers traveling between Grand, Zion, and Bryce Canyons. If, as rumored, the building really is haunted, its ghosts are probably gorging on spicy dishes such as Mongolian beef and kung pao chicken; vegetarian fare (including spicy tofu and snow peas with black mushrooms); and sizzling platters of meat and shrimp. In addition to serving good food, this restaurant dispenses liquor—a rarity in Kanab. Be forewarned, however, that the wine list is ghastly. Your choices: Almaden, Almaden, and Almaden.

7 Havasu Canyon & Supai

70 miles N of Hwy. 66; 155 miles NW of Flagstaff; 115 miles NE of Kingman

In the heart of the 185,000-acre Havasupai Indian Reservation, south of the Colorado River in the central Grand Canyon, you'll find the town of Supai. It's nestled between the red walls of Havasu Canyon, alongside the spring-fed Havasu Creek. Two miles downstream are some of the prettiest waterfalls on earth.

ESSENTIALS

GETTING THERE   By Car   It isn't possible to drive all the way to Supai Village or Havasu Canyon. The nearest road, Indian Road 18, ends 8 miles from Supai at Hualapai Hilltop, a barren parking area where the trail into the canyon begins. The turnoff for Indian Road 18 is 6 miles east of Peach Springs and 21 miles west of Seligman on Route 66. Once you're on Indian Road 18, follow it for 60 paved miles to Hualapai Hilltop. There's no gas or water available anywhere in this area, so be sure to top off in either Seligman or Kingman.

By Helicopter   The easiest and fastest (and by far the most expensive) way to reach Havasu Canyon is by helicopter from the Grand

Canyon Airport. Charter flights linking Grand Canyon Airport and Supai are operated by **Papillon Grand Canyon Helicopters** (☎ 800/528-2418 or 520/638-2419). The round-trip fare from Papillon's heliport in Tusayan to Supai is $440. **Airwest Helicopters of Arizona** (☎ 602/516-2790) offers service linking Supai and Hualapai Hilltop from 10am to 1pm several days each week. Reservations are not accepted for these flights, which cost $65 each way.

By Horse or Mule   The next-easiest way to get to Havasu Canyon is by horse or mule. Both you and your luggage can ride to Supai from Hualapai Hilltop, the trailhead for Supai and Havasu Canyon. Pack and saddle horses can be rented through the **Havasupai Tourist Enterprise** (☎ 520/448-2121), which is based in Supai. Round-trip rates are $80 from Hualapai Hilltop to Supai village, $115.50 from Hualapai Hilltop to the campground. Day tours from the lodge in Supai to Havasu Falls are available for $45. Riders must weigh under 250 pounds, be at least 4 feet, 7 inches, be comfortable around large animals, and have at least a little riding experience. Be sure to confirm your horse reservation a day before driving to Hualapai Hilltop. Sometimes no horses are available, and it's a long drive back to the nearest town. Entrance ($20 per person) and camping ($10 per person per night) fees are not included in the mule trip price. One-way rates, costing half the round-trip fare, are also available. Many people who hike into the canyon decide that it's worth the money to ride out, or at least have their backpacks packed out. Pack mules, which can carry up to four articles weighing up to 130 pounds (total), are available for the same price as a mule ride. The gatekeeper at the campground can usually help you arrange for a ride out.

On Foot   To reach Supai on foot, you'll follow a trail that begins at Hualapai Hilltop and descends 8 miles and about 2,000 vertical feet to the village. It covers a shorter vertical drop than the rim-to-river trails in the canyon, but has no drinking water or rest rooms until you reach town. From Supai, it's another 2 miles, mostly downhill, to the campground. The steepest part of the trail is the first 1 1/2 miles from Hualapai Hilltop. After this section it's relatively gradual. See below for more information on the hike to Supai.

FEES & RESERVATIONS   There's a $20 per-person entry fee to Havasu Canyon, effective year-round. Everyone is required to register at the Tourist Office across from the sports field as you enter the village of Supai. Because it's a long walk in to the campground,

Making Reservations

The Havasupai ask that visitors secure reservations for camping or lodging before arriving at Hualapai Hilltop. To make camping or mule reservations, contact the **Havasupai Tourist Enterprise** at ☎ **520/448-2141.** After making reservations, you'll need to check in at the Tourist Enterprise office upon arriving in Supai, 8 miles into your hike. To make lodging reservations, call the lodge directly at ☎ **520/448-2111.** Don't enter the canyon without reservations; you may be forced to hike out. Also, be sure to get a map and full trail description of this area before starting your hike. The best is the *Havasu Trail Guide* written by Scott Thybony and published by the Grand Canyon Natural History Association.

be sure you have a confirmed reservation before setting out from Hualapai Hilltop. It's good to make reservations as far in advance as possible, especially for holiday weekends. The tourist enterprises at Supai accept Visa and MasterCard for both mule and camping reservations.

HIKING TO SUPAI & BEYOND TO THE WATERFALLS

Initially, the surroundings on the trail to Supai from Hualapai aren't particularly pleasant. Helicopters buzz overhead, bits of paper rot alongside the trail or hang impaled on cacti, and phone lines parallel the path. Unannounced by the wranglers trailing them, horses canter past, startling hikers.

The trail drops in switchbacks down the Coconino Sandstone cliffs below Hualapai Hilltop, then descends a long slope to the floor of Hualapai canyon. Most of the hike consists of a descent down the gravelly, gradually sloping creek bed at the bottom of the canyon. Usually dry, this wash is prone to flash flooding, so exercise caution during stormy weather. At the junction with Havasu Canyon, go left, following the blue-green waters of Havasu Creek downstream into the town of Supai.

When you see the two large hoodoos (rock spires) atop the red-rock walls, you'll know you're near town. The 450 Havasupai Indians living here believe that if either rock falls, disaster will befall their people. Unconcerned, children chase each other through town, ducking barbed wire strung between sticks, cottonwood trees, and metal poles. Prefabricated wood houses, some with windows boarded up, line the dirt paths that crisscross this sleepy community, which has a post office, a small grocery, a lodge (see information below), and a cafe.

Roughly 1¹/₂ miles past town you'll come to 75-foot-high **Navajo Falls,** then to 150-foot-high **Havasu Falls.** Just past the campground, more than 10 miles from the trailhead, is 300-foot-high **Mooney Falls,** named for a miner who fell to his death there in 1880. The milky water in the creek seems deceptively clear where shallow. It's turquoise where deeper and emerald at its deepest, under falls so lovely as to make a swimmer laugh with delight. The creek's milky appearance comes from calcium carbonate, which precipitates around the falls in formations resembling enormous drooping mustaches. These formations are colored brownish red by the mud and iron oxide contained in runoff.

Three miles past the campground is the smaller Beaver Falls. Below them, travertine repeatedly dams the river, forming a series of seductive swimming holes. Getting there requires doing one long and relatively tricky descent down a rock face, using a fixed rope for assistance, and several shorter climbs without ropes. Four miles past these dams, Havasu Creek empties into the Colorado River. The hike downstream from the campground involves numerous river crossings, so bring your river sandals in addition to your hiking boots.

OTHER AREA ACTIVITIES

Grand Canyon Caverns. On Rte. 66, 12 mi. east of Peach Springs. ☎ **520/ 422-3223.** Admission $8.50 adults, $5.75 kids 4–12. Open 8am–6pm in high season, 9am–5pm in low season. Tours every half hour. AE, DISC, MC, V.

In addition to visiting Havasu Canyon, you may want to tour the Grand Canyon Caverns. Discovered by a drunken cowboy in 1927, these caverns are notable not for pristine limestone formations but for sheer size. One cavern room is at least as large as a basketball court—or a football field, if the guides here can be believed.

The 45-minute tour recalls the days when entrepreneurs continually dreamed up new, more creative ways of luring tourists off Route 66. After descending 210 feet by elevator, you'll see an enormous fake ground sloth, a dead mountain lion that presumably fell into the hole and was preserved here, and an emaciated road-killed coyote, which the cavern's owners dragged into the cave in 1958 to test their theories on underground preservation. (They were wrong.) There are even some glowing rocks, which our tour guide told us had been "found elsewhere and brought down here strictly for your viewing."

The adjacent gift shop also has its share of novelties, including live rattlesnakes. The cafeteria serves tasty burgers and sells cold cans of beer for just $1.25.

WHERE TO STAY
IN HAVASU CANYON

Havasu Canyon Campground. 10 mi. from Hualapai Hilltop on the Havasu Canyon Trail. Havasupai Tourist Enterprise, General Delivery, Supai, AZ 86435. ☎ **520/448-2141.** Limit 350 campers. Apr 1–Oct 31, $15 per person entrance fee plus $10 per night; Nov 1–Mar 31, $12 entrance fee plus $9 per night. Open year-round. MC, V.

First, a few reasons for not coming: Dog-haters will want to avoid this campground, where dusty, scarred, but ultimately content canines nap under picnic tables by day and howl at their own echoes by night. The dozen-or-so outhouses, each of which seems to represent a step in the evolution of the modern composting toilet, seldom if ever have paper in them. And, oh yes, the crowds can be thick: On weekends from April to September, the Havasupai Tourist Enterprise packs the campground before cutting off reservations. There are no showers, public phones, fire pits, or grills. (Open fires are not allowed.)

When uncrowded, however, the campground is a delight. The milky creek flows past on one side, perfect for cooling off. Drinking water (purify for safety) is available at the aptly named Fern Spring, where a water-yielding pipe protrudes from a rock wall covered with maidenhair fern. The ground, dusty from heavy use, nonetheless is soft enough to make for excellent tenting, and cottonwood trees provide ample shade. And then there's the falls.

During stormy weather, be sure to pitch your tent on one of the higher spots in the campground. During my last visit, a half-dozen mangled picnic tables in Havasu Creek served as evidence of recent flash floods through the area. If you're seeking solitude, travel farther downstream from the campground's entrance. The camping area is nearly a half-mile long, and few people lug their packs all the way to the end nearest Mooney Falls.

Havasupai Lodge. General Delivery, Supai, AZ 86435. ☎ **520/448-2111.** 24 units. A/C. $80 double plus $20 per person entry fee. MC, V. No pets.

For a place halfway to the floor of the Grand Canyon and 8 miles from the nearest road, this motel is nice enough. The rooms, which open onto a grassy courtyard, are clean and pleasant, although some could use new fixtures and drapery. In-room air-conditioners will cool you during the summer months. Even if there were televisions, the best entertainment would be the waterfalls, which you can reach on horseback from the lodge for $45, or on foot for free. Sometimes the lodge's employees seem more hostile than hospitable. Try to keep your sense of humor. The Havasupai love to laugh, and a smile goes a long way.

The Havasupai Cafe, across from the general store, serves breakfast, lunch, and dinner. It's a casual place where people fritter time over french fries and fry bread. The food is relatively inexpensive despite the fact that all ingredients must be packed in by horse. Try the chocolate chip cookies, which taste great and are sold in bags of four for $1.

NEAR HUALAPAI HILLTOP

Grand Canyon Caverns Inn. P.O. Box 180 (on Hwy. 66, 12 mi. east of Peach Springs, 25 mi. west of Seligman), Peach Springs, AZ 86434. ☎ **520/ 422-3223.** Fax 520/422-4470. E-mail: gcc@seligmannet.com. 49 units. A/C TV TEL. Summer $49 double; winter $27. AE, DISC, MC, V. Pets accepted.

The closest lodging to Hualapai Hilltop, this motel sits as far off the beaten path as you can get in the Grand Canyon area. The rooms probably look much the same as they did in the 1950s. In mine, polished rocks and crystals had been mounted, framed, and hung on a wall that had striped wallpaper. The main attractions are the frosty outdoor swimming pool, the nearby caverns, and the space itself. Come sunset, that is more than enough to make the stay enjoyable.

7

A Nature Guide to Grand Canyon National Park

A photograph of the Grand Canyon may tell a thousand words, but a thousand words don't begin to tell the canyon's story, which spans more than 2 billion years. This chapter tells more of that story. The landscape section discusses the rock layers and how the canyon was carved. The flora section describes common plants, ranging from fir trees on the rims to barrel cacti on the canyon floor. The fauna section covers the creatures that flourish in the canyon's forbidding climes. And the ecology section explores a very recent development—the effects of humans.

1 The Ecosystem

Grand Canyon National Park is a continuation of the land around it—land that's far from pristine. Its air is clouded by distant industry and not-so-distant automobiles, its largest river constricted by dams, its silence shattered by high-flying jets and low-flying sightseeing planes. Theodore Roosevelt's dictum—to "leave it as it is"—now seems oversimple. In the 1990s, the canyon's ecology depends nearly as much on public policy as on nature.

EFFECTS OF THE GLEN CANYON RIVER DAM Some of the most significant changes in the ecology of the Grand Canyon result from the Glen Canyon Dam, which constricts the Colorado River just northeast of Grand Canyon. The dam, which began operating in 1963, provides large amounts of inexpensive hydroelectric power for cities such as Phoenix and recreational opportunities for an estimated 2.5 million boaters and fishers on Lake Powell every year.

Inside the canyon, however, it has completely altered the biological communities in and around the river. Water temperatures in the canyon used to fluctuate from near freezing in winter to 80°F or warmer in summer. A mere trickle in winter, the river surged during the spring snowmelt to levels five times higher than the largest floods today. Now penstocks 200 feet below the surface of Lake

Powell take in water that remains 48°F year-round, at a rate that hardly changes. And the water itself has been sanitized. In pre-dam days, the Colorado carried tons of reddish silt that had washed into it from the canyons of the Four Corners area (thus the name "Rio Colorado," Spanish for "red river"). Today, that silt settles to the bottom of the torpid waters of Lake Powell, and the river emerges from the dam as clear as a mountain brook.

These changes decimated the canyon's native fish, which had evolved to survive in the extreme temperatures, powerful flows, and heavy silt of the old river. Four of the eight native fish species died off, and one—the humpback chub—is breeding only where warmer tributaries enter the Colorado. In their places, rainbow trout, which were introduced below the dam for sport fishing, have flourished. Along the shores, tamarisk and coyote willow choke riverbanks that pre-dam floods once purged of vegetation. This vegetation now is home to a variety of small lizards, mammals, and waterfowl, which, in turn, attract birds of prey such as the peregrine falcon.

Another effect of the dam has been the loss of an estimated 45% of the beaches along the Colorado River. Before the dam was built, the canyon's huge floods lifted sand off the bottom of the river and deposited it in large beaches and sandbars. The post-dam flows are generally too weak to accomplish this.

In March 1996, the Bureau of Reclamation, the National Park Service, and a group of concerned environmental groups sought to find out whether a man-made flood released from the dam would restore some of the beaches. For 7 days in March and April 1996, the dam unloosed a sustained flow of 45,000 cubic feet per second—the maximum it could safely release. Although the flood packed only a fraction of the force of pre-dam deluges, it restored parts of 80 canyon beaches, and most scientists initially deemed the experiment—known as the Beach Habitat Restoration Flood—to be a success. A shorter, smaller controlled flood was conducted in October 1997.

Still, the long-term prognosis for the beaches isn't good. Because sand now washes into the river only from its tributaries below the dam, years can pass before enough of it accumulates for a productive man-made flood. And the new sand that was deposited on beaches during the 1996 flood eroded faster than expected— 85% of it had washed away within 6 months. Today, most scientists value the project for what it revealed about spiked flows, but as little more than a Band-Aid in restoring beaches and natural aquatic habitats.

The Hoover Dam, near Las Vegas, also affects the canyon. The last 35 miles of the Colorado River in the Grand Canyon are submerged in the still waters of Lake Mead, the reservoir above Hoover Dam.

EFFECTS OF AIR TRAFFIC   While the dams control the river, airplanes and helicopters break the natural silence. In 1998, 821,000 people took sightseeing flights over Grand Canyon, according to Federal Aviation Administration (FAA) estimates. For years, planes and helicopters were free to fly anywhere over the canyon and below the rims. Then, after a collision between sightseeing aircraft killed 25 people in 1986, the FAA established strict flight corridors for the aircraft and forced helicopters and planes to fly at different altitudes.

Although sightseeing flights have long been forbidden over Grand Canyon Village, the flight corridors still come within earshot of popular destinations, and public opinion supports reductions in noise. In July 1999, the FAA proposed a new set of regulations for sightseeing flights over Grand Canyon. These rules would freeze the maximum number of flights per year at the number between May 1997 and April 1998, tighten requirements for the reporting of flights, and slightly expand the flight-free area of the park. If approved, the new rules will be in enacted in the year 2000.

Unfortunately, they will do little to reduce aircraft noise in the park. Although the flight-free zone would be expanded, the busiest flight corridors would still thrive. Only a small part of the canyon would be out of earshot of aircraft noise, which travels an average of 16 miles in the eastern canyon and even farther in the west. However, the cap on flights would ensure that, at the very least, the problem wouldn't worsen in the future.

The proposed rules may also help lead to more significant changes in the long run. By keeping the amount of air traffic constant, the new laws would help National Park Service scientists determine how much human-generated noise is affecting different parts of the park. This data could then be used to design new regulations aimed at achieving Congress's goal of restoring "natural quiet" to at least 50% of the park at least 75% of the time by the year 2008.

AIR POLLUTION   Another factor affecting the canyon's ecology is air pollution, which on some days decreases the visibility over the canyon from more than 200 miles to less than 50. In summer, much of the air pollution comes from urban areas in southern California, southern Arizona, and northern Mexico. In winter, during periods

Protecting the Environment

Here are a few things you can do during your stay to protect Grand Canyon National Park:

- **Respect the animals.** When accustomed to handouts, wild animals are nuisances at best, dangerous at worst. Deer will sometimes butt, kick, or gore people who have food; squirrels, which may carry rabies and even bubonic plague, won't hesitate to bite the hand that feeds them. And human food isn't good for wildlife. In recent years, the park has been forced to shoot deer that have become sickly from eating human food. So don't feed the critters. With your cooperation, they can live in the park in something akin to a natural state.

- **Report sightings of California condors and stay at least 300 feet away from them.** The endangered California condor, the largest land bird in North America, was reintroduced to the wild just north of Grand Canyon in 1996. By 1999, many of the condors had begun venturing to crowded areas on the South Rim. If the condors—identifiable by their grayish-black coloration, orangish heads, and triangular white patches under each wing—become accustomed to people, their survival will be jeopardized. The park asks that visitors stay at least 300 feet from the birds and report any sightings to a ranger.

- **Stay on designated trails.** Short-cutting is riskier on the steep trails at Grand Canyon than at other parks. Besides falling, people who cut trails often kick off rockfall dangerous to those below. Short-cutting also digs paths that channel water during storms, causing unnecessary erosion of desert soils. Through-

of calm weather, nearby pollution sources, including power generating stations, play a more significant role.

The federal Clean Air Act mandates that natural visibility eventually be restored to all National Parks and Wilderness Areas. In the Grand Canyon area, the EPA hopes to restore natural visibility by 2065. Seeking to accomplish this, the National Park Service regularly takes part in a commission that includes state and Environmental Protection Agency regulators, Native American tribal leaders, industry representatives, and other interested parties.

out the canyon, off-trail hikers frequently trample cryptogamic soils—delicate plants that take as long as 100 years to form.

- **Pack it out.** Even when day-hiking, remember to pack out anything that you bring.
- **Avoid littering and recycle.** Even small bits of litter such as cigarette butts can add up to a big mess in the crowded areas on the rim. Pieces of paper that blow into the canyon can take decades to decay in the dry desert air. So can seemingly harmless organic material such as orange and banana peels and apple cores. Also note that plastic, glass, and aluminum are recycled in bins alongside trash receptacles throughout the park.
- **Leave plants, rocks, and artifacts in place.** Removing any of these things not only detracts from the beauty of the park but is against the law. While it may seem innocuous to pick a flower, imagine what would happen if each of the park's 5 million visitors did so.
- **Use the shuttles.** Grand Canyon Village, the West Rim Drive, and Yaki and Yavapai points are accessible via free shuttles, all of which pass through the Maswik Transportation Center. By using the shuttle, you can ease congestion, noise, and air pollution.

If you'd like to do something extra to help the park, sign up for the canyon's **Habitat Restoration Program,** which works to restore the natural environment. Activities include seed gathering, the removal of exotic species, and revegetating areas where the soils have been disturbed. To find out more, call Frank Hays at ☎ 520/638-7857.

The park's air quality should improve somewhat after late 1999, when scrubbers will be installed at the Navajo Generating Station in Page, Arizona. This coal-burning station may have been responsible for as much as half the canyon's air pollution in winter, according to Park Service estimates. Yet the problem extends far past obvious polluters in the immediate area. For natural visibility to be restored, pollution sources ranging from automobile emissions in Los Angeles to factories in Mexico must be addressed.

FOREST FIRES   Even as National Park Service scientists fret over air quality, they know that more forest fires are needed in the ponderosa pine forest on the canyon rims. Before humans began suppressing forest fires, these areas experienced low-intensity blazes every 7 to 10 years. These fires made the forest healthier by burning excess undergrowth and deadfall, thinning tree stands, and returning nutrients to the soil. After fire suppression began, however, deadfall and excess undergrowth accumulated on the forest floors, and trees grew too close together. With so much "fuel" available, the fires that did occur burned much hotter than before—hot enough, even, to kill old-growth ponderosas, which tend to be fire-resistant. Once dead, stands of these grand old trees were often supplanted by faster-growing aspen and fir trees.

In the late 1990s, Congress appropriated additional federal funding for land agencies to manage fire for ecological benefits, either through prescribed burns or what the government calls "fire-use fires"—naturally triggered blazes that are allowed to burn. The new funds will enable the National Park Service to burn more areas, more often, improving the health of its forests. Taking into account factors such as visibility, weather, location, fire-danger level, and available manpower, Grand Canyon National Park hopes to eventually do prescribed burns on 10,000 acres per year, far above levels in the early '90s. Visitors to the park will sometimes smell the smoke.

WELL-DRILLING   Another concern is possible damage by well-drilling outside the park on the South Rim. According to a Forest Service study, water wells for new development around Grand Canyon could deplete the flows from springs inside the canyon. Depending on the location of the wells, Havasu Creek, Hermit Spring, Indian Garden Spring, or other smaller springs may lose water. Many of these are irreplaceable water sources for both wildlife and backcountry hikers.

When the Forest Service in 1999 approved a preliminary plan allowing a large new development, Canyon Forest Village, just outside the park's south entrance, the developer agreed to transport water for the community from far outside the area. Under the plan, ground water from the rim would be used only for construction and during emergencies. This should help protect the canyon's springs. However, new development and well-drilling continues in outlying communities, and Grand Canyon National Park is nearing the limits of its own water supply, which comes from a spring below the North Rim.

2 The Landscape

If you could observe 2 billion years pass in an hour, you'd see the land from which the Grand Canyon is carved wander across the globe, traveling as far south as the equator and perhaps even farther. You'd see it dip below sea level, rise as mountains, dry into dunes, and smother under swamps. You'd watch as different sediments such as silt, mud, and sand, were deposited (usually by water) atop it. Out of sight, compacted from above and cemented together by minerals, these sediments would eventually form *sedimentary* rocks such as sandstone, siltstone, limestone, and shale. Some of these rocks would resurface later, only to be eroded by wind and water. Others would remain safely buried. Because the canyon itself may be as little as 6 million years old, you probably wouldn't recognize it until the last 11 seconds of the hour, when two or more rivers began to cut down through the rocks of the Colorado Plateau. All of human history would require only a quarter second at the end of the hour.

Although you can't personally experience the canyon's 2-billion-year history, the layers of rock in the Grand Canyon record much of what happened during that time. Because the rocks are both well preserved and exposed down to very deep layers, the canyon is one of the best places in the world for geologists to learn about the Paleozoic era—and even earlier.

The record starts with the **Vishnu Formation,** consisting of schist, gneiss, and granite. The oldest and deepest layer in the canyon, it's the black rock draped like a wizard's robe directly above the Colorado River. Originally laid down as sedimentary rock, the layer was driven deep into the earth underneath a mountain range more than 1.7 billion years ago. There, it was heated to temperatures so extreme (1,100°F) and under pressure so great that its chemical composition changed, making it a *metamorphic* rock that's much harder and glossier than the others.

The Grand Canyon Supergroup, a group of sedimentary and *igneous* (volcanic) rocks laid down between 1.25 billion and 600 million years ago, appears directly above the schist in numerous locations in the canyon. These pastel-colored layers stand out because they're tilted at about 20°F. **Desert View** is one good place to see them. Once part of a series of small mountain ranges, the Supergroup was shaved off by erosion, disappearing from many parts of the canyon.

Where the Supergroup has disappeared, the **Tapeats Sandstone layer** is just above the Vishnu Formation, even though a gap of over a billion years separates the two layers. Caused by erosion, this huge gap is commonly referred to as the **Great Unconformity.** Because of it, the layers have little in common. While the Vishnu Formation predates atmospheric oxygen, the Tapeats Sandstone contains fossils of sponges and trilobites that date to the Cambrian explosion of life. It also tells us about the beginnings of an incursion of the Tapeats Sea 545 million years ago. At that time, the water was so shallow and so turbulent that only the heaviest particles—sand—could sink. That sand eventually formed the sandstone.

The Bright Angel Shale forms the gently sloping blue-gray layer (known as the Tonto Platform) above the Tapeats Sandstone. It tells of a Tapeats Sea that had become deeper and considerably calmer in this area. Some 530 million years ago, the water was calm enough to let fine-grained sediment settle to the bottom. The sediment formed a muck that eventually became the shale.

Above it is the **Muav Limestone,** which dates back 515 million years. The Muav layer recalls a Tapeats Sea that was deeper still—so deep that feathery bits of shell from tiny marine creatures sank. These bits of shell, together with other calcium carbonate that precipitated naturally out of the water, created limestone. Because it crops up at the base of the Redwall and is stained a similar color, the Muav can be difficult to single out. Only way to tell it apart from the Redwall is by its horizontal beds, which tend to be thinner than the Redwall's. Where not stained by the layers above, the Muav appears as a yellowish cliff. (In parts of the canyon, a layer known as Temple Butte limestone appears above the Muav.)

About halfway between rim and river, the **Redwall Limestone** forms some of the canyon's steepest cliffs—800 feet in places. This imposing rock layer tells us about a Mississippian-age sea that deposited layers of calcium carbonate across all of what is now North America from 360 to 320 million years ago. Silvery gray under the surface, the Redwall is stained red by iron oxide from the red rocks above. To see the true color of the Redwall, look for places where pieces have recently broken off.

Just above the Redwall is the **Supai Group.** Formed about 285 million years ago, these layers of sandstone, shale, and siltstone were deposited in tidal flats along shorelines. They usually form a series of red ledges just above the Redwall cliffs. Right above them, and even deeper red, is the Hermit Shale, which was deposited in the flood plain of one or more great rivers around 265 million years ago. This soft shale forms a gentle slope or platform directly below the **Coconino Sandstone.**

The Coconino may be the easiest layer in the canyon to identify. The third layer from the top, it's the color of desert sand and forms cliffs that are nearly as sheer as those of the Redwall. The Coconino was laid down as dunes in a Sahara-like desert that covered this land about 270 million years ago. Everywhere in this layer, you'll see the slanted lines caused by cross-bedding—places where new dunes blew in atop old ones. While the other layers display fossils that become increasingly complex through time (the Supai contains fossils of insects and ferns, and marine invertebrates are common in the Redwall), the only imprints in the Coconino are lizard and arthropod tracks that always go uphill. This seems odd until you watch a lizard on sand. It digs in while going up, making firm imprints in the process, then smears its tracks coming down. Some of these fossils are visible along the South Kaibab Trail.

On the top sit the canyon's youngest rocks—the yellow-gray **Toroweap Formation** and the cream-colored **Kaibab Formation,** which forms the rim rock. Both were deposited by the same warm, shallow sea from 260 to 250 million years ago, when this land was roughly 100 meters below sea level. Younger rock layers once laid atop the Kaibab Formation, but they have eroded off in most areas around the canyon. However, a few remnants of these layers remain. To see them, look east from Desert View to nearby Cedar Mountain or northeast to the Vermilion and Echo cliffs.

MOVING MOUNTAINS   Today, the ancient rocks are all part of the **Colorado Plateau.** Between 65 and 38 million years ago, this land was lifted by a process known as subduction. When a continental plate butts up against an oceanic plate, the heavier, denser oceanic plate slips underneath it. Like an arm reaching under a mattress, this slipping—or subduction—can elevate land (on the upper plate) that's far inland from the continental margins. This happened in the Four Corners area during an event known as the Laramide Orogeny. At that time, the Pacific plate was subducted under the North American plate, pushing the land in a 130,000-square-mile area in the Four Corners area to elevations ranging from 5,000 to 13,000 feet. This area, which consists of many smaller individual plateaus and landforms, is today known as the Colorado Plateau. The Grand Canyon area has six plateaus—the Coconino and Hualapai on the South Rim; and the Kaibab, Kanab, Uinkaret, and Shivwits on the North Rim—that are part of the larger Colorado Plateau. These plateaus are slightly higher than the surrounding areas.

Because the earth's crust is very thick under the Grand Canyon area, the layers of rock here rose without doing much collapsing or shearing. In those places where significant faulting did take place, the rocks sometimes folded instead of breaking. Places where rocks bend in a single fold are known as **monoclines.** As you drive your car up the 4,800-vertical-foot climb from Lee's Ferry to Jacob Lake on the North Rim, you'll ascend the East Kaibab monocline. As you drive east from Grandview Point, you'll descend the Grandview monocline. In both cases, you'll remain on the same rock layer, the Kaibab Formation, the whole time.

The Colorado Plateau is an excellent place for canyon formation for three reasons. First, it sits at a minimum of 5,000 feet above sea level, so water has a strong pull to saw through the land. This makes the rivers here more active than, say, the Mississippi, which descends just 1,670 feet over the course of 2,350 miles. With an average drop of 8 feet per mile, the Colorado River in Grand Canyon is 11 times steeper than the Mississippi. Second, its desert terrain has little vegetation to hold it in place, so it erodes quickly during rains. Third, those rains often come in monsoons that fall hard and fast, cutting deep grooves instead of eroding the land more evenly, as softer, more frequent rains would.

The different layers and types of rock make the resulting canyons more spectacular, perhaps, than any in the world. In addition to being different colors, the rocks vary in hardness and erode at different rates. Known as **differential erosion,** this phenomenon is responsible for the **stair-step effect** one finds at the Grand Canyon.

Here's how it works: The softer rocks—usually shales—erode fastest, undercutting cliffs of harder rock above them. During melt-freeze cycles in winter, water seeps into cracks in these now-vulnerable cliffs, freezes, and expands, chiseling off boulders that collapse onto the layers below. These collapsed rocks tumble down into boulder fields such as those at the bases of the canyon's temples. The biggest rock slides sometimes pile up in ramps that make foot descents possible through cliff areas. Where soft rock has eroded off of hard rock underneath it, platforms are formed. One such platform, known as the Esplanade, is obvious in the western canyon. The end result is a series of platforms and cliffs.

Runoff drives the process, and more of it comes from the North Rim. This happens for two reasons. First, the land through which the canyon is cut slopes gently from north to south. So runoff from the North Rim tends to drain into the canyon while runoff from the South Rim drains away from it. And more precipitation falls at the higher elevations on the North Rim—25 inches, as opposed to 16 for the South Rim. As this water makes its way—often along fault lines—to the Colorado River, it cuts side canyons that drain into the main one.

These side canyons tend to become longer and more gradual through time. Since the runoff can't cut any lower than the Colorado River, it tends to eat away the land near the top of each side canyon. As this happens, the head of each canyon slowly moves closer to its water source—a process known as headward erosion. If you're standing at Grand Canyon Village looking down the Bright Angel fault, you may notice that the gorge formed along it is longer on the north side of the Colorado River. This is typical of the side canyons in the Grand Canyon. Because more water comes off the North Rim, more erosion has taken place on that side of the river, and longer canyons have been formed.

AND THEN CAME THE FLOODS   The eroded material has to go somewhere. The rocks that fall into the side canyons are swept into the Colorado River, usually by flash floods that occur during the canyon's August monsoon season. While it may be hard to imagine a current this strong in what is usually a dry or nearly dry side canyon, look again at how thousands of tiny drainages converge like capillaries into a single significant creek bed. In most cases, several square miles of hard land drains into one relatively narrow rock chute. When a downpour falls at the canyon, it can generate floods that are immensely powerful and very dangerous. It's not unusual for flash floods to be caused by isolated storms that never even reach the Colorado River. Hikers in the inner canyon sometimes have little warning other than distant thunder or, worse still, the roar of the rapidly approaching water.

Below each significant side canyon are boulders, swept into the Colorado River by these floods. These boulders form dams in the larger river, creating rapids where the water spills over them. The water above each set of rapids usually looks as smooth as a reservoir. Below the first rocks, however, it cascades downstream, crashing backward in standing waves against large boulders. Before Glen Canyon dam was built, the Colorado River broke up many of the biggest rocks during its enormous spring floods. These floods, which commonly reached levels five times higher than an average flow today, swept along small rocks, which would in turn chip away and break apart boulders, eventually moving *them* downstream. For the canyon to have reached its present size, the river had to sweep away more than 1,000 cubic miles of debris. Now, with the enormous spring floods a thing of the past, less debris is being moved, and the rapids have become steeper and rockier.

While it's fairly easy to explain how the side canyons cut down to the level of the Colorado River, it's much harder to say how the Colorado cut through the plateaus around the Grand Canyon. Unless the river was already in place when these adjoining plateaus started rising roughly 60 million years ago, it would have had to first climb 3,000 feet uphill before it could begin cutting down. The explorer John Wesley Powell, who mapped the Colorado River in 1869, assumed that the river had cut down through the land as the land rose. The river in the eastern canyon may indeed be old enough to have accomplished this. The western canyon, however, is much younger. In fact, there's no evidence of a through-flowing Colorado River in the western Grand Canyon before about 5 million years ago.

Geologists have proposed a number of theories about how the river assumed its present course, none of which is supported by a strong body of evidence. Most center around the idea of an ancestral Colorado River that flowed through the eastern canyon, exiting the canyon via a channel different from its current one. The ancestral Colorado River would have been diverted onto its present course by a another, smaller river that probably reached it via headward erosion. Depending on the theory you choose, this "pirate" river may have cut headward all the way from the Gulf of California, or it may have originated on the Kaibab Plateau during a period when the climate was wetter than it is today. No one is sure what happened, and the debate is still open.

3   The Flora

C. Hart Merriam, an American zoologist who studied the plant life around the canyon in 1889, grouped the species here in geographical ranges that he called "life zones." According to Merriam, different life zones resulted from "laws of temperature control" that corresponded to changes in elevations. Each life zone began and ended at a particular elevation, much like the rock layers that ring the canyon walls.

Merriam's theory was a good one at the time, but he didn't immediately recognize the significance of other variables. Today, naturalists understand that the Grand Canyon's flora are strongly affected by factors such as air currents, water flows, soil types, slope degree, and slope aspect. Most naturalists now prefer to talk about biological communities, avoiding the mistake of fixing species in any particular "zone."

However, if your goal is to identify a few major plant species and the general areas where you might find them, life zones still work fairly well. So we'll use them, with thanks to Dr. Merriam. The canyon's five life zones are: **Boreal,** from 8,000 to 9,100 feet; **Transition,** from 7,000 to 8,000 feet; **Upper Sonoran,** from 4,000 to 7,500 feet; **Lower Sonoran,** from the bottom of the canyon to 4,000 feet; and **Riparian,** along the banks of the Colorado River and its tributaries. Some of the more common or unusual plants in each zone are as follows:

BOREAL ZONE

Douglas fir   Found on the North Rim and on isolated north-facing slopes below the South Rim, the Douglas fir grows up to 130 feet high and 6 feet in diameter. You'll often find it in areas very close to the North Rim itself. Its soft 1-inch-long needles generally grow in pairs. Its hanging cones, which grow to about 3 inches long, each have three-pronged bracts (or "mouse tails") between their scales. The Douglas fir is built for cold weather. Its branches, while cupped, are flexible enough to slough off snow.

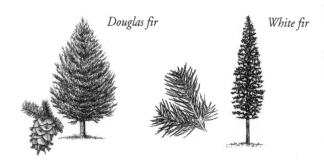

Douglas fir   *White fir*

White fir   You'll know you've moved into spruce-fir forest when you start tripping over deadfall and running into low branches. One of the more common trees in this high-alpine forest, the white fir has smooth, gray bark; cones that grow upright to about 4 inches long; and 2-inch-long, two-sided curving needles. The white fir closely resembles the subalpine fir. But the branches of the subalpine fir, unlike those of the white fir, grow to ground level, and its needles are about an inch shorter. Another common tree in this forest is the blue spruce, recognizable by its blue color and sharp needles.

TRANSITION ZONE

Big sagebrush   More common on the rims than in the canyons, this fuzzy gray-green plant grows to 4 feet high on thick wood stalks. To make sure you haven't misidentified it as rabbit brush (another gray-green plant of comparable size), look at a leaf—it should have three tiny teeth at the end. Or simply break off a sprig (outside the park) and smell it. If it doesn't smell divine, it's not sagebrush. Some Indian tribes burned sage bundles during purification rituals.

Big sagebrush

Gambel oak

Gambel oak   To find Gambel (or scrub) oak on the South Rim in winter, look for the bare one. The only deciduous tree in the immediate vicinity of the South Rim, its leaves turn orange before falling. To find Gambel oak in summer, look for its acorns, its long (up to 6 inches) lobed leaves, and its gray trunk. It grows in thick clumps that clutter the otherwise open floor of the ponderosa pine forest. A plant with a similar name, shrub oak, grows lower in the canyon and has sharp, hollylike leaves.

Indian paintbrush   You should be able to identify this plant from the name alone. Many of its leaves are colored red or orange at their tips, making them look as if they've been dipped in paint.

Lupine   Common on both rims, this purple flower blooms from spring to late summer. You can spot lupine by its palmate leaves and tiny purple flowers growing in clusters at the top of its main stem.

Ponderosa pine   Found on both rims and in isolated places in the canyon, this tree can withstand forest fires, provided the fires come often enough to keep the fuel on the forest floor to a minimum. Its

Indian paintbrush

Lupine

thick bark shields the inside of the tree from the heat. When the fires are over, the ponderosa thrives on the nutrients in the ash-covered soil. Once the tree's low branches have burned off, fires can no longer climb to the crown. So the trees that survive grow stronger. To spot a mature ponderosa pine, look for its thick red-orange bark (younger ones have blackish bark), its 6-inch-long needles in groups of three, and its absence of low branches. Once you've identified one, smell its bark—you'll be rewarded with a rich vanilla-like scent.

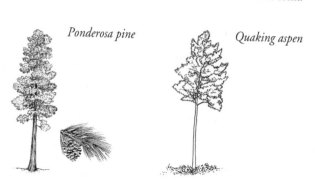

Ponderosa pine

Quaking aspen

Quaking aspen   The ponderosa pine may smell the best, but tree-huggers should save the last dance for the quaking aspen, which grows alongside it in many North Rim forests. Its cool, dusty white bark feels great against your cheek on a hot day. Its leaves, on long, twisted stems, shudder at the very idea of a breeze. If you hug one aspen you're probably hugging many. Dozens and sometimes hundreds of these trees have been known to sprout from a common root system, meaning they're technically one plant. In fact, one of the world's largest organisms is a quaking aspen in Utah.

UPPER SONORAN

Brittlebush   This round, downy, silver-blue bush is most common in the lower reaches of the canyon and most conspicuous in spring, when it sprouts yellow, daisylike flowers that last only until the canyon gets hot. Growing to about 3 feet tall and with simple, broad leaves, it is the easiest to recognize of the many species of yellow composites (plants where many florets are packed together in heads resembling flowers) in the canyon.

Brittlebrush

Cliff rose & Apache plume   These flowering shrubs, which grow both on the rims and in the canyon, have much in common. Both are members of the rose family, grow tiny five-lobed leaves, and send up numerous delicate flowers from which feathery plumes sometimes protrude. However, a few differences do exist: Cliff rose is the larger of the two, growing to a maximum of 25 feet, compared to 5 feet for the Apache plume. Its flowers are a creamy yellow, as opposed to white for the Apache plume. And its leaves, unlike those of the Apache plume, are hairless. The Apache plume blooms a few weeks longer—from early spring into October.

Cliff rose

Apache plume

Mormon tea   Common throughout the park, this virtually leafless plant has hundreds of jointed, needlelike stems that point skyward. Once the plants are full-grown, they remain largely unchanged for as long as 500 years. Photos of desert scenes taken more than 50 years apart show the same Mormon tea plants with every stem still in place. The only difference between young and old plants is color—the older plants are yellow-green or even yellow-gray; the younger ones are light green. Both the early Mormon pioneers and the Indians used the stems, which contain pseudoephedrine and tannin, for medicine.

Piñon pine   Wherever a new juniper tree sprouts, a piñon pine usually follows, growing to about the same size (30 feet) as the juniper. Shorter and rounder than most pines, the piñon pine grows 1-inch-long needles, usually in pairs. It commonly takes root in the shadows of juniper trees, which are more heat-tolerant. Their system has worked well. Together, the piñon pine and the Utah juniper dominate much of the high desert in the Southwest. Packing 2,500 calories per pound, piñon (or pine) nuts have always been a staple for the Indians in this area, and today they're also popular in Italian restaurants, where they're used to make pesto.

Piñon pine

Utah agave & banana yucca   The plants consisting of 3-foot-long spikes are most often agave or yucca. Agave leaves have serrated edges, while yucca leaves have rough, sandpaper-like sides. The Indians in the canyon used fibers and leaves from these plants to make sandals, baskets, and rope. If you were to break off a particularly sharp leaf and peel away the fibers from its edge, you would eventually end up with a thread with a needlelike tip. The agave blooms only once every 15 to 25 years. When it does, it's easy to spot—its spiky base sends up a wooden stalk, about 14 feet high, atop which yellow flowers grow. Because this flourish occurs so rarely, the agave is often referred to as the century plant. After flowering, it dies. Some naturalists theorize that the agave, whose leaves become rich in nutrients just before it flowers, evolved to bloom rarely so that animals would not grow accustomed to eating it. This trick didn't fool the Ancestral Puebloans, who discovered that the roasted hearts of the plant were always nutritious. Unlike the agave, the banana yucca blooms every 2 to 3 years, sending up 4-foot-high stalks on which yellow flowers hang. Its fruit, which tastes a bit like banana, ripens later in summer.

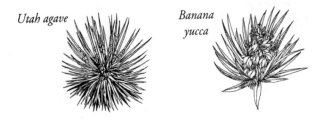

Utah agave

Banana yucca

Utah juniper   This tree, which seldom grows higher than 30 feet, *looks* like it belongs in the desert. Its scraggy bark is as dry as straw, its tiny leaves are tight and scalelike, and its gnarled branches appear to have endured, well, everything. Burned in campfires since the dawn of time, juniper wood releases a fragrant smoke that evokes the desert as much as the yipping of coyotes. Its dusty-looking blue berries are actually cones, each with one or two small seeds inside.

Utah juniper

LOWER SONORAN

Barrel cactus   The barrel cactus does indeed resemble a small green barrel. One of the more efficient desert plants, it can survive for years without water. Contrary to the popular myth, however, there's no reservoir of drinking water inside.

Barrel cactus

Blackbrush   The blue-gray color of the Tonto Platform (above the Tapeats Sandstone) doesn't derive solely from the Bright Angel Shale. It also comes from blackbrush, a gray, spiny, 3-foot-high plant that dominates the flora atop the platform. Blackbrush grows leathery half-inch-long leaves on tangled branches that turn black when wet. Because the plant's root system is considerably larger than the plant itself, each blackbrush bush commands plenty of area. There's usually 10 to 15 feet between plants.

Hedgehog cactus   The hedgehog cactus looks like a cluster of prickly cucumbers standing on end. Of the four species in the canyon, the most colorful is the claret cup, which sprouts crimson flowers every spring.

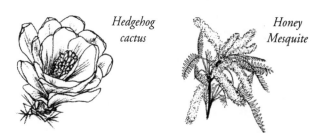

*Hedgehog
cactus*

*Honey
Mesquite*

Honey mesquite & catclaw acacia   These two species of tree, which favor the walls above rivers or creek beds, show us the heights reached by the Colorado River's pre-dam floods. After a flood recedes, acacia and mesquite seedlings take root in the moist soil. Later, the maturing trees send pipelike roots down to the river or creek bed. Both species have dark branches and leaves with small paired leaflets, reach heights of about 20 feet, and grow seedpods several inches long. The mesquite's leaflets, however, are longer and narrower than the acacia's. And while the acacia has tiny barbs like cat claws for protection, the mesquite grows paired inch-long thorns where the leaves meet the stems. Mesquite beans were a staple for the Ancestral Puebloans.

Opuntia cactus   Most members of this family are known as prickly pear. Although prickly pear do grow on the South Rim, the most impressive are lower in the canyon. There, the prickly pear's flat oval pads link up in formations that occasionally sprawl across 40 or more square feet of ground. Look closely at each pad and you'll notice that even in the most contorted formations the narrow side always points up, cutting down on the sunlight received. Because this cactus tends to hybridize, it produces a variety of yellow, pink, and magenta flowers from April to June. Put a finger inside one of these flowers, and the stamens will curl around it, a reflex designed to coat bees with pollen. Prickly pear pads can be roasted and eaten, and the fruit, which ripens in late summer, is often used to make jelly. There are several species of opuntia, ranging from very prickly (grizzly bear) to spineless (beavertail).

*Opuntia cacuts/
prickly pear*

RIPARIAN

Fremont cottonwood   To cool off, look for the bright green canopy of this tree, which grows near many of the tributaries to the Colorado River but seldom by the large river itself. The tree's spreading branches and wide, shimmering leaves shade many of the canyon's springs. Covered with grooved, ropelike bark, the cottonwood's trunk can grow as wide as a refrigerator. Its flowers, which bloom in spring, drop tiny seeds that look like cotton. A nice grove of these trees shelters the picnic area at Indian Garden.

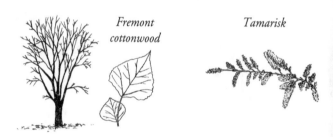

Fremont cottonwood

Tamarisk

Tamarisk   This exotic species was once used for flood-bank control by the CCC. Today, it is the plant that boaters and hikers love to hate. Before the Glen Canyon dam was built, the Colorado River's annual spring floods thinned or wiped out most of the tamarisk along its banks. Now tamarisk and coyote willow have taken over many beaches, creating thickets that can make hiking miserable. Other animals don't mind the thickets, as they're home to a diverse population of birds, lizards, and insects. Soft as ostrich feathers, the plant's stems grow tiny scalelike leaves and sprout small white flowers in spring. While young tamarisk consists of skinny, flexible stalks, the older plants have wood trunks.

4   The Fauna

To view wildlife during your stay at Grand Canyon, bring a flashlight. Most desert animals are either *nocturnal* (active at night) or *crepuscular* (active at dawn and dusk). By laying low during the day, they avoid the powerful sun, cutting their water needs and enabling them to forage or hunt without overheating. All have specialized mechanisms to survive this harsh environment, and many, if provoked, can be as prickly as the plants around them.

MAMMALS

Bats   The **western pipestral** is the most common bat at Grand Canyon. At sunset you'll see them flutter above the rim, rising and falling as if on strings. Gray with black wings, they send out supersonic sounds that echo differently off of different objects. The bats then "read" the echoes to determine what they're approaching. If it's an insect, they know what to do. They'll sometimes eat 500 bugs in an hour.

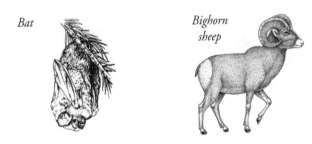

Bat

Bighorn sheep

Bighorn sheep   If there's a hint of a foothold, a bighorn sheep will find it. Its hooves are hard and durable on the outside but soft and grippy underneath, a perfect design for steep, rocky terrain. You'll often hear them clattering before you spot their stocky, gray-brown bodies and white rumps. Six feet long, the males weigh up to 300 pounds. Their horns are coiled; the females' are straight. Look for bighorn sheep in side canyons that have water, and sometimes on the rims.

Coyote

Coyotes Coyotes will eat almost anything—bugs, carrion, plants, rodents, and bird eggs included. Their versatile diet has helped them flourish, and today you'll find them everywhere in and around the canyon. They look like lanky midsized dogs. But their noses are more sharply pointed, and their tails hang between their legs when they run. During summer, their bodies are tan, their bellies white, and their legs rust-colored. In winter, the ones on the rim turn mostly gray. If you camp during your visit, you'll probably hear their squeaky yips and howls at sunset. Look for them at dusk in the meadows on the North Rim or at daybreak around the Tusayan garbage dumpsters.

Desert cottontails Common even in the canyon's most populated areas, these oval-eared rabbits feed on grasses, twigs, juniper berries, and leaves. Their bodies are mostly tan, but sometimes all you'll see is their white tails as they dash away from coyotes and bobcats.

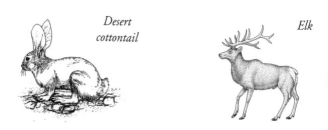

Desert cottontail

Elk

Elk Merriam's elk, which were native to this area, were hunted off in the 1920s. Transplanted from Yellowstone, Roosevelt elk have flourished on both rims. Their bodies are tan; their heads and necks dark brown and shaggy. These long-legged, thick-bodied animals grow to enormous sizes. The bulls weigh as much as 1,000 pounds and stand up to 5 feet high at the shoulders; the cows average 550 pounds. Unlike deer, which prefer bushes and shrubs, elk feed primarily on grasses on the forest floor. Rather than migrate far, they'll dig through snow for forage. Every year the bulls grow large racks, used to battle one another for the cows. In fall, during mating season the bulls can be dangerously aggressive. At this time, you may hear their high-pitched "bugling" inside the park. Herds of elk can often be seen roaming the National Forest on the South Rim near Grandview Point, and less commonly along the North Rim entrance road.

Mountain lions   These solitary cats, whose legs are as powerful as springs, will probably see you before you see them. Sightings around the canyon are rare, even among people who have spent their lives studying them. This isn't because the animals are small—they grow up to 6 feet long and weigh 200 pounds, with cylindrical tails as long as 3 feet. Their coat is tawny everywhere except the chest and muzzle, which are white. Their retractable claws let them alternately sprint across rocks and dig in on softer slopes—bad news for deer and elk, on which they prey. Hunted to near extirpation in this area in the early 1900s, the mountain lion has recovered of late, especially on the North Rim, where over 100 are believed to live.

Mountain lion

Mule deer

Mule deer   These tan or gray ungulates, which grow to as much as 200 pounds, are common everywhere in the park, including developed areas. They summer on the rims, then move into the canyon or lower on the plateaus in winter, when their fur turns grayish-white. Every year the bucks grow antlers, then shed them in March after battling other males during mating season. Mule deer browse on a variety of bushes and shrubs, but their favorite food may be cliff rose. Active at night, they frequently dart in front of cars, making night driving risky.

Raccoons   Recognizable by their gray bodies, tails with black stripes, and black "bandit" masks, raccoons are common around the rim campgrounds.

Ringtails   A relative of the raccoon, ringtails frequently raid campsites near the Colorado River. Their tails have luminous white bands. Their ears are pink and mouselike, their bodies gray-brown. They're smart enough and dexterous enough to untie knots. If

Raccoon

Ringtail

cornered, they may spray a foul-smelling mist like skunks do. When not raiding campsites, they feed on mice and other small animals.

Squirrels   The Kaibab and Aberts squirrels were once the same species sharing the same ponderosa pine forest. After the canyon separated the squirrels, subtle genetic differences between the groups took hold in later generations. Although both still have tufts of fur rising above their ears, the Kaibab squirrel, which lives only on the North Rim, is gray with a white tail. The Aberts squirrel, on the South Rim, has a gray body, a reddish back, and a dark tail with white sides. Both still nest in, and feed on the bark of, ponderosa pines, and both are notoriously clueless (even by squirrel standards) around cars. Among the other species, the grayish-brown squirrels seen begging along the rim are rock squirrels. The ones that look like oversized chipmunks are golden-mantled ground squirrels.

Kaibab squirrel

Aberts squirrel

BIRDS

Bald eagles   It's hard to mistake a mature bald eagle for any other bird. Dark plumage, a white head and tail, and yellow beak combine to give this bird, with its 6-foot wingspan, a look as distinctive as America itself. During winter, bald eagles frequently sit in trees along the river in the eastern canyon, where they like to fish for trout.

Bald Eagle

Common raven

Common ravens   These shiny blue-black birds soar like raptors above the rims when not walking like people around the campgrounds. They're big—up to 27 inches long—and smart. In addition to unzipping packs and opening food containers, they've been known to team up and take trout from bald eagles.

Golden eagles   Golden-brown from head to talon, this bird is commonly spotted soaring above the rims, its wings spanning to 6 feet or more. Wings tucked, the golden eagle can dive at speeds approaching 100 m.p.h. Although known to kill fawns, it usually prefers smaller mammals. It sometimes can be mistaken for an immature bald eagle.

Golden eagle

Great Horned Owl

Great horned owls   This bird often perches in trees along the rims. Look for black circles around its eyes, puffy white feathers on its chest, and feathery tufts that resemble horns above its ears.

Peregrine falcons   Identifiable by its gray back, black-and-white head, and pointed, sickle-shaped wings, this bird frequently preys on waterfowl, sometimes knocking them out of the air. Once endangered, the peregrine has benefited from the presence of Glen

Canyon dam, which has created a new habitat for waterfowl. The canyon is now home to the largest population of peregrines in the continental United States.

*Peregrine
falcon*

*Red-tailed
hawk*

Red-tailed hawks   One of the more commonly sighted raptors, the red-tailed hawk flies with its wings on a plane the way an eagle does, but has a smaller (4-foot) wingspan. Identifiable by its white underside, reddish tail, brown head, and brown back, the red-tailed hawk sometimes drops rattlesnakes from great heights to kill them.

Swifts and swallows   Two small birds—**white-throated swifts** and **violet-green swallows**—commonly slice through the air above the rims, picking off bugs. The swift's black-and-white colored body is uniformly narrow from head to tail. Its wings, which curve back toward its tail, seem to alternate strokes as it flies. The swallow, which has a rounder body and green feathers on its back and head, flies more steadily than the swift.

*Violet-green
swallow*

Turkey vultures   If you see a group of birds circling, their wings held in "Vs," rocking in the wind like unskilled hang-glider pilots, you're watching a group of turkey vultures. Up close, look for the dark plumage and bald red head. The turkey vulture feeds on carrion on the canyon floor.

Wild turkeys　Growing to 4 feet long, the males of this species are easiest to spot. They have bare blue heads, red wattles, and 6-inch-long feathered "beards" on their chests. The females are smaller and less colorful. Common on both rims but seen most often in the meadows on the North Rim, wild turkeys were once raised in pens by the Ancestral Puebloans.

Turkey vulture

Wild turkey

INVERTEBRATES

Black widows　These black spiders often spin their irregularly shaped, sticky webs in crevices in the Redwall Limestone. Although they're most active at night, you can occasionally spy one in the shadows. Their large, round abdomens give them a unique appearance. Only the females, recognizable by the red hourglass shape under the abdomen, are poisonous, with bites lethal enough to endanger small children.

Scorpions　Like a crayfish, each scorpion has two pincers and a long tail that curls toward its head like a whip. At the end of the tail is a stinger. Of the two species commonly found in the canyon, the most numerous by far is the giant hairy scorpion. Three to 4 inches long, this tan-colored scorpion inflicts a bite that's usually no worse than a bee sting. The bark (or sculptured) scorpion is more dangerous. Up to 2 inches long and straw-colored, it injects a neurotoxic venom much stronger than that of its larger counterpart. These bites are very painful and can be deadly in rare cases. The best way to see scorpions is to shine an ultraviolet light on the canyon floor at night—in this light, they glow!

Scorpion

REPTILES

Chuckwallas   Common in the lower parts of the canyon, chuck-wallas look as if they've just completed a crash diet, leaving them with skin that's three sizes too big. When threatened, they inflate that loose skin, wedging themselves into crevices in rock piles and cliffs. From 11 to 16 inches long, chuckwallas have black heads and forelegs.

Chuckwalla

Collard lizard

Collared lizards   At the middle and lower elevations of the canyon, you'll see a variety of collared lizards, all of which grow to 14 inches long and have big heads, long tails, and two black bands across their shoulders. Usually tan, black-collared lizards change shades when the temperature shifts. Western collared lizards are among the more colorful in the park, with blue, green, and yellow markings supplementing the black bands. These lizards are not the least bit shy around people. Sometimes, they'll stare you down for hours.

Rattlesnakes   If something rattles at you below the rim, it's prob-ably the Grand Canyon rattlesnake, the most common rattler inside the canyon. Its pinkish skin with dark blotches blends well with the canyon's soil. Like other rattlers, it has a triangular head, heat-sensing pits between its eyes, and a rattle used to warn larger animals. To maintain an acceptable body temperature, this snake becomes active only when the temperature along the ground approaches 78°F. At other times it's sluggish. It may sun itself on a ledge or curl up under a rock pile or log. Although venomous, the Grand Canyon rattlesnake is more reluctant to bite than other rattlesnakes. They're often seen near water, where they prey on small rodents. Other rattlesnake species are found closer to the rims. On the South Rim, the only common rattlesnake is the Hopi rattlesnake; on the North Rim, it's the Great Basin rattlesnake.

Rattlesnake

Short-horned lizards   These lizards can be found sunning themselves or scurrying across the forest floors on the canyon rims. With horizontal spines on their heads and rows of barbs on their backs, these short, stout lizards look like tiny dinosaurs or "horny toads," as they're commonly called. They'll sometimes ooze blood from their eyes at attackers.

Short-horned lizard

Sonoran gopher snake

Sonoran gopher snakes   The "wannabe" of the snake world, the gopher snake likes to pretend that it's a rattler. To bluff its way out of trouble, it flattens its usually narrow head into a triangular shape and shakes its tail, which (alas) has no rattle. (Some rattlesnakes lose their rattles, so don't take chances.)

See also separate Accommodations and Restaurant indexes, below.

ACCOMMODATIONS